Praise for *A Developer's Guide to Data Modeling for SQL Server*

"Eric and Joshua do an excellent job explaining the import⸱ to do it correctly. Rather than relying only on academic co⸱ amples to illustrate the important concepts that many datab⸱⸱⸱⸱⸱⸱⸱velop- ers tend to ignore. The writing style is conversational and ⸱⸱⸱⸱⸱⸱⸱ ⸱⸱n database design novices and seasoned pros alike. Readers who are respon⸱⸱⸱⸱. designing, imple- menting, and managing databases will benefit greatly from Joshuas and Eric's expertise."

—**Anil Desai,** Consultant, Anil Desai, Inc.

"Almost every IT project involves data storage of some kind, and for most that means a relational database management system (RDBMS). This book is written for a database- centric audience (database modelers, architects, designers, developers, etc.). The authors do a great job of showing us how to take a project from its initial stages of requirements gathering all the way through to implementation. Along the way we learn how to handle some of the real-world design issues that typically surface as we go through the process.

"The bottom line here is simple. This is the book you want to have just finished read- ing when your boss says 'We have a new project I would like your help with.'"

—**Ronald Landers,** Technical Consultant, IT Professionals, Inc.

"The Data Model is the foundation of the application. I'm pleased to see additional books being written to address this critical phase. This book presents a balanced and pragmatic view with the right priorities to get your SQL server project off to a great start and a long life."

—**Paul Nielsen,** SQL Server MVP, SQLServerBible.com

"This is a truly excellent introduction to the database design methodology that will work for both novices and advanced designers. The authors do a good job at explaining the ba- sics of relational database modeling and how they fit into modern business architecture. This book teaches us how to identify the business problems that have to be satisfied by a database and then proceeds to explain how to build a solid solution from scratch."

—**Alexzander N. Nepomnjashiy,** Microsoft SQL Server DBA, NeoSystems North-West, Inc.

"*A Developer's Guide to Data Modeling for SQL Server* explains the concepts and prac- tice of data modeling with a clarity that makes the technology accessible to anyone build- ing databases and data-driven applications.

"Eric Johnson and Joshua Jones combine a deep understanding of the science of data modeling with the art that comes with years of experience. If you're new to data model- ing, or find the need to brush up on its concepts, this book is for you."

—**Peter Varhol,** Executive Editor, *Redmond Magazine*

A Developer's Guide to Data Modeling for SQL Server

COVERING SQL SERVER 2005 AND 2008

A Developer's Guide to Data Modeling for SQL Server

COVERING SQL SERVER
2005 AND 2008

Eric Johnson

Joshua Jones

Addison-Wesley

Upper Saddle River, NJ • Boston • Indianapolis • San Francisco
New York • Toronto • Montreal • London • Munich • Paris • Madrid
Capetown • Sydney • Tokyo • Singapore • Mexico City

Many of the designations used by manufacturers and sellers to distinguish their products are claimed as trademarks. Where those designations appear in this book, and the publisher was aware of a trademark claim, the designations have been printed with initial capital letters or in all capitals.

The authors and publisher have taken care in the preparation of this book, but make no expressed or implied warranty of any kind and assume no responsibility for errors or omissions. No liability is assumed for incidental or consequential damages in connection with or arising out of the use of the information or programs contained herein.

The publisher offers excellent discounts on this book when ordered in quantity for bulk purchases or special sales, which may include electronic versions and/or custom covers and content particular to your business, training goals, marketing focus, and branding interests. For more information, please contact:

U.S. Corporate and Government Sales
(800)382-3419
corpsales@pearsontechgroup.com

For sales outside the United States please contact:

International Sales
international@pearsoned.com

 This Book Is Safari Enabled

The Safari® Enabled icon on the cover of your favorite technology book means the book is available through Safari Bookshelf. When you buy this book, you get free access to the online edition for 45 days.

Safari Bookshelf is an electronic reference library that lets you easily search thousands of technical books, find code samples, download chapters, and access technical information whenever and wherever you need it.

To gain 45-day Safari Enabled access to this book:

- Go to informit.com/onlineedition
- Complete the brief registration form
- Enter the coupon code BZG7-GAAI-IAAQ-R6IB-DCI8

If you have difficulty registering on Safari Bookshelf or accessing the online edition, please e-mail customer-service@safaribooksonline.com.

Visit us on the Web: informit.com/aw

Library of Congress Cataloging-in-Publication Data

Johnson, Eric, 1978–
  A developer's guide to data modeling for SQL server : covering SQL server
2005 and 2008 / Eric Johnson and Joshua Jones. — 1st ed.
      p. cm.
  Includes index.
  ISBN 978-0-321-49764-2 (pbk. : alk. paper)
  1. SQL server.   2. Database design.   3. Data structures (Computer science)
I. Jones, Joshua, 1975- II. Title.

  QA76.9.D26J65 2008
  005.75'85—dc22   2008016668

ISBN-13: 978-0-321-49764-2
ISBN-10:   0-321-49764-3
Text printed in the United States on recycled paper at Courier in Stoughton, Massachusetts.
First printing, June 2008

For Michelle and Evan—Eric

To my wife and children; I have time to play now—Josh

Contents

PREFACE

As database professionals, we are frequently asked to come into existing environments and "fix" existing databases. This is usually because of performance problems that application developers and users have uncovered over the lifetime of a given application. Inevitably, the expectation is that we can work some magic database voodoo and the performance problems will go away. Unfortunately, as most of you already know, the problem often lies within the design of the database. We often spend hours in meetings trying to justify the cost of redesigning an entire database in order to support the actual requirements of the application as well as the performance needs of the business. We often find ourselves tempering good design with real-world problems such as budget, resources, and business needs that simply don't allow for the time needed to completely resolve all the issues in a poorly designed database.

What happens when you find yourself in the position of having to redesign an existing database or, better yet, having to design a new database from the ground up? You know there are rules to follow, along with best practices that can help guide you to a scalable, functional design. If you follow these rules you won't leave database developers and DBAs cursing your name three years from now (well, no more than necessary). Additionally, with the advent of enterprise-level relational database management systems, it's equally important to understand the ins and outs of the database platform your design will be implemented on.

There were two reasons we decided to write this book, a reference for everyone out there who needs to design or rework a data model that will eventually sit on Microsoft SQL Server. First, even though there are dozens of great books that cover relational database design from top to bottom, and dozens of books on how to performance-tune and write T-SQL for SQL Server, there wasn't anything to help a developer or designer cover the process from beginning to end with the right mix of theory and practical experience. Second, we'd seen literally hundreds of poorly designed databases left behind by people who had neither the background in database theory nor the experience with SQL Server to design an effective data model. Sometimes, those databases were well designed for the technology they were implemented on; then they were simply copied and pasted (for lack of a more accurate term) onto SQL Server, often with disastrous results. We thought that a book that discussed design for SQL Server would be helpful for those people redesigning an existing database to be migrated from another platform to SQL Server.

We've all read that software design, and relational database design in particular, should be platform agnostic. We do not necessarily disagree with that outlook. However, it is important to understand which RDBMS will be hosting your design, because that can affect the capabilities you can plan for and the weaknesses you may need to account for in your design. Additionally, with the introduction of SQL Server 2005, Microsoft has implemented quite a bit of technology that extends the capabilities of SQL Server beyond simple database hosting. Although we don't cover every piece of extended functionality (otherwise, you would need a crane to carry this book), we reference it where appropriate to give you the opportunity to learn how this functionality can help you.

Within the pages of this book, we hope you'll find everything you need to help you through the entire design and development process—everything from talking to users, designing use cases, and developing your data model to implementing that model and ensuring it has solid performance characteristics. When possible, we've provided examples that we hope will be useful and applicable to you in one way or another. After spending hours developing the background and requirements for our fictitious company, we have been thinking about starting our own music business. And let's face it—reading line after line of text about the various uses for a varchar data type can't always be thrilling, so we've tried to add some anecdotes, a few jokes, and even a paraphrased movie quote or two to keep it lively.

Writing this book has also been an adventure for both of us, in learning how the publishing process works, learning the finer details of writing for a mass audience, and learning that even though we are our own worst critics, it's hard to hear criticism from your friends, even if they're right; but you're always glad that they are.

ACKNOWLEDGMENTS

We have always enjoyed training and writing, and this book gave us the opportunity to do both at the same time. Many long nights and weekends went into this book, and we hope all the hard work has created a great resource for you to use.

We cannot express enough thanks to our families—Michelle and Evan, and Lisa, Braydon, and Sydney. They have been very supportive throughout this process and put up with our not being around. We love you very much.

We would also like to thank the team at Addison-Wesley, Joan Murray and Kim Boedigheimer. We had not written a book before this one, and Joan had enough faith in us to give us the opportunity. Thanks for guiding us through the process and working with us even when things got tricky.

A big thanks goes out to Embarcadero (embarcadero.com) for setting us up with copies of ERStudio for use in creating the models you will see in this book.

We also want to thank Microsoft for creating SQL Server and providing the IT community with the ability to host databases on such a robust platform.

Finally, we would be amiss if we didn't thank you, the reader. Without you there would be no book.

About the Authors

Eric Johnson (Microsoft SQL MVP) is the co-founder of Consortio Services and the primary database technologies consultant. His background in information technology is diverse, ranging from operating systems and hardware to specialized applications and development. He has even done his fair share of work on networks. Because IT is a way to support business processes, Eric has also acquired an MBA. All in all, he has ten years of experience with IT, much of it working with Microsoft SQL Server. Eric has managed and designed databases of all shapes and sizes. He has delivered numerous SQL Server training classes and Webcasts as well as presentations at national technology conferences. Most recently, he presented at TechMentor on SQL Server 2005 replication, reporting services, and integration services. In addition, he is active in the local SQL Server community, serving as the president of the Colorado Springs SQL Server Users Group. He is also the co-host of *CS Techcast*, a weekly podcast for IT professionals at www.cstechcast.com. You can find Eric's blog at www.consortioservices.com/blog.

    Joshua Jones (MCTS, SQL Server 2005; MCITP, Database Administrator) is operating systems and database systems consultant with Consortio Services in Colorado Springs. There he provides training, administration, analysis, and design support for customers using SQL Server 2000 and 2005. In his seven years as an IT professional, he has worked in many areas of information technology, including Windows desktop support, Windows 2000 and 2003 server infrastructure design and support (AD, DNS, MS Exchange), telephony switch support, and network support. Josh has spoken at various PASS sponsored events about SQL Server topics such as 64-bit SQL Server implementation, reporting services administration, and performance tuning. He is also a co-host of *CS Techcast*, a weekly podcast for IT professionals at www.cstechcast.com.

DATA MODELING THEORY

CHAPTER 1

DATA MODELING OVERVIEW

What exactly is this thing called data modeling? Simply put, **data modeling** is the process of figuring out how to store digitized information in a logically structured computer database. It may sound easy, but a lot goes into the process of developing a sound data model. Data modeling is a technical process that involves understanding and mapping business information to logical objects that can eventually be stored in a database. This means that a data modeler must wear many hats to do the job effectively. You not only must understand the process by which the model is built, but you also must be a data detective. You must be good at asking questions and finding out what is really important to your customer.

In data modeling, as in many areas of information technology, customers know what they want, but they don't always know what they need. It's your job to figure out what they need. Suppose you're dealing with Tom, a project manager for an appliance distribution company. Tom understands that his company orders refrigerators, dishwashers, and the like from the manufacturers and then takes orders and sells those appliances to its customers (retail stores). What Tom doesn't know is how to take that information, model it, and ultimately store it in a database so that it can be leveraged to help the company make decisions or control a process.

In addition to finding out what information your customer cares about and getting it into a database, you must find out how the customer intends to use the information. Is it for historical purposes, or will the company use the data in its daily operations? Will it be used only to produce reports, or will an application need to manipulate the data regularly? As if that weren't enough, you eventually have to think about turning your data model into a physical database.

There are many choices on the market when it comes to database management products. These products are similar in that they allow you to store, secure, and use information in databases; however, each product implements features in its own way, so you must also make the best use of these features to provide a solution that best meets the needs of your customer.

Our goal in this book is to give you the know-how and skills you need to design and implement data models. There is plenty of information out there on database theory, so that is not our focus; instead, we want to look at real-world scenarios and focus your modeling efforts on optimizing your design for Microsoft SQL Server 2008. The concepts and topics we discuss are applicable to older versions of Microsoft SQL Server, but some features are available only in SQL Server 2008. Where we encounter this problem we will point out the key differences or at least let you know that the topic applies only to SQL Server 2008.

Before we go much further, there are a few terms you should be familiar with. Many of these terms you probably already know, but we want to make sure that we are all on the same page.

Databases

What is a database? The simple answer is that a **database** is anything that contains information. A database can be either logical or physical (or both). You will hear many companies refer to any internal information as the company's database. In fact, I once had a discussion with a manager of mine as to whether a napkin could be a database. If you think about it, I could indeed write something on a napkin and it could be a record. Because it is storing data, you could call it a database. So why don't we store all of our important information on napkins? The main reason is that we don't want to lose a customer's order in the washing machine.

Seriously, when we store data we need a database that can hold information in a logical way and allow data retrieval. When you think of a database, you should really think of something with tables that are made up of rows and columns. Each **table** contains information pertaining to a single "topic," and each **row** contains data about a single instance of that topic. Figure 1.1 shows a simple logical model containing information about employees and their computers.

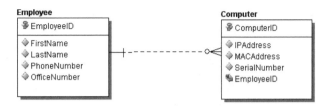

FIGURE 1.1 A simple relational database containing employee and computer information

The Employee table holds all the pertinent data about employees, and each row in it contains all the information for a single employee. Similarly, **columns** hold the data of the same type for each row. For example, the PhoneNumber column holds only phone numbers of employees. Many databases contain other objects, such as views, stored procedures, functions, and constraints, among others; we get into those details later.

Taking the definition one step further, we need to look at relational databases. A **relational database,** the most common type of database in use, is one in which the tables relate to one another in some way. Looking at our Employee table, we might also want to track which computers we give to which employees. In this case we would have a Computer table that would relate to the Employee table, as in the statement, "An employee owns or has a computer." Once we start talking about relational databases, we knock other databases off the list. Things like spreadsheets, text files, or napkins inherently stand alone and cannot be related to other objects. From this point forward, when we talk about databases, we are referring to relational databases that contain collections of tables that can relate to one another.

Relational Database Management Systems

A **relational database management system** (RDBMS) is a software product that stores relational databases. In addition to storing databases, RDBMSs provide many other functions. They give you a way to secure the databases and manage user access. They also have functions that allow you to manage your databases, functions such as backup and restore, index management, data loading utilities, and even reporting.

A number of RDBMS products are available, ranging from freely available open source products such as MySQL to enterprise-level solutions such as Oracle, Microsoft SQL Server, or IBM's DB2. Which system you use depends largely on your specific environment and requirements. This book focuses on Microsoft SQL Server 2008. Although a data model can be implemented on any system, it needs to be tweaked to fit that product. If you know ahead of time that you will be deploying on SQL Server 2008, you can start that tweaking from step 1 and end up with a database that will take full advantage of the features that SQL Server offers.

Why a Sound Data Model Is Important

Data modeling is a long process, and doing it correctly requires many hours. In fact, when a team sits down to start building an application, data modeling can easily be the single most time-consuming part. This large time investment means that the process will be scrutinized by managers, application developers, and the customer. The temptation is to cut the modeling process short and move on to creating the database. All too often we have seen applications built with a "We will build the database as we go" attitude. This is the wrong way to go about building any solution that includes a database. Data modeling is extremely important, and it is vital that you take the time to do it correctly. Failure to do things right in the beginning will cause you to revisit the database design many times over the course of a project.

Data modeling is the plan by which the database will eventually be built. If the plan is flawed, it will be impossible to build a good database. Compare it to building a house. You start with blueprints, which show how the house will be built. If the blueprints are incorrect or incomplete, you wouldn't expect to be able to build the house. Data modeling is the same. Given that data modeling is important to the success of the database, it is equally important to do it correctly. Well-designed data models not only serve as your blueprint but also help you avoid some common database problems. Let's explore some of the benefits that a sound data model gives you.

Data Consistency

A solid data model provides **data consistency.** Without data consistency, you could find that you have all the data you could ever want, but you can't garner helpful information from it. What do I mean by data consistency?

Let's assume that the company you work for stores all of its information in spreadsheets. In a spreadsheet world, your data is only as good as the people who record it.

What does that mean for data consistency? Suppose you store all your customer information in a single workbook in your spreadsheet. You want to know a few pieces of basic information about each customer: name, address, phone number, and e-mail address. That seems easy enough, but now let's introduce the human element into the scenario. Your customer service employees are required to add information to the workbook for each new customer they work with. Because your customer service reps are human, how they record the information will vary from person to person. For example, a rep may record the customer's information as shown in row 1 of Table 1.1, and another may record the same customer's information a different way, as shown in row 2 of Table 1.1.

Table 1.1 The Same Customer's Information as Entered
by Two Customer Service Reps

Name	Address	City	State	ZIP	Phone	Email
John Doe	123 Easy Street	SF	CA	94134	(415) 555-1956	jdoe@abcnetwork.com
J. Doe	123 Easy St.	San Fran	CA	94134	5551956	jdoe@abcnetwork.com

These are subtle differences to be sure, but if you look closely you'll see some problems. First, if you want to run a report to count all of your San Francisco-based customers, how would you go about it? Sure, a human can tell that "SF" and "San Fran" are shorthand for San Francisco, but a computer can't make that assumption without help. To run your report, you would need to look for all the possible ways that someone could key in San Francisco, to include all the ways it can be misspelled. Next, let's look at the customer's name. For starters, are we sure it's the same person? "J. Doe" could be Jane Doe or Javier Doe. Although the e-mail address is the same on both records, I have seen my fair share of families with only one shared e-mail address. Additionally, the second customer service representative omitted the customer's area code, and that means you must spend time looking it up if you ever need to call the customer.

For data to be useful, it must be consistent; I cannot stress this enough. This means that when you store a piece of data, it is stored in the same way each and every time. The city is always stored as San Francisco, and the phone number always has the area code. If your data isn't consistent, you (or the users of the system you design) will spend too much time trying to figure it out and too little time leveraging it. Granted, you probably won't spend a lot of time modeling data to be stored in a spreadsheet, but these same kinds of things can happen in a database.

Scalability

When all is said and done, you want to build a database that the customer can use immediately and also for the foreseeable future. No matter how good a job you do on the data model, things change and new data becomes available. A sound data model will provide for **scaling.** This means that customers can continue to add records to the database, and the model will not run into problems. Similarly, adding new information to existing entities should be no harder than adding an attribute (discussed later in this chapter). In contrast, a poorly modeled database will be difficult or even impossible to alter. Take as an example the entity in Figure 1.2 (entities are discussed later in this chapter). This entity holds the data relating to a customer, including the customer's address information.

FIGURE 1.2   A simple customer entity containing address data

This design works well if each customer has only a single address. In the real world, customers have multiple addresses for work, home, vacation homes, or Grandma's house. How can we change this model to store the extra addresses? Because of the way this model was built, the easiest way to add the data is to add attributes (Address1, Address2, Address3), as shown in Figure 1.3.

FIGURE 1.3   A simple customer entity expanded to support three addresses

This method has several problems. We now have three sets of attributes in the same entity that hold the same data. This is bad from a normalization standpoint, and it is also confusing. We can't tell which address is the customer's home or work address. We also don't know why the customer had these addresses on file in the first place. The model, as it exists in Figure 1.3, is not very scalable, and this is the kind of problem that can occur when you need to expand the model. An alternative, more scalable model is shown in Figure 1.4.

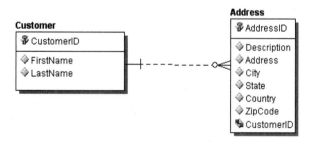

FIGURE 1.4   An expanded customer model to include a separate address entity

As you can see, this model solves all our scalability problems. In fact, this new model doesn't need to be scaled. We can still enter one address for each customer, but we can also easily enter more addresses when the need arises. Additionally, each address can be labeled so that we can tell what the address is for.

Meeting Business Requirements

Many big, expensive solutions have been implemented over the years that serve no real purpose—IT only for the sake of IT. Some people thought that if they bought the biggest and best computer system, all their problems would be solved. Experience tells us that things just don't work that way: Technology is more successful when it's deployed to solve a business problem.

With data modeling, it's easy to fall into implementing something that the business doesn't need. To make your design work, you need to take a big step back and try to figure out what the business is trying to accomplish and then help it achieve its goals. You need to take the time to do data modeling correctly, and really dig into the company's requirements. Later, we look specifically at how to get the requirements you need. For now, just keep in mind that if you do your job as a data modeler correctly, you will meet the needs, and not only the wants, of your customer.

Easy Data Retrieval

Once you have data stored in a database, it is useful only if users can retrieve it. A database serves no purpose if it has a ton of great information but it's hard to retrieve it. In addition to thinking about how you will store data, it's crucial to design a model that lends itself to getting the data back out.

One of the worst databases I have ever seen, I designed. (Because this book is written by two authors, I'm forced to acknowledge that the author speaking here is Eric Johnson.) I am not proud of it, but it was a great learning experience. Years before I was properly introduced to the world of relational database management systems, I started, as many people do, by playing with Microsoft Access to build a database for a small Visual Basic application I was writing. I was working as a trainer and just starting to take Microsoft certification exams to become a Microsoft Certified Systems Engineer (MCSE).

As part of my job as a trainer, I had to find a way to test the students to make sure they were learning the material. The first few classes got a typical multiple-choice test. This test was delivered on paper and graded by hand. This was time consuming, and it wasn't much fun. Because I was a budding technology geek, I wanted a better way.

Enter my Visual Basic testing application, complete with the Access back end, which in my mind would look similar to the Microsoft tests I myself had recently been taking. All the questions would be either multiple-choice or true-false. At this point, I hadn't done much with Access—or any database application for that matter—so I just started doing what seemed to work. I had a table that held student records, which was straightforward, and a table that held information about the exams. These two tables were just about perfect; they had a purpose, and all the information they contained pertained to the entity the table represented. These two tables were also the only two tables in the database that were easy to navigate and retrieve data from.

That brings me to the Question table, which, as the name suggests, stored the questions for the exams. This table also stored the possible answers the students could choose. As you can see in Figure 1.5, this table had problems.

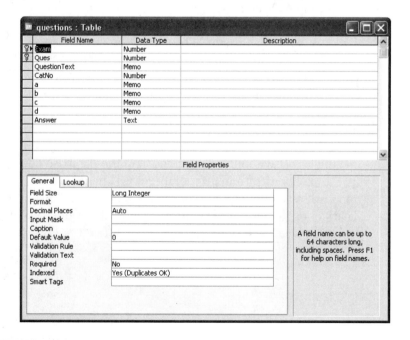

FIGURE 1.5 An example of a poorly designed Question table for a testing application

Let's take a look at what makes this a bad design and how that affects data retrieval. The first four columns are OK; they store information about the question, such as the test where it appears and the question's category. The problems start to become obvious in the next five columns. Columns a, b, c, and d store the text that is displayed to the user for the multiple-choice options. The Answer column contains the correct letter or letters that make up the correct answer. How do you determine the correct answer for the question? It's not too hard for a human to figure out, but computers have a hard time comparing rows to columns.

The other problem with this table is that there are only four options; you simply cannot have a question with five options unless you add a column to the table. When delivering the test, instead of getting a nice neat result set, I had to write code to walk the columns for each row to get the options for each question. Data retrieval ease was not one of this table's strong suits.

It gets even better (or worse, depending on how you look at it); take a look at Figure 1.6. This is the table that held the students' responses to the questions. When you are finished rolling on the floor laughing, we will continue.

This table is an example of one of the worst data modeling traps you can fall into: using columns when you should be using rows. It is similar to the problem we saw earlier in Figure 1.3. This table not only contains the answer the student provided (in a string format)—I was literally storing the letters they picked—but it also has a column for each question. You can't see it in the figure, but this table goes all the way up to a column called Ques61. In fact, my application dynamically added columns if you were creating a test with more questions than the database could support.

To be honest, I don't remember how I made any use of this data. The application is a bunch of spaghetti code that I can't even follow anymore. That's enough self-deprecation for now, but I wanted to show you how a bad model can make data retrieval very difficult.

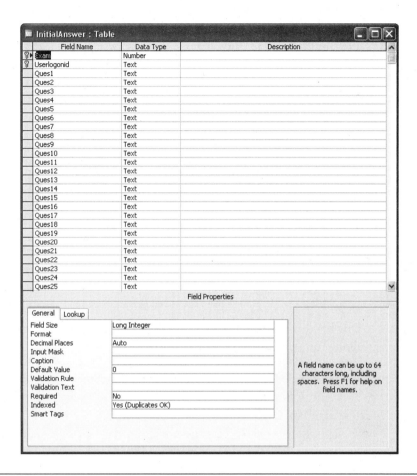

FIGURE 1.6 An example of a poorly designed response table for a testing application

Performance Tuning

In my experience, when a database performs poorly it seldom stems from transaction load or limited hardware resources; often, it's because of poor database design. Another hallmark of the IT industry is to throw money at a problem in the hope that things will improve. Sure, if you go out and buy the most expensive server known to humans and load it up with gigs upon gigs of RAM—and as many processors as you can without setting the thing on fire—you will get your database to perform better. But many design decisions are about trade-offs: do you really want to spend hundreds or thousands of dollars for a 10 percent performance boost?

In the long run, a better solution can be to redesign a poorly designed database. The horrible testing database we discussed probably wouldn't have scaled very well. The application had to do many tricks in order to save and retrieve the data. This created far more work than would have been required in a well-designed system. Don't get me wrong—I am not saying that all performance problems stem from bad design, but often bad design causes problems that can't be corrected without a redesign. If the data model is sound from the get-go, you can focus your energy on actually tuning the database using indexes, statistics, or even access methods. Again, just like a house, a database that has a solid foundation lets you repair the problems that occur.

The Process of Data Modeling

This book is written as a step-by-step, process-oriented look at data modeling. You will walk through a real-world project from start to finish. Your journey will follow Mountain View Music, a fictitious small online music retailer that is in the process of redesigning its current system. You will start with a little theory and work toward the final implementation of the new database on Microsoft SQL Server 2008.

The main topic of this book is not data modeling theory, but we give you enough information on theory to start constructing a sound model. We focus on the things you need to be aware of when designing a model for SQL Server.

This book is divided into four parts; each one builds on the preceding one as we walk you through our retailer scenario. In the first four chapters we look at theory, such as logical and physical elements and normalization. In Part II, we explain how to gather and interpret the requirements of the company. Part III finds us actually building the logical model. Finally, in Part IV, we build the physical model and implement it on SQL Server.

Throughout this book we focus on the fact that we are designing this data model to ultimately be implemented on SQL Server. For that reason, we point out the correct decisions to make based on the capabilities of SQL Server that will help to produce an efficient model for that platform. We go through all this in detail throughout the book, but let's take a brief look at each area and see what lies ahead.

Modeling Theory

Everything begins with a theory, and in IT, the theory is the way things would be done in a perfect world. Unfortunately, we do not live in a perfect world, and things must be adapted for them to be successful. That said, you still have to understand the theory so that you can come as close as possible. There is always a reason behind a theory, and understanding these underlying reasons will make you a better data modeler.

Data modeling is not a new idea, and there are many resources on database design theory and methodology; a few titles focus on nothing more than the symbols you can use to draw diagrams. That being the case, we do not focus on the methodology and theory; instead we discuss the most important components of the theory and focus on putting these theories into practice.

Logical Elements

When you start modeling, you begin with the logical modeling. The **logical model** is a representation of the data in a way that can be presented to the business as well as serve as a road map for the physical implantation. The main elements of a logical model are entities, attributes, and relationships. **Entities** are logical groupings of data, such as all the information that describes a customer. **Attributes** are the pieces of information that make up entities. For a customer, the attributes might be things like name, address, or phone number. **Relationships** describe how one entity is related to another. For example, the relationship "customers place orders" describes the fact that customers "own" the orders they place. We dive deeper into logical elements and explain how they are used in Chapter 2, Elements Used in Logical Data Models.

Physical Elements

Once the logical model is constructed you create the physical model. Like the logical model, the physical model is made up of various elements. Tables are where everything is stored. Tables have columns, which contain the information about the data in the table rows. SQL Server also provides primary and foreign keys (defined in Chapter 2), which allow you to define the relationship between two tables.

At first glance, tables, columns, and keys might seem to be the same as the logical elements, but there are important differences. **Logical**

elements simply describe the groupings of data as they might exist in the real world; in contrast, **physical elements** actually store the data in a database. A single entity might be stored in only one table or in multiple tables. In fact, sometimes more than one entity wind up being stored in one table. The various physical elements and the ways they are used are the topics of Chapter 3, Physical Elements of Data Models.

Normalization

A well-designed data model has some level of normalization. In short, **normalization** is the process of separating data into logical groupings. Normalization is divided into **levels,** and each successive level builds on the preceding level.

First normal form, notated as 1NF, is the most basic form of normalization. In essence, in 1NF the data is stored in a table and each column contains one type of data. This means that any given column in the table stores the same piece of information, such as a phone number. Additionally, 1NF requires that your data have a primary key. A **primary key** is the column or columns that uniquely identify the row. Normalization can go up to six levels; however, most well-built models conform to third normal form.

Generally, in this book we talk about topics in linear order; you must do the current one before the next one. Normalization is the exception to this rule, because there is not really a specific time during modeling when you sit down and normalize the model, nor are you concerned with the level your model conforms to. For the most part, normalization takes place throughout your modeling. When you start defining entities that your model will have, you will have already started normalizing your model. Sound transactional models are normalized, and normalization helps with many of the other areas we have discussed. Normalized data is easier to retrieve, is consistent, is scalable, and so on. You must understand this concept in order to build models, and we cover it in detail in Chapter 4, Normalizing a Data Model.

Business Requirements

In Part II, we focus on gathering business requirements. I have said it before and you can be sure I will say it again: You are building a database for a reason, and that reason should be to solve a business problem. To that end, you must be able to extract the requirements from the company and turn those requirements into a usable database. We attack this topic in two phases: requirements gathering and requirements interpretation. In this part, we talk through the requirements of Mountain View Music and describe how we went about extracting them.

Requirements Gathering

In Chapter 5, Requirements Gathering, we look at methods for gathering requirements and explain which sort of information is important. The techniques range from interviewing the end users to reverse-engineering an existing application or system. No matter what methods you use, the goal is the same: to determine what the business needs. It may sound easy, but I have yet to sit down with a customer and have him tell me exactly what he needs. He can answer questions about the company's processes and business, but you must drill down to the core of the problem.

In fact, a lot of the time, your job is to act like a three-year-old, continually asking, "Why?" For example, the customer will tell you he wants a button; you ask why, and he will tell you it's to open a door. Why must you open a door? The door must open in order to get product out of the warehouse. Why does the product need to leave the warehouse? We have to get the product into the hands of our customers. The bottom line is that he wants a button in order to sell products to the customer. This is the basic need of the business, and it's this information that is important. If you meet this need, the customer won't really care whether you did it with a button or a switch or a magic password.

Often, it's easy to focus our attention on making customers happy at the cost of giving them what they really need. We simply give the customer exactly what she asks for; in her mind, widget Z is what she needs, but in reality widget Z may work beautifully as designed but not solve the actual business problem. The worst feeling ever is at the end of a project when the customer says, "It's exactly what we asked for, but it's not what we need." In Chapter 5 we go over several options for requirements gathering so that you can avoid the problem of not meeting your customers' needs.

Requirements Interpretation

Once you have the first cut of the requirements, you start turning them into a data model. In Chapter 6, Interpreting Requirements, we look at how you take the requirements, which are in human language, and turn them into a data model. We look not only at extracting the information required for the model, but also at extracting business rules.

Business rules are policies enforced by a company for its various business processes. For example, the company might require that each purchase be approved by three people holding specific titles (purchasing agent, manager of accounts payable, project manager). Business rules may or may not be implemented in your model, but they need to be documented because eventually you need to implement them somewhere. Whether you implement them as a relationship in the model, use a trigger in SQL Server, or even implement them through an application, it is important to understand them early, because the model design will be driven by the business rules that it needs to support. In Chapter 6 we also look at the iterative process of working with stakeholders in the company. They not only have to sign off on the initial model, but both you (as the designer) and they (as the customer) will have changes that need to be made as the process moves forward.

Next, we discuss the business review of the model. It's crucial to get your customers' buy in and sign-off of the logical model. Once the customer has approved the model, you can document releases and work toward the agreed-upon system.

We cannot reiterate this point enough: You cannot skip this step. It will save you days of pain down the line if the company needs to make changes to the requirements. If you have agreed-upon release cycles, then you can simply add new changes at the expense of the project's time line or of other requirements. Without this agreement, you will be engaged in discussions, even arguments, about the changes, and either your customer or your modeling team will end up dissatisfied with the outcome.

Building the Logical Model

In Part III, we get to the actual building of the model. By this time, you will have a grasp of the requirements and it will be time to translate them into the model. We will walk you through the thought process you go through when building a model and translate the requirements from Mountain View Music.

Creating the Logical Model

The first step in building the logical model is to sit down and create the model from the requirements. This is the bulk of the work of building the logical model. In Chapter 7, Creating the Logical Model, we look at how you determine which entities your model will need and how these entities are related. In addition we look at the attributes you need and explain how to determine which type of data the attributes will store. We also go over the diagramming method used in building the model. There are many techniques for creating the data diagram, but we stick to one method throughout this project.

Common Modeling Problems

In Chapter 8, Common Data Modeling Problems, we look at several common traps that are easy to fall into when you build your model. There are many ways to build a logical model, and no single method is always the correct one. However, there are many practices that are always wrong, and you can avoid them. Many aspects of data modeling are counterintuitive, and following your intuition can lead to some of these problems. We go through these problems and talk about why people fall into these traps, how you can avoid them, and the appropriate ways to work around them. Additionally, we look at a few things, such as subtype and supertype modeling, that aren't necessarily problems but can be tricky.

Building the Physical Model

Once you have the logical model hammered out, you translate it into a physical model, and we turn to that topic in Part IV. A physical model is made up of the tables and other physical objects of your RDBMS. Much of the work of creating your database has been completed during the logical modeling, but that doesn't mean you should take the physical model lightly. Logical models are meant to map to logical, real-world entities, whereas the physical model defines how the data will be stored in the database. At this point the focus is on ways to store data in the database to meet the business requirements for data retrieval. This is where an intimate knowledge of the specific RDBMS system is invaluable.

Creating the Physical Model

The first step is to create the model. In Chapter 9 we look at how you determine which tables and keys you need based on your logical model. In some cases you will end up with more than one table to represent a single logical entity, whereas in other cases you will roll up multiple entities onto a single table.

Additionally, you will probably end up with tables that contain data not represented in your logical model. We call these **supporting tables.** They are used to support the use of the database but do not necessarily store data that the business cares about. Supporting tables might be lookup tables or tables to support application code, or they might support business rules. For example, suppose that the business requires that all users belong to a group, and their group membership determines the access they have in an application. This security model can be stored in tables and referenced by the application.

Except for these differences, building the physical model is similar to building the logical model. You still need to determine the needed tables, columns, primary keys, and foreign keys, and diagram them in a model.

SQL Server has other objects in addition to tables. Objects such as views, stored procedures, user-defined functions, user-defined data types, constraints, and triggers can also be used in your physical model. We look at these objects in detail in Chapter 3, and we describe how to build a physical model in Chapter 9, Creating the Physical Model with SQL Server.

Indexing

The next big part of implementing your database on SQL Server is indexing: **Indexes** are structures that are placed on tables in a physical database to help enhance performance by giving the database engine reference points to find the data on disk. Deciding what types of indexes to use and where to use them is a bit of a black art, but it is a critical part of your database. Index requirements are largely driven by business rules and usage information. What data does the business need to retrieve quickly? Will a given table typically be written to or read from? Answering these questions goes a long way toward determining your indexes. We look at indexes and explore considerations for implementing them in Chapter 10, Indexing Considerations.

Creating an Abstraction Layer

Another important, and often overlooked, part of database design is the abstraction layer. An **abstraction layer** provides a level of access to the database without giving users direct access to the tables. To create an abstraction layer, you create views, stored procedures, and functions to access the data in the underlying tables.

Abstraction layers are created for several reasons. The first is security. If you have a good abstraction layer, you can more easily control who has access to specific types of information. Another reason for an abstraction layer is to shield users and applications from database changes. If you re-arrange tables, as long as you update the abstraction layer to point at the new table structure, your users and applications will never be the wiser. This means less broken code and easier migration of code when changes need to be made. We talk in great detail about the benefits of an abstraction layer and explain how to build one in Chapter 11, Creating an Abstraction Layer in SQL Server.

Summary

Data modeling is one of the most important tasks in the process of database-oriented application design. It's no trivial task to design a logical model and then create and implement a physical model. However, using a straightforward, standardized approach will help ensure that the resulting models are understandable, scalable, and accurate. Without a sound data model that is rooted in practical business requirements, the implementation of a relational database can be clumsy, inefficient, and extremely difficult to maintain. This book provides you with the background, processes, and guidance to effectively design and implement relational databases using Microsoft SQL Server 2008.

CHAPTER 2

ELEMENTS USED IN LOGICAL DATA MODELS

Imagine, for a moment, that you've been asked to build a house. One of the first questions you'd ask yourself is, "Do I have all the tools and materials I need?" To answer this question, you need a plan for building the house. The plan, a construction blueprint, will provide the information on the required tools and materials. So step 1 is to design a blueprint. If you've never done this before, you'll probably need to do some research to make sure you understand the overall process of designing the blueprint.

Like a blueprint, the logical database model you build will be the source for all the development of the physical database. Additionally, the logical model provides the high-level view of the database that can be presented to the key project stakeholders. For these reasons, the logical model is generally devoid of RDBMS specifics; instead it contains the key information that defines how the model, and eventually the database, will meet business requirements. But before you can begin to construct a logical model, it's important to understand all the tools that you will need.

In this chapter, we cover the objects and concepts related to the creation of a logical data model; you'll use these objects in Chapter 7 to start building the data model for Mountain View Music. For now, let's talk about entities and attributes and see how relationships are built between them.

Entities

Entities represent logical groupings of data and are the central concept that defines how data will be stored in the database. Common examples of entities are customers, orders, and products. Each entity, which should represent a single type of information, contains a collection of occurrences, or instances, of the entity. An **instance** of an entity is very similar to a

23

record in a table; you often see the terms *instance, record,* and *row* used interchangeably in data modeling. For our purposes, an instance occurs in an entity, and a row or record occurs in a physical table or view.

It is often tempting to think of entities as tables (there is often a one-to-one relationship between entities and tables), but it's important to remember that a logical entity may be represented by multiple physical tables or a single table may represent multiple entities. The purpose of an entity is to identify the various pieces of data whose attributes will be stored in the database.

One way to identify what qualifies as an entity is to think of entities as nouns. Entities tend to be objects that can be referenced as a noun; orders, cars, trumpets, and telephones are all real-world objects, and therefore they could be entities in a logical model. It's crucial to accurately identify the entities in your model, and it's a large part of the early design effort.

When choosing entities, you should first concern yourself primarily with the purpose of the entity and worry later about the attributes and other details (we talk about attributes in the next section). As part of the requirements gathering process (detailed in Chapter 5), interviews with users and other key stakeholders will reveal the common nouns used throughout the business, and therefore the key entities. Once you begin designing the model, you will use your notes to identify the entities you will need. You must take care to filter your notes and use only the information that is relevant to the current project.

Attributes

For each entity, there are specific pieces of information that describe it. These are the attributes of that entity. For example, suppose you need to create an entity to store all the pertinent information about hats. You name the entity Hats, and then you decide what information, or attributes, you need to store about hats: color, manufacturer, style, material, and the like. When you construct a model, you define a collection of attributes that stores the data for each entity. The definition of an attribute is made up of its name, description, purpose, and data type (which we talk about in the next section).

Be wary of attaching attributes to one entity that actually belong to another entity. One common mistake is to convert data from physical documentation (such as printed spreadsheets or manuals) into entities and attributes in a logical model. For example, it is common for customer information to be physically stored with order information. This practice could lead to the belief that customer data, such as address or phone number, is an attribute of an order. However, customer is an entity in and of itself, as is an order. Storing the customer attributes with the order entity would complicate storage and data retrieval and possibly lead to a design that is difficult to scale.

To model the attributes of your entities, you need to understand a few key concepts: data types, keys, domains, and values. In the next few sections we talk about these concepts in detail.

Data Types

In addition to the descriptive information, the definition of an attribute contains its data type. The **data type,** as the name implies, defines the type of information that is being stored in the attribute. For example, an attribute might be a string, a number, or a representation of a true or false condition.

In logical models, the specification of data types for attributes is not strictly required. Because a data type is a specification of the physical storage of data, sometimes you decide which data types to use when you create the physical model. However, there are benefits to specifying the data type during the logical modeling phase.

- Developers will have a guide to follow when building the physical model without having to research requirements (something that would be a duplication of effort).
- You will discover inconsistencies across multiple entities that contain the same type of data (e.g., phone numbers) before you create the physical model.
- To help facilitate the creation of the physical database, you can specify types that are specific to your RDBMS. You do this only when the target RDBMS is known before the data modeling process has begun.

Most available data modeling software allows you to select from the available data types of your RDBMS. Because we are working with Microsoft SQL Server, we reference its known data types. Now let's take a look at the various data types used in logical data modeling.

Alphanumeric

All data models contain **alphanumeric** data: any data in a string format, whether it is alphabetic characters or numbers (as long as they do not participate in mathematic operations). For example, names, addresses, and phone numbers are all string, or alphanumeric, types of data. The actual data types used for alphanumeric information are char, nchar, varchar, and nvarchar. As you can probably tell from the names, all these **char** data types store character data, such as letters, numbers, and special symbols.

For all these data types, you specify a length. Generally, the length is the total number of characters that the specified attribute can contain. If you are creating an attribute to contain abbreviations of U.S. state names, for example, you might choose to specify that the attribute is a char(2). This defines the attribute as an alphanumeric field that contains exactly two characters; char data types store exactly as many characters as they are defined to hold, no more and no less, no matter how much data is inserted.

You probably noticed that there are four kinds of char data types: two with a prefix of *var*, and two with an *n* prefix (one of which contains both prefixes). The *var* prefix means that a variable-length field is being specified. A **variable-length field** is defined as a field having no more than the number of characters specified in the length designation. To contrast char with varchar, specifying char(10) results in a field that contains ten characters, even if a specific instance of an entity has six characters in that specific attribute. The remaining four characters are padded. If the attribute is defined as a varchar(10), then there will be only six actual characters stored.

The *n* prefix specifies that the data is being stored in a Unicode format. **Unicode** is an international, platform-agnostic specification for the storage of character data. Using Unicode allows systems that work with characters from multiple languages to have a common storage format that can be read by any other system using the Unicode specification. If you need to store anything beyond basic ASCII text, you will need to have a Unicode data type.

The primary difference between Unicode and non-Unicode systems is that Unicode requires two bytes of physical storage for every character stored; non-Unicode systems generally use only one byte (sometimes more than one byte is needed when you start storing variable-length data). The problem with using only one byte for character storage is that one byte cannot adequately store certain character data, such as Japanese Kanji or Korean Hangul characters. Obviously, there are storage and performance trade-offs involved here, and they are covered in more depth in Chapter 3.

For now, keep in mind that Unicode may be required based on the character data you are storing.

Numeric

Numeric data is any data that needs to be stored as numerals. You can perform calculations on all the numeric data types. The general types of numeric data are integer, decimal, money, float, and real.

Integer data is stored as any whole number. It can store positive and negative numbers and generally comes in different sizes to accommodate the values needed. **Decimals** are numbers stored to the scale and precision specified. **Scale** in this case refers to the total number of numerals that are stored in the field, and **precision** refers to the number of those numerals stored to the right of the decimal point. **Money** is for the storage of currency and is accurate to different degrees based on the RDBMS being used. **Float** is an approximate number data type for use with floating-point data values. This is generally stored in scientific notation, and a designator can be specified with this data type that describes the number of bits that are used to store the number. **Real** is nearly identical to float; however, float can hold larger values.

As with the alphanumeric data types, the specific information regarding the physical storage of these data types is covered in Chapter 3.

Boolean

Boolean data types are data types that evaluate to TRUE, FALSE, or NULL. This is a logic-based data type; although the data being stored may be Boolean, the actual data type is bit. A **bit** data type stores a 1 or a 0 or NULL. This translates to true, false, and nothing, respectively. Boolean data types are used for logic-based evaluation of data and are often used as **switches** or **flags,** such as a designator to describe whether a vehicle is in or out of service.

BLOB and CLOB

Not all data stored in a database is in a human-readable format. For example, a database that houses product information for an online retailer not only holds the descriptive data about each product but may also store pictures of those products. The binary data that makes up the information about the image is not something that can be read as character data, but it can be stored in a database for retrieval by an application. This kind of data is generally called **binary large object** (BLOB) data.

This information is usually stored in SQL Server in one of the following data types: binary, varbinary, and image. As with the character data types, the existence of the *var* prefix denotes that the given attribute has variable-length values in the field. Therefore, **binary** defines a fixed-width attribute containing binary data, and **varbinary** specifies the *maximum* width of an attribute containing the binary data. The **image** data type simply specifies that the attribute contains variable-length binary data, similar to varbinary but with much greater storage potential.

Character data can also come in forms much longer than the standard alphanumeric data types described earlier. What if you need to store free-form text in a single field, such as raw resume information? Two **character large object** (CLOB) data types handle this information: **text** and **ntext.** These two data types are designed to handle large amounts of character data in a single field. Again, as with the other character data types, the *n* prefix indicates whether or not the data is being stored in the Unicode format. Choose these data types when you will have very large amounts of alphanumeric text stored as a single attribute in an entity.

Dates and Times

Nearly every data model in existence requires that some entities have attributes that are related to dates and times. Date and time data can be used to track the time a change was made to an order, the hire date for employees, or even the delivery time for products. Every RDBMS has its own implementations of date and time data types that store this data. For SQL Server 2008, there are now six data types for this purpose. This is an improvement over previous versions of SQL Server, which only had two data types: datetime and smalldatetime. Each data type stores date-oriented information; the difference is in the precision of the data and in the range of valid values.

First, let's look at the old standards. **Datetime** stores date and time data with 1 millisecond accuracy. For example, suppose you are inserting a record into a table that has a datetime column and the value inserted is

12/01/2006 6:00PM

The actual value that ends up in the database will be

```
12/01/2006 18:00:00.000
```

In contrast, **smalldatetime** would store the same value as

```
12/01/2006 18:00
```

Additionally, datetime stores any date between January 1, 1753, and December 31, 9999, whereas smalldatetime stores only values ranging from January 1, 1900, to June 6, 2079. It may seem strange that these date ranges where chosen; the reason lies in the storage requirements at the disk level and the way the actual data is manipulated internally in SQL Server.

As we mentioned, SQL Server 2008 provides four new date and time data types: date, time, datetime2, and datetimeoffset. These new data types store date and time data in more flexible ways than their predecessors. The **date** and **time** data types are the most straightforward; they store only the date portion or only the time portion of a given value. The **datetime2** data type, which is not cleverly named, is just like datetime except that you can specify a variable length for the precision of fractional seconds from 0 to 7. The **datetimeoffset** data type is similar to datetime except that in addition to the date and time, you specify an offset value. Your offset is not tied to any particular time zone, such as Greenwich Mean; instead you have to know the time zone you are using as the base from which to compare your values.

We have covered a lot of ground here, and again we refer you to Chapter 3 for a longer discussion of the reasons these data types store data the way they do.

It can be tempting, when you're designing a logical model, to quickly gloss over the chosen data types for each attribute. This practice can cause a number of design problems later in development. For one thing, most data modeling software can generate a physical design based on the logical model, so choosing inappropriate data types in the logical model can lead to confusion in the physical design, particularly when multiple developers are involved. Be sure to refer frequently to the business requirements to ensure that you are defining attributes based on the data that will be stored. This practice will also help when you're discussing the model with nontechnical stakeholders.

Primary and Foreign Keys

A **primary key** (PK) is an attribute or group of attributes that uniquely identifies each instance in an entity. The PK must always contain data; it cannot be null. Two examples of PKs are employee numbers and ISBNs. These numbers identify a single employee or a single book, respectively. When you're modeling, nearly every entity in your logical model should have a PK, even if you have to make one up using an arbitrary number.

If the data has no natural PK, it is often necessary to add a column for the sole purpose of acting as a PK. These kinds of PKs are called **surrogate keys.** Usually, this practice leans toward the physical implementation of a database instead of the logical model, but modeling a surrogate key will help you build relationships based on PKs. Such keys are often built on numbers that simply increase with each new record; in SQL Server these numbers are called **identities.**

Another modeling rule is to avoid using meaningful attributes for PKs. For example, social security numbers (SSNs) tend to be chosen as PKs for entities such as Employee. This is a bad choice for a number of reasons. First, SSNs are a poor choice because of privacy concerns. Many identity thefts occur because the thief had access to the victim's SSN. Second, although it is assumed that SSNs are unique, occasionally SSNs are reissued, so they are not always guaranteed to be unique.

Third, you may be dealing with international employees who have no SSN. It can be tempting to create a fake SSN in this case; but what if an international employee becomes a citizen and obtains a real SSN? If this happens, records in dependent entities could be tied to either the real SSN or the fake SSN. This not only complicates data retrieval but also could leave you with orphaned records.

In general, PKs should

- Be highly unlikely *ever* to change
- Be composed of attributes that will never be null
- Use meaningless data whenever possible

A close cousin to the PK is the **foreign key** (FK). FKs are attributes in a given entity that are actually based on a key, usually the PK, of another entity. Consider, for example, the Employee entity and a new entity called Vehicle. To know which vehicle the employee has been assigned, you must relate these two entities. In this case an FK exists on the Vehicle entity that points to the PK on the Employee entity. Simply put, an attribute in the

Vehicle table contains the Employee Number of the employee who has been assigned any given Vehicle. The actual attributes in the referencing entity can be either a key or a non-key attribute. That is, the FK in the referencing entity could be composed of the same attributes as its PK, or they could be a completely different set of attributes. This combination of PKs and FKs helps ensure consistency in the logical relationships between entities.

Domains

As you begin building a model, you'll likely notice that, within the context of the data you are working with, several entities share similar attributes. Often, application- or business-specific pieces of data must remain identical in all entities to ensure consistency. Status, Address, Phone Number, and Email are all examples of attributes that are likely to be identical in multiple entities. Rather than painstakingly create and maintain these attributes in each individual entity, you can use domains.

A **domain** is a definition of an attribute that is maintained as part of the logical model but outside a given entity. Whenever an attribute that is part of a domain is used, that domain is added to the entity. Generally, a data model does not provide a visual indication that a given attribute is actually part of a domain. Most data modeling tools provide a separate section or document, such as a **data dictionary,** to store domain information. Whenever there are changes to that domain, the related attributes in all entities are updated, as is the documentation that stores the domain information.

For example, consider the Phone Number attribute. Often, logical models are designed with localized phone numbers in mind; in the United States, this is generally notated with a three-digit area code, followed by a three-digit prefix, followed by a four-digit suffix (XXX-XXX-XXXX). If later in the design you decide to store international numbers as well, and if a phone number attribute has been added to multiple entities, it may be necessary to edit every entity to update the attribute. But if instead you create a Phone Number domain and add it to every entity that stores phone numbers, then updating the Phone Number domain to the new international format will update every entity in the model.

Thus, to reduce the chance that identical attributes will vary from entity to entity in a logical design, it's a good idea to use domains whenever possible. This practice will help enforce consistency and save design time, not only during the initial rollout but also throughout the lifetime of the database.

Single-Valued and Multivalued Attributes

All the attributes we've talked about thus far represent **single-valued at-tributes.** That is, for each unique occurrence of an item in an entity, there is only one value for each of the attributes. However, some attributes nat-urally have more than one potential value—for example, of the entity. These are known as **multivalued attributes.** Identifying them can be tricky, but handling them is fairly simple.

One common example of a potentially multivalued attribute is Phone Number. For example, when you're storing customer information, it's typ-ical to store at least one phone number; however, customers often have multiple phone numbers. Generally, you simply add multiple phone num-ber fields to the Customer entity, labeling them based either on arbitrary numbering (Phone1, Phone2, etc.), or on common usage (Home, Mobile, Office). This is a fine solution, but what do you do if you need to store mul-tiple office numbers for a single customer? This is a multivalued attribute: for one customer, you have multiple values for exactly the same attribute.

You don't want to store multiple records for a single customer merely to account for a different phone number; that defeats the purpose of using a relational database, because it introduces problems with data retrieval. Instead, you can create a new entity that holds phone numbers, with a relationship to the Customer entity (based on the primary key of the Customer), that allows you to identify all phone numbers for a single cus-tomer. The resultant entity might have multiple entries for each customer, but it stores only a unique identifier—CustomerID—and of course the phone number.

Using this kind of entity is the only way to resolve a true multivalued at-tribute problem. In the end, the physical implementation will benefit from this model, because it can take advantage of DBMS-specific search tech-niques to search the dependent entity separately from the primary entity.

Referential Integrity

One core aspect of a relational database is that data in one entity can ref-erence data in another entity. When this scenario occurs, there is almost al-ways a requirement that the relationship be maintained; the data must be consistent between the relevant entities. This concept, referred to as **ref-erential integrity** (RI), is usually enforced in the physical implementation using database objects such as constraints and keys. However, RI is documented in the logical model to ensure that business rules (as well as general data consistency) are followed within the database.

Suppose you are designing a database that stores information about the inventory of a library. In the logical model, you might have an Author entity, a Publisher entity, and a Title entity, among many others. Any given author may have more than one title in the inventory; in contrast, a title probably has been published by only one publisher, although one publisher may have published many titles. If users need to remove an author, simply deleting that author would leave at least one title orphaned. Similarly, deleting a publisher would leave at least one title orphaned.

Thus, you need to create definitions of the actions that are enforced when these updates occur. Referential integrity provides these definitions. With RI in place, you can specify that when an author is deleted, all related titles are also deleted. You could also specify that the addition of a title fails when there is no corresponding author. These might not be the most realistic examples, but they clearly illustrate the need to handle the interrelation between data in multiple entities.

You document referential integrity in the logical model via PK and FK relationships. Because each entity should have a key attribute that uniquely identifies each record the entity contains, you can relate key attributes in parent and child entities based on those keys. For example, take a look at Figure 2.1.

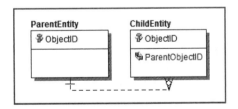

FIGURE 2.1   Primary key and foreign key

This example shows a basic relationship between two entities. After creating the relationship, you specify in its definition any constraints on data manipulation actions on the parent and child entities. For example, you can specify that any INSERT into the child entity should fail if there isn't already a parent instance with a matching primary key value. Similarly, you could specify that any DELETE statement against the parent entity fails unless all matching child entries are removed first. Table 2.1 describes the various options that can be set when an action takes place on a parent or child entity.

Table 2.1   Referential Integrity Options for a Relationship

Entity	Action	Available Actions
Parent entity	INSERT	None: Inserting a new instance has no effect on the child entity.
	UPDATE	None: This does not affect any records in the child entity, nor does it prevent updates that result in mismatched data between the parent and child entities.
		Restrict: Checks data in the primary key value of the parent entity against the foreign key value of the child entity. If the value does not match, prevents the update from taking place.
		Cascade: Duplicates changes in the primary key value of the parent entity to the foreign key value in the child entity.
		Null (Set Null): Similar to Restrict; if the value does not match, sets the child foreign key value to NULL and permits the update.
	DELETE	None: This does not affect any records in the child entity; it may result in orphaned instances in the child entity.
		Restrict: Checks data in the primary key value of the parent entity against the foreign key value of the child entity. If the value does not match, prevents the delete from taking place.
		Cascade: Deletes all matching entries from the child entity (in addition to the instance in the parent entity) based on the match of primary key value and foreign key value between the entities.
		Null (Set Null): Similar to Restrict; if the value does not match, sets the child foreign key value to NULL (or a specified default value) and permits the delete. This creates orphaned instances in the child entity.
Child entity	INSERT	None: Takes no action; enforces no restrictions.
		Restrict: Checks data in the primary key value of the parent entity against the foreign key value being inserted into the child entity. If the value does not have a match, prevents the insert from taking place.
	UPDATE	None: Takes no action; enforces no restrictions.
		Restrict: Checks data in the primary key value of the parent entity against the foreign key value being updated in the child entity. If the value does not have a match, prevents the update from taking place.
	DELETE	None: Allows any record to be deleted from the child entity.

Relationships

The term *relational database* implies the use of relationships, right? If you don't know how data is related, using a relational database to simply store information is no different from dumping all your receipts, paycheck stubs, and financial statements into a large trash bag for storage. Tax season would be a nightmare; sure, all the data is there, but how long would it take you to sort out the relevant information and file your taxes?

The real power of a relational database lies in the efficient and flexible storage and retrieval of data. Identifying and implementing the correct relationships in a logical model are two of the most critical design steps. To correctly identify relationships, it's important to understand all the possibilities, know how to recognize each one, and determine when each should be used.

Relationship Types

Logically, there are three distinct types of relationships between entities: one-to-one, one-to-many, and many-to-many. Each represents the way two entities logically relate to each other. It is important to remember that these relationships are *logical;* physical implementation is another step, as discussed later in Chapter 9.

One-to-One Relationships

Simply put, a **one-to-one** relationship between two entities is, as the name implies, a direct match between the entities. For each record in the first entity, there is one matching record in the second entity, no more and no less. For example, think of two people playing catch with a ball. There is one thrower and one receiver. There cannot be more than one thrower, and there cannot be more than one catcher (in terms of someone actually catching the ball).

Why would you choose to create a one-to-one relationship? Moreover, if there is only one matching record in each entity for a given piece of data, why wouldn't you combine the entities? Let's take a look at Figure 2.2.

For any given school, there is only one dean, and for any given dean, there is one school. In the example, all of the attributes of a Dean entity

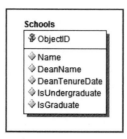

FIGURE 2.2 The Schools entity

are stored in the Schools entity. Although this approach consolidates all information in a single entity, it is not the most flexible solution. Whenever either a school *or* a dean is updated, the record must be retrieved and updated. Additionally, having a school with no dean (or a dean with no school) creates a half-empty record. Finally, it creates data retrieval problems. What if you want to write a report to return information about deans? You would have to retrieve school data as well. What if you want to track all the employees who work for the dean? In this case, you would have to relate the employees to the combined Deans/Schools entity instead of only to deans. Now consider Figure 2.3.

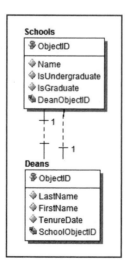

FIGURE 2.3 The Schools and Deans entities

In this example, there are two entities: Schools and Deans. Each entity has the attributes that are specific to those objects. Additionally, there is a reference in the Deans entity that notes which school the selected dean manages, and there is a reference in the Schools entity that notes the dean for the selected school. This design helps with flexibility, because Deans and Schools are managed separately. However, you can see that there is a one-to-one relationship, and you can constrain the data appropriately to avoid inconsistent or erroneous data.

One-to-Many Relationships

In **one-to-many** relationships, the most common type, a single record in the first entity has zero or more matching records in the second entity. There are numerous examples of this type of relationship, most notably in the header-to-detail scenario. Often, for example, orders are stored with a **header** record in one entity and a set of **detail** records in a second entity. This arrangement allows one order to have many line items without storing multiple records containing the high-level information for that order (such as order date, customer, etc.).

To continue our Schools and Deans scenario, what if a university decides to implement a policy whereby each school has more than one dean? This instantly creates a one-to-many relationship between Schools and Deans, as shown in Figure 2.4.

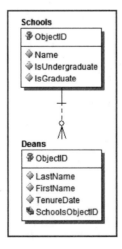

FIGURE 2.4 Schools and Deans entities, a one-to-many relationship

You can see that there is a relationship between the entities such that you *might* have more than one dean for each school. This relationship is inherently scalable, because the separate entities can be updated and managed independently.

Many-to-Many Relationships

Of the logical relationships, many-to-many relationships, also called non-specific relationships, are the most difficult concept, and possibly the most difficult to design. To simplify, in a **many-to-many** relationship the objects in an entity can be related to more than one object in a secondary entity, and the secondary objects can be related to more than one object in the initial entity. Imagine auto parts, specifically something simple like seats. Any given vehicle probably has more than one type of seat, perhaps two bucket seats for the front passenger and driver and a single bench seat in the rear. However, automakers almost always reuse seats in multiple models of vehicles. So, as entities, Seats can be in multiple Vehicles, and Vehicles can have multiple Seats.

Back to our university. What if the decision is made that a single dean can manage multiple schools or even that one school can have more than one dean? In Figure 2.5, we've arranged the Schools and Deans entities so that either entity can have multiple links to the other entity.

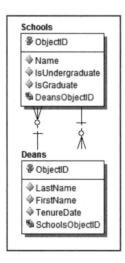

FIGURE 2.5   The Schools and Deans entities, many-to-many relationship

From a conceptual standpoint, all relationships exist between exactly two entities. Logically, we have a relationship between Schools and Deans. Technically, you could leave the notation with these two entities showing that there are two one-to-many relationships, one in each direction. Alternatively, you can show a single relationship that shows a "many" at both ends. However, from a practical standpoint, it may be easier to use a third entity to show the relationship, as shown in Figure 2.6.

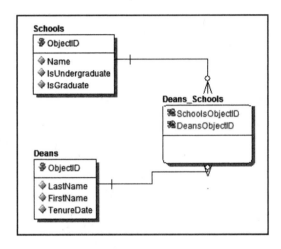

FIGURE 2.6 The Schools and Deans entities, many-to-many relationship with third entity

Arguably, this is a violation of the ideal that a logical model contain no elements of physical implementation. The use of a third entity, whereby we associate Deans and Schools by ID, duplicates the physical implementation method for many-to-many relationships. Physically, it is impossible to model this relationship without using a third table, sometimes called a **junction** or **join** table. So using it in the model may not conform to strict logical modeling guidelines; however, adding it in the logical model can help remind you why the relationship is there, as well as aid future modelers in understanding the relationship in the logical model.

Additionally, using the third entity can let you use additional attributes that actually describe each instance of the relationship. For example, you can use the Deans_Schools entity to note how long a specific dean has been in charge of a given school. If you have multiple combinations, the length of tenure for a dean at a given school may vary, so this attribute could be very useful.

Many-to-many relationships are widely used, but you should approach them with caution and carefully document them to ensure that there is no confusion as you move forward with the physical implementation.

Relationship Options

Now that you know about the various types of relationships, we need to cover some options that can vary from relationship to relationship within each type. These options will help you further refine the behavior of each relationship.

Identifying versus Non-Identifying Relationships

When the primary key of a child entity requires that the primary key of its parent entity be included, then the relationship between the entities is said to be **identifying.** This is because the child entity's unique attribute relies on the parent entity's unique attribute to correctly identify the corresponding instance. If this requirement is not in place, the relationship is defined as **non-identifying.**

In an identifying relationship, the primary key from the parent entity is literally one of the attributes in the child entity's primary key. Therefore, the foreign key in the child entity is actually also a part of, or the entirety of, its primary key. In a non-identifying relationship, the primary key from the parent entity is simply a non-key attribute in the child entity.

Few relationships are identifying relationships, because most child entities can be referenced independently of the parent entity. Many-to-many relationships often use identifying relationships, because the additional entity ties together the primary key values of the parent and child entities. For example, as shown earlier in Figure 2.6, the Deans_Schools entity shows SchoolsObjectID and DeansObjectID as the attributes in its primary key.

Note that this is always the case with many-to-many relationships; the join table's primary key is made up of the other tables' primary keys. Because the primary key attributes from the parent and child primary keys are present, you can tell visually that these are identifying relationships.

Non-identifying relationships, being far more prevalent, can be recognized when the primary key attribute of the parent entity is a non-key attribute in the child entity. Unless you have a specific requirement for an identifying relationship, most of your relationships will be non-identifying.

Optional versus Mandatory Relationships

Every relationship in a database needs to be defined as either optional or mandatory. It helps to think of **mandatory** relationships as "must have" relationships, and **optional** relationships as "may have" relationships. For example, if you have an Employee entity and an Office entity, an employee "must have" a home office. The relationship between these two entities defines the home office for an employee. In this case, we have a non-identifying relationship, and because we can't have a null value for the foreign key reference to the Office entity in the Employee entity, this relationship is also described as being mandatory. The relationship defines that every employee has a single home office, and although an employee may work in other offices, only one office is considered his or her home office.

Now consider a business that assigns vehicles to some employees. That business practice is reflected in the data model as an Employee entity and a Vehicle entity, with a relationship between them. You can see that an employee "may have" a vehicle, thus fitting our definition of an optional relationship.

Cardinality

In every relationship we've discussed, we've specified only the general type of relationship—one-to-one, one-to-many, and many-to-many. In each case, the description of the relationship is a specification of the number of records in a parent entity in relation to the number of records in a child entity. To more clearly model the actual relation of the data, you can be more specific when defining these relationships. What you are specifying is the **cardinality** of the relationship.

With a one-to-one relationship, the cardinality is implied. You are clearly stating that for every one record in the parent entity, there might be one record in the child entity. It would be more specific to say that there is "zero or one record in the child entity for every one record in the parent entity." But if you mean to say that there absolutely must be a record in each entity, then the relationship's cardinality would be "one record in the child entity for every one record in the parent entity." The cardinality of a one-to-one relationship is notated as [1:1].

In a one-to-many relationship, notated as [1:M], the cardinality implied is "one or more records in the child entity for every one record in the parent entity." But if the intent is that there doesn't need to be a record in the child entity, then the alternative definition is "zero or more records in the child entity for every one record in the parent entity." In most relationships, the "zero or more to many" interpretation is correct, so be sure to specify and document the alternative definition if it's used in your model.

A many-to-many relationship could be defined as "zero or more to zero or more records." In this case, the "zero or more to zero or more records" cardinality is almost always implied, although you could specify that there must be at least one record in each entity. In this case, show a many-to-many as [M:M].

In some data modeling software, you can specify that there be an explicit cardinality, such as "eight records in the child entity for every one record in the parent entity." For example, you may want to model managers to direct reports (business lingo for "people who report directly to that manager"). The company may state that to be a manager you must have at least four and no more than twenty direct reports. In this example, the cardinality would be "at least four and no more than twenty to one." Be sure to document this type of cardinality if your business requirements dictate it, because most people will assume the cardinality based on the definitions given here.

Using Subtypes and Supertypes

When you are determining the entities to be used in a data model, occasionally you may discover a single entity that seems to consist of a number of other complete entities. When this happens, it can be confusing when you try to determine which attributes belong to which entities and how to relate them. The answer to this dilemma is to use a supertype.

Supertypes and Subtypes Defined

A **supertype** is an entity that has multiple child entities, known as **subtypes,** which describe variations of the same type of entity. A collection of a supertype with its subtypes is sometimes referred to as a **subtype cluster.** These most commonly occur when you're dealing with categories of specific things, as shown in the simple example in Figure 2.7.

Assume that we're tracking information about broadband products. In this example, BroadBand is an entity, with appropriate attributes and a primary key. However, we want to divide the types of broadband into their

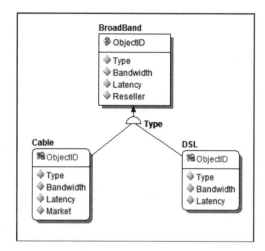

FIGURE 2.7   Simple subtype cluster

own entities, because we offer cable broadband to residential and commercial customers, and we offer DSL only to residential customers. Both cable and DSL *could* be stand-alone entities, but we wouldn't be seeing the entire relationship. There are attributes in the BroadBand entity that we don't track in each of the child entities, and attributes in the child entities that we don't track in the BroadBand entity. And we need to leave the design open to add more broadband types in the future without having to alter existing records.

To solve this problem, we designate BroadBand as a supertype, and the Cable and DSL entities as subtypes. To do this, first we create the child entities with their specific attributes, *without* a primary key. Then we create a required identifying relationship between the parent entity and each child entity; this relationship designates that the primary key from BroadBand be the primary key for each child. Finally, we choose a **discriminator,** which is an attribute in the parent entity whose value determines which subtype a given record belongs to; the discriminator can be a key or non-key attribute. In this case, our discriminator is Type, which contains a string value of either "DSL" or "Cable."

If a subtype cluster contains all possible subtypes for the supertype for which they are defined, the subtype cluster is said to be **complete.** Alternatively, if it includes only some of the possible subtypes, the cluster is **incomplete.** The designation is mostly a documentation concern, but as with most design considerations, documenting the specifics can be helpful in the future for other developers working from this model.

Generally, physical implementation of a subtype cluster must be determined on a case-by-case basis. Subtype clusters can be implemented in a one-to-one relationship of entities to tables, or some combination of tables and relationships. The most important aspects to remember are the propagation of the primary key among all the entities, as well as constraints on the discriminator to ensure that all the records end up in the correct tables.

When to Use Subtype Clusters

Inevitably, every data model contains entities that contain attributes that hold information about a small subset of the records in the entity. Whenever you find this happening in a data model, investigate further to see whether these attributes would be good candidates for a subtype cluster. However, be careful not to try to force a supertype/subtype relationship; doing so leads to a confusing data model that has more entities than necessary. Additionally, the existence of superfluous subtype clusters can lead to confusion in the physical implementation, often resulting in unnecessary tables and constraints. This could ultimately lead to poor performance and the inability to maintain the database efficiently.

Subtype clusters can be a very powerful tool to build flexibility into a data model. Because modeling data in this type of generalized hierarchy can allow future modifications without the need to change existing entities, searching for logical relationships where you can use subtype clusters should be considered time well spent.

Summary

In this chapter, we've covered the tools used to build a logical data model. Every data model consists of the objects necessary to describe the data being stored, definitions of how individual pieces of data are related to one another, and any constraints that exist on that data.

Now that we've covered the building blocks of the logical data model, Chapter 3 will help you bridge the gap between the logical objects and the physical implementation. Later you will use this theory to build a data model for the Mountain View Music company.

PHYSICAL ELEMENTS OF DATA MODELS

Now that you have a grasp of the logical elements used to construct a data model, let's look at the physical elements. These are the objects that you use to build the database. Most of the objects you build into your physical model are based on objects you created in the logical model. Many physical elements are the same no matter which RDBMS you are using, but we look at all the elements available in SQL Server 2008. It is important to know SQL Server's capabilities so that you can build your model with them in mind.

In this chapter, we cover all the physical SQL Server objects in detail and walk you through how to use each type of object in your physical model. You will use these elements later in Chapter 9.

Physical Storage

First, we'll start with the objects that allow you to store data in your database. You'll build everything else on these objects. Specifically, these are tables, views, and data types.

Tables

Tables are the building blocks on which relational databases are built. Underneath everything else, all data in your database ends up in a table. Tables are made up of rows and columns. Like a single instance in an entity, each row stores information pertaining to a single record. For example, in an employee table, each row would store the information for a single employee.

The columns in the table store information about the rows in the table. The FirstName column in the Employee table would store the first names of all the employees. Columns map to attributes from your logical model, and, like the logical model, each column has a data type assigned. Later in this chapter we look at the SQL Server data types in detail.

When you add data to a table, each column must either contain data (even if it is an empty string) or specify a NULL value, NULL being the complete absence of data. Additionally, you can specify that each column have a default value. The **default value** is used if you add data without specifying a value for that column. A default can be a fixed value, such as always setting a numeric column to the value of 12, or it can be a function that returns a value of the appropriate data type. If you do not have a default value specified and you insert data without specifying a value for a column, SQL Server attempts to insert a NULL value. If the column does not allow NULL values, your insert will fail.

You can think of a table as a single spreadsheet in an application such as Microsoft Excel. In fact, an Excel spreadsheet is a table, but Excel is not a relational database management system. A database is really nothing more than a collection of tables that store information. Sure, there are many other objects in a database, but without tables you would not have any data. Using Transact-SQL, also known as T-SQL, you can manipulate the data in a table. The four basic Data Manipulation Language (DML) statements are defined as follows:

- SELECT: Allows users to retrieve data in a table or tables
- INSERT: Allows users to add data to a table
- UPDATE: Allows users to change data in a table
- DELETE: Allows users to remove data from a table

How SQL Server Stores Tables

In addition to understanding what tables are, it's important that you understand how SQL Server stores them; the type of data your columns store will dictate how the table is stored on disk, and this can directly affect the performance of your database. Everything in SQL Server is stored on *pages*. **Pages** are 8K contiguous allocations of information on the disk, and there are different kinds of pages depending on what is on the page. For our purposes, we will focus on **data pages**: pages that store table data. Each row you add to a table is stored on a page, and depending on the size of the data in the row, the row can be stored either on a page with other rows, or on its own page or pages.

Before SQL Server 2005, data and overhead for a single row could not exceed 8,060 bytes (8K). This was a hard limit that you had to account for when designing tables. In SQL Server 2005, this limit has been overcome, in a manner of speaking. Now, if your row exceeds 8,060 bytes, SQL Server moves one or more of your variable-length columns onto a new page and leaves a 24-byte pointer in its place. This does not mean that you have an unlimited row size, nor should you make all your rows bigger than 8,060 bytes. Why not? First, notice that we said SQL Server will move *variable-length* columns. This means that you are still limited to 8,060 bytes of *fixed-length* columns. Additionally, you are still limited to 8K on your primary data page for the row. Remember the 24-byte pointer we mentioned? In theory you are limited to around 335 pointers on the main page. As ridiculous as a 336-column varchar(8000) table may sound, we have seen far stranger.

If SQL Server manages all this behind the scenes, why should you care? Here's why. Although SQL Server moves the variable-length fields to new pages after you exceed the 8K limit, the result is akin to a fragmented hard drive. You now have chunks of data that need to be assembled when accessed, and this adds processing time. As a data modeler you should always try to keep your rows smaller than the 8K limit for performance reasons. There are a few exceptions to this rule, and we look at them more closely later in this chapter when we discuss data types. Keep in mind that there is a lot more complexity in the way SQL Server handles storage and pages than we cover here, but your data model can't affect the other variables as much as it can affect table size.

Views

Views are simply stored T-SQL that uses SELECT statements to display data from one or more tables. The tables referenced by views are often referred to as the view's **base tables.** Views, as the name implies, allow you to create various pictures of the underlying information. You can reference as many or as few columns from each base table as you need to make your views. This capability allows you to slice up data and display only relevant information.

You access views in almost the same way that you access tables. All the basic DML statements work against views in the same way they do on tables, with a few exceptions. If you have a view that references more than one base table, you can use only INSERT, UPDATE, or DELETE statements that reference columns from one base table. For example, let's assume that we have a view that returns customer data from two tables. One table stores the customer's information, and the other holds the address data for that customer. The definition of the customer_address view is as follows:

```
CREATE VIEW customer_address
AS
SELECT customer.first_name,
     customer.last_name,
     customer.phone,
     address.address_line1,
     address.city,
     address.state,
     address.zip
FROM customer
JOIN address
     ON address.customer_id = customer.customer_id
WHERE address.type = 'home'
```

You can perform INSERT, UPDATE, and DELETE operations against the customer_address view as long as you reference only the customer table *or* the address table.

You may be asking yourself, "Why would I use a view instead of just referencing the tables directly?" There are several reasons to use views in your database. First, you can use a view to obscure the complexity of the underlying tables. If you have a single view that displays customer and address information, developers or end users can access the information they need from the view instead of needing to go to both tables. This technique eliminates the need for users to understand the entire database; they can focus on a single object. You gain an exponential benefit when you start working with many base tables in a single view.

Using views also allows you to change the tables or the location where the data is stored without affecting users. In the end, as long as you update the view definition so that it accommodates the table changes you made, your users will never need to know that there was a change. You can also use views to better manage security. If you have users who need to see some employee data but not sensitive data such as social security numbers or salary, you can build a view that displays only the information they need.

Finally, consider how using views can save you time when querying your database. Every time you run T-SQL code, SQL Server must first compile the code. This transforms the human-readable SELECT statement into a form that the SQL Server engine can understand, and the resulting code is an **execution plan.** Execution plans for running views are stored in SQL Server, and the T-SQL code behind them is compiled. This process takes time, but with views, the compilation is done only when the view is created. This saves you processing each time you call the view. The first time a view is called, SQL Server figures out the best way to retrieve the data from the base tables, given the table structure and the indexes in place. This execution plan is cached and reused the next time the view is called.

In our humble opinion, views are probably the most underused feature in SQL Server. For some reason, people tend to avoid the use of views or use them in inefficient ways. In Chapter 11 we look at some of the most beneficial uses for views.

Data Types

As mentioned earlier, every column in each of your tables must be configured to store a specific type of data. You do this by associating a data type with the column. Data types are what you use to specify the type, length, precision, and scale of data that can be stored in the column. SQL Server 2008 gives you several general categories of data types, with each category containing specific data types. Many of these data types are similar to the types we looked at in Chapter 2. In this section, we look at each of the SQL Server data types and talk about how the SQL Server engine handles and stores them.

When you build your model, it is important to understand how much space each data type requires. The difference between a data type that needs 2 bytes versus one that requires 4 bytes may seem insignificant, but when you multiply the extra 2 bytes over millions or billions of rows, you could end up needing tens or hundreds of gigabytes of additional storage.

SQL Server 2008 has functionality (parts of which were introduced in SQL Server 2005 Service Pack 2) that allows the SQL Server storage engine to compress data at the row and page levels. However, this functionality is limited to the Enterprise Edition and is, in general, more of an administrative concern. Your estimate of data storage requirements, which is based on the numbers we talk about here, should be limited to the uncompressed storage requirements. Enabling data compression in a database is something that a database administrator will work on with the database developer after the database has been built. With that said, let's look at the data types available in SQL Server 2008.

Numeric Data Types

Our databases need to store many kinds of numbers that we use day to day. Each of these numbers is unique and requires us to store varying pieces of data. These differences in numbers and requirements dictate that SQL Server be able to support 11 numeric data types. Following is a review of all the numeric data types available in SQL Server. Also, Table 3.1 shows the specifications on each numeric data type.

Table 3.1   Numeric Data Type Specifications

Data Type	Value Range	Storage
bigint	–9,223,372,036,854,775,808 through 9,223,372,036,854,775,807	8 bytes
bit	0 or 1	1 byte (minimum)
decimal	Depends on precision and scale	5–17 bytes
float	–1.79E+308 through –2.23E–308, 0, and 2.23E–308 through 1.79E+308	4 or 8 bytes
int	–2,147,483,648 to 2,147,483,647	4 bytes
money	–922,337,203,685,477.5808 to 922,337,203,685,477.5807	8 bytes
numeric	Depends on precision and scale	5–17 bytes
real	–3.40E+38 to –1.18E–38, 0, and 1.18E–38 to 3.40E+38	4 bytes
smallint	–32,768 to 32,767	2 bytes
smallmoney	–214,748.3648 to 214,748.3647	4 bytes
tinyint	0 to 255	1 byte

Int

The int data type is used to store whole integer numbers. Int does not store any detail to the right of the decimal point, and any number with decimal data is rounded off to a whole number. Numbers stored in this type must be in the range of –2,147,483,648 through 2,147,483,647, and each piece of int data requires 4 bytes to store on disk.

Bigint

Bigint is just what it sounds like: a big integer number. When you need larger numbers than supported by the int data type, you can use bigint. Using bigint expands your range from the paltry 2 billion of an int and allows you to store numbers from approximately negative 9 quintillion all the way to 9 quintillion. (A quintillion is a 1 followed by 18 zeros.) Bigger numbers require more storage; bigint data requires 8 bytes.

Smallint

On the other side of the int data type, we have smallint. Smallint can hold numbers from –32,768 through 32,767 and requires only 2 bytes of storage.

Tinyint

Rounding out the int family of data types is the tinyint. Requiring only 1 byte of storage and capable of storing numbers from 0 through 255, tinyint is perfect for status columns. Note that tinyint is the only int data type that cannot store negative numbers.

Bit

The bit data type is the SQL Server equivalent of a flag or a Boolean. The only valid values are 0, 1, or NULL, making the bit data type perfect for storing on or off, yes or no, or true or false. Bit storage is a bit more complex (pardon the pun). Storing a 1 or a 0 requires only 1 bit on disk, but the minimum storage for bit data is 1 byte. For any given table, the bit columns are lumped together for storage. This means that when you have 1-bit to 8-bit columns they collectively take up 1 byte. When you have 9- to 16-bit columns, they take up 2 bytes, and so on. SQL Server implicitly converts the strings TRUE and FALSE to bit data of 1 and 0, respectively.

Decimal and Numeric

In SQL Server 2008, the decimal and numeric data types are exactly the same. Previous versions of SQL Server do not have a numeric data type; it was added in SQL Server 2005 so that the terminology would fall in line with other RDBMS software. Both these data types hold numbers complete with detail to the right of the decimal. When using decimal or numeric, you can specify a precision and a scale. Precision sets the total number of digits that can be stored in the number. Precision can be set to any value from 1 through 38, allowing decimal numbers to contain 1 through 38 digits. Scale specifies how many of the total digits can be stored to the right of the decimal point. Scale can be any number from 0 to the precision you have set. For example, the number 234.67 has a precision of 5 and a scale of 2. The storage requirements for decimal and numeric vary depending on the precision. Table 3.2 shows the storage requirements based on precision.

Table 3.2   Decimal and Numeric Storage Requirements

Precision	Storage
1 through 9	5 bytes
10 through 19	9 bytes
20 through 28	13 bytes
29 through 38	17 bytes

Money and Smallmoney

Both the money and the smallmoney data types store monetary values to four decimal places. The only difference in these two types is that money can store values from about –922 trillion through 922 trillion and requires 8 bytes of storage, whereas smallmoney holds only values of –214,748.3648 through 214,748.3647 and requires only 4 bytes of storage. Functionally, these types are similar to decimal and numeric, but money and smallmoney also store a currency symbol such as $ (dollar), ¥ (yen), or £ (pound).

Float and Real

Both float and real fall into the category of approximate numbers. Each holds values in scientific notation, which inherently causes data loss because of a lack of precision. If you don't remember your high school chemistry class, we briefly explain scientific notation. You basically store a small subset of the value, followed by a designation of how many decimal places should precede or follow the value. So instead of storing 1,234,467,890 you can store it as 1.23E+9. This says that the decimal in 1.23 should be moved 9 places to the right to determine the actual number. As you can see, you lose a lot of detail when you store the number in this way. The original number (1,234,467,890) becomes 1,230,000,000 when converted to scientific notation and back.

Now back to the data types. Float and real store numbers in scientific notation; the only difference is the range of values and storage requirements for each. See Table 3.1 for the range of values for these types. Real requires 4 bytes of storage and has a fixed precision of 7. With float data, you can specify the precision or the total number of digits, from 1 through 53. The storage requirement varies from 4 bytes (when the precision is less than 25) to 8 bytes (when the precision is 25 through 53).

Date and Time Data Types

When you need to store a date or time value, SQL Server provides you with six data types. Knowing which type to use is important, because each date and time data type provides a slightly different level of accuracy, and that can make a huge difference when you're calculating exact times, as well as durations. Let's look at each in turn.

Datetime and Smalldatetime

The datetime and smalldatetime data types can store date and time data in a variety of formats; the difference is the range of values that each can store. Datetime can hold values from January 1, 1753, through December 31, 9999, and can be accurate to 3.33 milliseconds. In contrast, smalldatetime can store dates only from January 01, 1900, through June 6, 2079, and is accurate only to 1 minute. For storage, datetime requires 8 bytes, and smalldatetime needs only 4 bytes.

Date and Time

New in SQL Server 2008 are data types that split out the date portion and the time portion of a traditional date and time data type. Literally, as the names imply, these two data types account for either the date portion (month, day, and year), or the time portion (hours, minutes, seconds, and nanoseconds). Thus, if needed, you can store only one portion or the other in a column.

The range of valid values for the date data type are the same as for the datetime data type, meaning that date can hold values from January 1, 1753, through December 31, 9999. From a storage standpoint, date requires only 3 bytes of space, with a character length of 10.

The time data type holds values 00:00:00.0000000 through 23:59:59.9999999 and can hold from 8 characters (hh:mm:ss) to 16 characters (hh:mm:ss:*nnnnnnn*), where *n* represents fractional seconds. For example, 13:45:25.5 literally means that it is 1:45:25 and one-half second p.m. You can specify the scale of the time data type from 0 to 7 to designate how many digits you can use for fractional seconds. At its maximum, the time data type requires 5 bytes of storage.

Datetime2

Another new data type in SQL Server 2008 is the datetime2 data type. This is very similar to the original datetime data type, except that datetime2 incorporates the precision and scale options of the time data type. You can specify the scale from 0 to 7, depending on how you want to divide and store the seconds. Storage for this data type is fixed at 8 bytes, assuming a precision of 7.

Datetimeoffset

The final SQL Server 2008 date and time data type addition is datetime-offset. This is a standard date and time data type, similar to datetime2 (because it can store the precision). Additionally, datetimeoffset can store a plus or minus 14-hour offset. It is useful in applications where you want to store a date and a time along with a relative offset, such as when you're working with multiple time zones. The storage requirement for datetime-offset is 10 bytes.

String Data Types

When it comes to storing string or character data, the choice and variations are complex. Whether you need to store a single letter or the entire text of *War and Peace,* SQL Server has a string data type for you. Fortunately, once you understand the difference between the available string data types, choosing the correct one is straightforward.

Char and Varchar

Char and varchar are probably the most used of the string data types. Each stores standard, non-Unicode text data. The differences between the two lie mostly in the storage of the data. In each case, you must specify a length when defining a column as char or varchar. The length sets the limit on the number of characters the column can hold.

Here's the kicker: The char data type always requires the same number of bytes for storage as you have specified for the length. If you have a char(20), it will always require 20 bytes of storage, even if you store only a 5-character word in the column. With a varchar, the storage is always the actual number of characters you have stored plus 2 bytes. So a varchar(20) with a 5-character word will take up 7 bytes, with the extra 2 bytes holding a size reference for SQL Server. Each type can have a length of as many as 8,000 characters.

When do you use one over the other? The rule of thumb is to use char when all the data will be close to the same length, and use varchar when the data will vary a great deal. Following this rule should make for optimum storage.

Another tip is to avoid using varchar for short columns. We have seen databases use varchar(2) columns, and the result is wasted space. Let's assume you have 100 rows in your table and the table contains a varchar(2) column. Assuming all the columns are NULL, you still need to store the 2 bytes of overhead, so without storing any data you have already taken up as much space as you would using char(2).

One other special function of varchar is the **max** length option. When you specify max as the length, your varchar column can store as much as $2^{31}-1$ bytes of data, which is about 2 trillion bytes, or approximately 2GB of string data. If you don't think that's a lot, open your favorite text editor and start typing until you reach a 2GB file. Go on, we'll wait. It's a lot of information to cram into a single column. Varchar(max) was added to SQL Server in the 2005 release and was meant to replace the text data type from previous versions of SQL Server.

Nchar and Nvarchar

The nchar and nvarchar data types work in much the same way as the char and varchar data types, except that the *n* versions store Unicode data. Unicode is most often used when you need to store non-English language strings that require special characters such as the Greek letter beta (β). Because Unicode data is a bit more complex, it requires 2 bytes for each character, and thus an nchar requires double the length in bytes for storage, and nvarchar requires double the actual number of characters plus the obligatory 2 bytes of overhead.

From our earlier discussion, recall that SQL Server stores tables in 8,060-byte pages. Well, a single column cannot span a page, so some simple math tells us that when using these Unicode data types, you will reach 8,000 bytes when you have a length of 4,000. In fact, that is the limit for the nchar and nvarchar data types. Again, you can specify nvarchar(max), which in SQL Server 2005 replaced the old ntext data type.

Binary and Varbinary

Binary and varbinary function in exactly the same way as char and varchar. The only difference is that these data types hold binary information such as files or images. As before, varbinary(max) replaces the old image data type. In addition, SQL Server 2008 allows you to specify the filestream attribute of a varbinary(max) column, which switches the storage of the BLOB. Instead of being stored as a separate file on the file system, it is stored in SQL Server pages on disk.

Text, Ntext, and Image

As mentioned earlier, the text, ntext, and image data types have been replaced with the max length functionality of varchar, nvarchar, and varbinary, respectively. However, if you are running on an older version or upgrading to SQL Server 2005 or SQL Server 2008, you may still need these data types. The text data type holds about 2GB of string data, and ntext holds about 1GB of Unicode string data. Image is a variable-length binary field and can hold any binary data, up to about 2GB. When using these data types, you must use certain functions to write, update, and read to the columns; you cannot just do a simple update. Keep in mind that these three data types have been replaced, and Microsoft will likely remove them from future releases of SQL Server.

Other Data Types

In addition to the standard numeric and string data types, SQL Server 2008 provides several other useful data types. These additional types allow you to store XML data, globally unique identifiers (GUIDs), hierarchical identities, and spatial data types. There is also a new file storage data type that we'll talk about shortly.

Sql_variant

A column defined as sql_variant can store most any data that can be stored in the other SQL Server data types. The only data you cannot put into a sql_variant are text, ntext, image, xml, timestamp, or the max length data types. Using sql_variant you can store various data types in the same column of a table. As you will read in Chapter 4, this is not the best practice from a modeling standpoint. That said, there are some good uses for sql_variant, such as building a staging table when you're loading less-than-perfect data from other sources. The storage requirement for a sql_variant depends on the type of data you put in the column.

Timestamp

This data type has a somewhat misleading name. In fact timestamp does not store any sort of time or date information. Instead, timestamp is a binary number that is automatically incremented each time an insert or update happens to a table containing the timestamp column. The counter for the timestamp column is stored for the entire database, and each table is allowed to have only a single timestamp column. In this way, you can tell in what order various operations have happened in your database, or you can implement row versioning.

We once used timestamp to archive a large database. Each night we would run a job to grab all the rows from all the tables where the timestamp was greater than the last row copied the night before. Timestamps require 8 bytes of storage, and remember, 8 bytes can add up fast if you add timestamps to all your tables.

Uniqueidentifier

The uniqueidentifier data type is probably one of the most interesting data types available, and it is the topic of much debate. Basically, a uniqueidentifier column holds a GUID—a string of 32 random characters in blocks separated by hyphens. For example, the following is a valid GUID:

```
45E8F437-670D-4409-93CB-F9424A40D6EE
```

Why would you use a uniqueidentifier column? First, when you generate a GUID, it will be a completely unique value and no other GUID in the world will share the same string. This means that you can use GUIDs as PKs on your tables if you will be moving data between databases. This technique prevents duplicate PKs when you actually copy data.

When you're using uniqueidentifier columns, keep in mind a couple of things. First, they are pretty big, requiring 16 bytes of storage. Second, unlike timestamps or identity columns (see the section on primary keys later in this chapter), a uniqueidentifier does not automatically have a new GUID assigned when data is inserted. You must use the NEWID function to generate a new GUID when you insert data. You can also make the default value for the column NEWID(). In this way, you need not specify anything for the uniqueidentifier column; SQL Server will insert the GUID for you.

Xml

The xml data type is a bit outside the scope of this book, but we'll say a few words about it. Using the xml data type, SQL Server can hold Extensible Markup Language (XML) data in a column. Additionally, you can bind an XML schema to the column to constrain the XML data being stored. Like the max data types, the xml data type is limited to 2GB of storage.

Table

A table data type can store the result set of T-SQL statements for processing later. The data is stored in a similar fashion to the way an entire table is stored. It is important to note that the table data type *cannot* be used on columns; it can be used only in variables in T-SQL code. Programming in SQL Server is beyond the scope of this book, but the table data type plays an important role in user-defined functions, which we discuss shortly.

Table variables behave in the same way as base tables. They contain columns and can have check constraints, unique constraints, and primary keys. As with base tables, a table variable can be used in SELECT, INSERT, UPDATE, and DELETE statements. Like other local variables, table variables exist in the scope of the calling function and are cleaned up when the calling module finishes executing. To use table variables, you declare them like any other variable and provide a standard table definition to the declaration.

Hierarchyid

The hierarchyid data type is a system-provided data type that allows you to store hierarchical data, such as organizational data, project tasks, or file system–style data in a relational database table. Whenever you have self-referencing data in a tiered format, hierarchyid allows you to store and query the data more efficiently. The actual data in a hierarchyid is represented as a series of slashes and numerical designations. This is a specialized data type and is used only in very specific instances.

Spatial Data Types

SQL Server 2008 also introduces the spatial data types for relational storage. The first of the two new data types is geometry, which allows you to store planar data about physical locations (distances, vectors, etc.). The other data type, geography, allows you to store round earth data such as latitude and longitude coordinates. Although this is oversimplifying, these data types allow you to store information that can help you determine the distance between locations and ways to navigate between them.

User-Defined Data Types

In addition to the data types we have described, SQL Server allows you to create user-defined data types. With **user-defined data types,** you can create standard columns for use in your tables. When defining user-defined data types, you still must use the standard data types that we have described here as a base. A user-defined data type is really a fixed definition of a data type, complete with length, precision, or scale as applicable.

For example, if you need to store phone numbers in various tables in your database, you can create a phone number data type. If you create the phone number data type as a varchar(25), then every column that you define as a phone number will be exactly the same, a varchar(25). As you recall from the discussion of domains in Chapter 2, user-defined data types are the physical implementation of domains in SQL Server. We highly recommend using user-defined data types for consistency, both during the initial development and later during possible additions to your data model.

Referential Integrity

We discussed referential integrity (RI) in Chapter 2. Now we look specifically at how you implement referential integrity in a physical database.

In general, data integrity is the concept of keeping your data consistent and helping to ensure that your data is an accurate representation of the real world and that it is easy to retrieve. There are various kinds of integrity; referential integrity ensures that the relationships between tables are adhered to when you insert or update data. For example, suppose you have two tables: one called Employee and one called Vehicle. You require that each vehicle be assigned to an employee; this is done via a relationship, and the rule is maintained with RI. You physically implement this relationship using primary and foreign keys.

Primary Keys

A primary key constraint in SQL Server works in the same way as a primary key does in your logical model. A primary key is made up of the column or columns that uniquely identify the row in any given table.

The first step in creating a PK is to identify the columns on which to create the key; most of the time this is decided during logical modeling. What makes a good primary key in SQL Server, and, more importantly, what makes a poor key? Any column or combination of columns in your table that can uniquely identify the row are known as **candidate keys.** Often there are multiple candidate keys in a table. Our first tip for PK selection is to avoid string columns. When you join two tables, SQL Server must compare the data in the primary key to the data in the other table's foreign key. By their nature, strings take more time and processing power to compare than do numeric data types.

That leaves us with numeric data. But what kind of numeric should you use? Integers are always good candidates, so you could use any of the int data types as long as they are large enough to be unique given the table's potential row count. Also, you can create a composite PK (a PK that uses more than one column), but we do not recommend using composite PKs if you can avoid it. The reason? If you have four columns in your PK, then each table that references this table will require the same four columns. Not only does it take longer to build a join on four columns, but also you have a lot of duplicate data storage that would otherwise be avoided.

To recap, here are the rules you should follow when choosing a PK from your candidate keys.

- Avoid using string columns.
- Use integer data when possible.
- Avoid composite primary keys.

Given these rules, let's look at a table and decide which columns to use as our PK. Figure 3.1 shows a table called Products. This table has a couple of candidate keys, the first being the model number. However, model numbers are unique only to a specific manufacturer. So the best option here would be a composite key containing both Model Number and Manufacturer. The other candidate key in this table is the SKU. An SKU (stock-keeping unit) number is usually an internal number that can uniquely identify any product a company buys and sells regardless of manufacturer.

Products

SKU	INTEGER	NOT NULL
Model Number	VARCHAR(25)	NOT NULL
Name	VARCHAR(100)	NOT NULL
Manufacturer	VARCHAR(25)	NOT NULL
Description	VARCHAR(255)	NOT NULL
WarrantyDetails	VARCHAR(500)	NOT NULL
Price	MONEY(10,0)	NOT NULL
Weight	DECIMAL(5,2)	NOT NULL
Shipping Weight	DECIMAL(5,2)	NOT NULL
Height	DECIMAL(4,2)	NOT NULL
Width	DECIMAL(4,2)	NOT NULL
Depth	DECIMAL(4,2)	NOT NULL
Is Serialized	BIT	NOT NULL
Status	TINYINT	NOT NULL

FIGURE 3.1 A Products table in need of a primary key

Let's look at each of the candidates and see whether it violates a rule. The first candidate (Model Number and Manufacturer) violates all the rules; the data is a string, and it would be a composite key. So that leaves us with SKU, which is perfect; it identifies the row, it's an integer, and it is a single column.

Now that we have identified our PK, how do we go about configuring it in SQL Server? There are several ways to make PKs, and the method you use depends on the state of the table. First, let's see how to do it at the same time you create the table. Here is the script to create the table, complete with the PK.

```
CREATE TABLE Products(
    sku                 int             NOT NULL    PRIMARY KEY,
    modelnumber         varchar(25)     NOT NULL,
    name                varchar(100)    NOT NULL,
    manufacturer        varchar(25)     NOT NULL,
    description         varchar(255)    NOT NULL,
    warrantydetails     varchar(500)    NOT NULL,
    price               money           NOT NULL,
    weight              decimal(5, 2)   NOT NULL,
    shippingweight      decimal(5, 2)   NOT NULL,
    height              decimal(4, 2)   NOT NULL,
    width               decimal(4, 2)   NOT NULL,
    depth               decimal(4, 2)   NOT NULL,
    isserialized        bit             NOT NULL,
    status              tinyint         NOT NULL
)
```

You will notice the PRIMARY KEY statement following the definition of the sku column. That statement adds a PK to the table on the sku column, something that is simple and quick.

However, this method has one inherent problem. When SQL Server creates a PK in the database, every PK has a name associated with it. Using this method, we don't specify a name, so SQL Server makes one up. In this case it was PK_Products_30242045. The name is based on the table name and some random numbers. On the surface, this doesn't seem to be a big problem, but what if you later need to delete the PK from this table? If you have proper change control in your environment, then you will create a script to drop the key and you will drop the key from a quality assurance server first. Once tests confirm that nothing else will break when this key is dropped, you go ahead and run the script in production. The problem is that if you create the table using the script shown here, the PK will have a different name on each server and your script will fail.

How do you name the key when you create it? What you name your keys is mostly up to you, but we provide some naming guidelines in Chapter 7. In this case we use pk_product_sku as the name of our PK. As a best practice, we suggest that you always explicitly name all your primary keys in this manner. In the following script we removed the PRIMARY KEY statement from the sku column definition and added a CONSTRAINT statement at the end of the table definition.

```
CREATE TABLE Products(
    sku                 int             NOT NULL,
    modelnumber         varchar(25)     NOT NULL,
    name                varchar(100)    NOT NULL,
    manufacturer        varchar(25)     NOT NULL,
    description         varchar(255)    NOT NULL,
    price               money           NOT NULL,
    weight              decimal(5, 2)   NOT NULL,
    shippingweight      decimal(5, 2)   NOT NULL,
    height              decimal(4, 2)   NOT NULL,
    width               decimal(4, 2)   NOT NULL,
    depth               decimal(4, 2)   NOT NULL,
    isserialized        bit             NOT NULL,
    status              tinyint         NOT NULL,
CONSTRAINT pk_product_sku PRIMARY KEY (sku)
)
```

Last, but certainly not least, what if the table already exists and you want to add a primary key? First, you must make sure that any data already in the column conforms to the rules of a primary key. It cannot contain NULLs, and each row must be unique. After that, another simple script will do the trick.

```
ALTER TABLE Products
ADD CONSTRAINT pk_product_sku PRIMARY KEY (sku)
```

But wait—there's more. Using the sku column as we have done here is fine, but there are other PK options we need to discuss. If you were to go through your entire database and define PKs as we have done on the Products table, you would likely end up with a different column name in each table that holds the primary key. This is not necessarily a bad thing, but it means that you must look up the data type and column name whenever you want to add another column with a foreign key or you need to write a piece of code to join tables.

Wouldn't it be nice if all your tables had their PKs in columns having the same name? For example, every table in your database could be given a column named objectid and that column could simply have an arbitrary unique integer. In this case, you can use an identity column in SQL Server to manage your integer PK value. An **identity column** is one that automatically increments a number with each insert into the table. When you make a column an identity, you specify a **seed,** or starting value, and an **increment,** which is the number to add each time a new record is added. Most commonly, the seed and increment are both set to 1, meaning that each new row will be given an identity value that is 1 higher than the preceding row.

Another option for an arbitrary PK is a GUID. GUIDs are most often used as PKs when you need to copy data between databases and you need to be sure that data copied from another database does not conflict with existing data. If you were instead to use identities, you would have to play with the seed values to avoid conflicts; for example, the number 1,000,454 could easily have been used in two databases, creating a conflict when the data is copied. The disadvantages of GUIDs are that they are larger than integers and they are not easily readable for humans. Also, PKs are often clustered, meaning that they are stored in order. Because GUIDs are random, each time you add data it ends up getting inserted into the middle of the PK, and this adds overhead to the operation. In Chapter 10 we talk more about clustered versus nonclustered PKs.

Of all the PK options we have discussed, we most often use identity columns. They are easy to set up and they provide consistency across tables. No matter what method you use, carefully consider the pros and cons. Implementing a PK in the wrong way not only will make it difficult to write code against your database but also could lead to degraded performance.

Foreign Keys

As with primary keys, foreign keys in SQL Server work in the same way as they do in logical design. A foreign key is the column or columns that correspond to a primary key and establish a relationship. Exactly the same columns with the same data as the primary key exist in the foreign key. It is for this reason that we strongly advise against using composite primary keys; not only does it mean a lot of data duplication, but also it adds overhead when you join tables. Going back to our employee and vehicle example, take a look at Figure 3.2, which shows the tables with some sample data.

Table - dbo.employee

objid	first_name	last_name	phone
1	Tim	Smith	719-555-1234
2	Eric	Johnson	719-555-4321
3	Josh	Jones	719-555-7896
4	Dennis	Regan	303-555-8888

Table - dbo.vehicle

objid	make	model	year	employee_objid
2	Nissan	Maxima	2000	2
3	Ford	Taurus	2002	3

FIGURE 3.2   Data from the employee and vehicle tables showing the relationship between the tables

As you can see, both tables have objid columns. These are identity columns and serve as our primary key. Additionally, notice that the vehicle table has an employee_objid column. This column holds the objid of the employee to whom the car is assigned. In SQL Server, the foreign key is set up on the vehicle table, and its job is to ensure that the value you enter in the employee_objid column is in fact a valid value that has a corresponding record in the employee table.

The following script creates the vehicle table. You will notice a few things that are different from the earlier table creation script. First, when we set up the objid column, we use the IDENTITY(1,1) statement to create an identity, with a seed and increment of 1 on the column. Second, we have a second CONSTRAINT statement to add the foreign key relationship. When creating a foreign key, you specify the column or columns in the referencing table that contain the foreign key as well as the referenced table and columns that contain the primary key.

```
CREATE TABLE dbo.vehicle(
    objid int IDENTITY(1,1) NOT NULL,
    make varchar(50) NOT NULL,
    model varchar(50)NOT NULL,
    year char(4) NOT NULL,
    employee_objid int NOT NULL,
 CONSTRAINT PK_vehicle PRIMARY KEY (objid),
 CONSTRAINT FK_vehicle_employee
    FOREIGN KEY(employee_objid)
    REFERENCES employee (objid)
)
```

Once your primary keys are in place, the creation of the foreign keys is academic. You simply create the appropriate columns on the referencing table and add the foreign key. As stated in Chapter 2, if your design requires it, the same column in a table can be in both the primary key and a foreign key.

When you create foreign keys, you can also specify what to do if an update or delete is issued on the parent table. By default, if you attempt to delete a record in the parent table, the delete will fail because it would result in orphaned rows in the referencing table. An **orphaned row** is a row that exists in a child table that has no corresponding parent. This can cause problems in some data models. In our employee and vehicle tables, a NULL in the vehicle table means that the vehicle has not been assigned to an employee. However, consider a table that stores orders and order details; in this case, an orphaned record in the order detail table would be useless. You would have no idea which order the detail line belonged to.

Instead of allowing a delete to fail, you have options. First, you can have the delete operation **cascade,** meaning that SQL Server will delete all the child rows along with the parent row you are deleting. Be very careful when using this option. If you have several levels of relationships with cascading delete enabled, you could wipe out a large chunk of data by issuing a delete on a single record.

Your second option is to have SQL Server set the foreign key column to NULL in the referencing table. This option creates orphaned records, as discussed. Third, you can have SQL Server set the foreign key column back to the default value of the column, if it has one. Similar options are also available if you try to update the primary key value itself. Again, SQL Server can either (1) cascade the update so that the child rows still point to the correct parent rows with the new key, (2) set the foreign key to NULL, or (3) set the foreign key back to its default value.

Changing the values of primary keys isn't something we recommend you do often, but in some situations you may find yourself needing to do just that. If you find yourself in that situation often, you might consider setting up an update rule on your foreign keys.

Constraints

SQL Server contains several types of constraints to enforce data integrity. **Constraints,** as the name implies, are used to constrain the values that can be entered into columns. We have talked about two of the constraints in SQL Server: primary keys and foreign keys. Primary keys constrain the data so that duplicates and NULLs cannot exist in the columns, and foreign keys ensure that the entered value exists in the referenced table. There are several other constraints you can implement to ensure data integrity or enforce business rules.

Unique Constraints

Unique constraints are similar to primary keys; they ensure that no duplicates exist in a column or collection of columns. They are configured on columns that do not participate in the primary key. How does a unique constraint differ from a primary key? From a technical standpoint, the only difference is that a unique constraint allows you to enter NULL values; however, because the values must be unique, you can enter only one NULL value for the entire column. When we talked about identifying primary keys, we talked about candidate keys. Because candidate keys should also be able to uniquely identify the row, you should probably place unique constraints on your candidate keys. You add a unique constraint in much the same way as you add a foreign key, using a constraint statement such as

```
CONSTRAINT UNQ_vehicle_vin UNIQUE NONCLUSTERED (vin_number)
```

Check Constraints

Check constraints limit the values that can be entered into a column by using a logical expression. A **logical expression** is any SQL expression that can evaluate to TRUE or FALSE. The expression can be any valid SQL expression, from simple comparisons to something more complex such as calling a function. For example, say we want to limit the values that can be entered for salary in our employee table. The expression we would use to evaluate the data would be something like this:

```
salary >= 10000 and salary <=150000
```

This line rejects any value less than 10,000 or greater than 150,000.

Each column can have multiple check constraints, or you can reference multiple columns with a single check. When it comes to NULL values, check constraints can be overridden. When a check constraint does its evaluation, it allows any value that does not evaluate to false. This means that if your check evaluates to NULL, the value will be accepted. Thus, if you enter NULL into the salary column, the check constraint returns unknown and the value is inserted. This feature is by design, but it can lead to unexpected results, so we want you to be aware of this.

Check constraints are created in much the same way as keys or unique constraints; the only caveat is that they tend to contain a bit more meat. That is, the expression used to evaluate the check can be lengthy and therefore hard to read when viewed in T-SQL. We recommend you create your tables first and then issue ALTER statements to add your check constraints. The following sample code adds a constraint to the Products table to ensure that certain columns do not contain negative values.

```
ALTER TABLE dbo.Products
ADD CONSTRAINT chk_non_negative_values
CHECK
(
weight >= 0
AND (shippingweight >= 0 AND shippingweight >= weight)
AND height >= 0
AND width >= 0
AND depth >= 0
)
```

Because it doesn't make sense for any of these columns to contain negative numbers (items cannot have negative weights or heights), we add this constraint to ensure data integrity. Now when you attempt to insert data with negative numbers, SQL Server simply returns the following error and the insert is denied. This constraint also prevents a shipping weight from being less than the product's actual weight.

```
The INSERT statement conflicted with the CHECK constraint
"chk_non_negative_values"
```

As you can see, we created one constraint that looks at all the columns that must contain non-negative values. The only downfall to this method is that it can be hard to find the data that violated the constraint. In this case, it's pretty easy to spot a negative number, but imagine if the constraint were more complex and contained more columns. You would know only that some column in the constraint was in violation, and you would have to go over your data to find the problem. On the other hand, we could have created a constraint for each column, making it easier to track down problems. Which method you use depends on complexity and personal preference.

Implementing Referential Integrity

Now that we have covered PKs, FKs, and constraints, the final thing we need to discuss is how to use them to implement referential integrity. Luckily it's straightforward once you understand how to create each of the objects we've discussed.

One-to-Many Relationships

One-to-many relationships are the most common kind of relationship you will use in a database, and they are also what you get with very little additional work when you create a foreign key on a table. To make the relationship required, you must make sure that the column that contains your foreign key is set to not allow NULLs. Not allowing NULLs requires that a value be entered in the column, and adding the foreign key requires that the value be in the related table's primary key. This type of relationship implements a cardinality of "one or more to one." In other words, you can have a single row but you are not limited to the total number of rows you can have. (Later in this chapter we look at ways to implement advanced cardinality.) Allowing NULL in the foreign key column makes the relationship optional—that is, the data is not required to be related to the reference table. If you were tracking computers in a table and using a relationship to define which person was using the computer, a NULL in your foreign key would denote a computer that is not in use by an employee.

One-to-One Relationships

One-to-one relationships are implemented in exactly the same way as one-to-many relationships—sort of. You still create a primary key and a foreign key; the problem is that at this point SQL Server still allows users to insert many rows into the foreign key table that reference the primary key table.

There is no way, by default, to constrain the data to one-to-one. To implement a one-to-one relationship that is enforced, you must get a little creative.

The first option is to write a stored procedure (more on stored procedures later in this chapter) to do all your inserting, and then add logic to prevent a second row from being added to the table. This method works in most cases, but what if you need to load data directly to tables without a stored procedure? Another option to implement one-to-one relationships is to use a trigger, which we also look at shortly. Basically, a **trigger** is a piece of code that can be executed after or instead of the actual insert statement. Using this method, you could roll back any insert that would violate the one-one relationship.

Additionally—and this is probably the easiest method—you can add a unique constraint on the foreign key columns. This would mean that the data in the foreign key would have to be a value from the primary key, and each value could appear only once in the referencing table. This approach effectively creates a one-to-one relationship that is managed and enforced by SQL Server.

Many-to-Many Relationships

One of the most complex relationships when it comes to implementation is the many-to-many relationship. Even though you can have a many-to-many relationship between two entities, you cannot create a many-to-many relationship between only two tables. To implement this relationship, you must create a third table, called a **junction table,** and two one-to-many relationships.

Let's walk through an example to see how it works. You have two tables—one called Student and one called Class—and both contain an identity called objid as their PK. In this situation you need a many-to-many relationship, because each student can be in more than one class and each class will have more than one student. To implement the relationship, you create a junction table that has only two columns: one containing the student_objid, and the other containing the class_objid. You then create a one-to-many relationship from this junction table to the Student table, and another to the Class table. Figure 3.3 shows how this relationship looks.

You will notice a few things about this configuration. First, in addition to being foreign keys, these columns are used together as the primary key for the Student_Class junction table. How does this implement a many-to-many relationship? The junction table can contain rows as long as they do

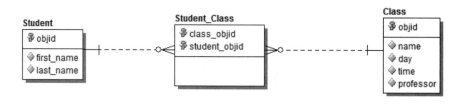

FIGURE 3.3   Many-to-many relationship between a Student and a Class table

not violate the primary key. This means that you can relate each student to all the classes he attends, and you can relate all the students in a particular class to that class. This gives you a many-to-many relationship.

It may sound complex, but once you create a many-to-many relationship and add some data to the tables, it becomes pretty clear. The best way to really understand it is to do it. When we build our physical model in Chapter 9, we look more closely at many-to-many relationships, including ways to make them most useful.

Implementing Advanced Cardinality

In Chapter 2, we talk about cardinality. Cardinality simply describes the number of rows in a table that can relate to rows in another table. Cardinality is often derived from your customer's business rules. As with one-to-one relationships, SQL Server does not have a native method to support advanced cardinality. Using primary and foreign keys, you can easily enforce one-or-more-to-many, zero-or-more-to-many, or one-to-one cardinality as we have described previously.

What if you want to create a relationship whereby each parent can contain only a limited number of child records? For example, using our employee and vehicle tables, you might want to limit your data so that each employee can have no more than five cars assigned. Additionally, employees are not required to have a car at all. The cardinality of this relationship is said to be zero-to-five-to-many. To enforce this requirement, you need to be creative. In this scenario you could use a trigger that counts the number of cars assigned to an employee. If the additional car would put the employee over five, the insert could be reversed or rolled back.

Each situation is unique. In some cases you might be able to use check constraints or another combination of PKs, FKs, and constraints to implement your cardinality. You need to examine your requirements closely to decide on the best approach.

Programming

In addition to the objects that are used to store data and implement data integrity, SQL Server provides several objects that allow you to write code to manipulate your data. These objects can be used to insert, update, delete, or read data stored in your database, or to implement business rules and advanced data integrity. You can even build "applications" completely contained in SQL Server. Typically, these applications are very small and usually manipulate the data in some way to serve a function or for some larger application.

Stored Procedures

Most commonly, when working with code in SQL Server you will work with a **stored procedure** (SP). SPs are simply compiled and stored T-SQL code. SPs are similar to views in that they are compiled and they generate an execution plan when called the first time. The difference is that SPs, in addition to selecting data, can execute any T-SQL code and can work with parameters. SPs are very similar to modules in other programming languages. You can call a procedure and allow it to perform its operation, or you can pass parameters and get return parameters from the SP.

Like columns, **parameters** are configured to allow a specific data type. All the same data types are used for parameters, and they limit the kind of data you can pass to SPs. Parameters come in two types: input and output. **Input parameters** provide data to the SP to use during their execution, and **output parameters** return data to the calling process. In addition to retrieving data, output parameters can be used to provide data to SPs. You might do this when an SP is designed to take employee data and update a record if the employee exists or insert a new record if the employee does not exist. In this case, you might have an EmployeeID parameter that maps to the employee primary key. This parameter would accept the ID of the employee you intend to update as well as return the new employee ID that is generated when you insert a new employee.

SPs also have a return value that can return an integer to the calling process. **Return values** are often used to give the calling process information about the success of the stored procedure. Return values differ from output parameters in that return values do not have names and you get only one per SP. Additionally, SPs always return an integer in the return value, even if you don't specify that one be returned. By default, an SP returns 0 (zero) unless you specify something else. For this reason, 0 is often used to designate success and nonzero values specify return error conditions.

SPs have many uses; the most common is to manage the input and retrieval of your data. Often SPs are mapped to the entities you are storing. If you have student data in your database, you may well have SPs named sp_add_student, sp_update_student, and sp_retrieve_student_data. These SPs would have parameters allowing you to specify all the student data that ultimately needs to be written to your tables.

Like views, SPs reduce your database's complexity for users and are more efficient than simply running T-SQL repeatedly. Again, SPs remove the need to update application code if you need to change your database. As long as the SP accepts the same parameters and returns the same data after you make changes, your application code does not have to change. In Chapter 11 we talk in great detail about using stored procedures.

User-Defined Functions

Like any programming language, T-SQL offers functions in the form of **user-defined functions** (UDFs). UDFs take input parameters, perform an action, and return the results to the calling process. Sound similar to a stored procedure? They are, but there are some important differences. The first thing you will notice is a difference in the way UDFs are called. Take a look at the following code for calling an SP.

```
DECLARE @num_in_stock int

EXEC sp_check_product_stock    @sku = 4587353,
        @stock_level = @num_in_stock OUTPUT

PRINT @num_in_stock
```

You will notice a few things here. First, you must declare a variable to store the return of the stored procedure. If you want to use this value later, you need to use the variable; that's pretty simple.

Now let's look at calling a UDF that returns the same information.

```
DECLARE @num_in_stock int

SET @num_in_stock = dbo.CheckProductStock (4587353)

PRINT @num_in_stock
```

The code looks similar, but the function is called more like a function call in other programming languages. You are probably still asking yourself, "What's the difference?" Well, in addition to calling a function and putting its return into a variable, you can call UDFs inline with other code. Consider the following example of a UDF that returns a new employee ID. This function is being called inline with the insert statement for the employee table. Calling UDFs in this way prevents you from writing extra code to store a return variable for later use.

```
INSERT INTO employee (employeeid, firstname, lastname)
VALUES (dbo.GetNewEmployeeID(), 'Eric', 'Johnson')
```

The next big difference in UDFs is the type of data they return. UDFs that can return single values are known as **scalar functions.** The data the function returns can be defined as any data type except for text, ntext, image, and timestamp. To this point, all the examples we have looked at have been scalar values.

UDFs can also be defined as **table-valued functions:** functions that return a table data type. Again, table-valued functions can be called inline with other T-SQL code and can be treated just like tables. Using the following code, we can pass the employee ID into the function and treat the return as a table.

```
SELECT * FROM dbo.EmployeeData(8765448)
```

You can also use table-valued functions in joins with other functions or with base tables. UDFs are used primarily by developers who write T-SQL code against your database, but you can use UDFs to implement business rules in your model. UDFs also can be used in check constraints or triggers to help you maintain data integrity.

Triggers

Triggers and constraints are the two most common ways to enforce data integrity and business rules in your physical database. Triggers are stored T-SQL scripts, similar to stored procedures, that run when a DML statement (other than SELECT) is issued against a table or view. There are two types of DML triggers available in SQL Server.

With an **AFTER trigger,** which can exist only on tables, the DML statement is processed, and after that operation completes, the trigger code is run. For example, if a process issues an insert to add a new employee to a table, the insert triggers the trigger. The code in the trigger is run after the insert as part of the same transaction that issued the insert. Managing transactions is a bit beyond the scope of this book, but you should know that because the trigger is run in the same context as the DML statement, you can make changes to the affected data, up to and including rolling back the statement. AFTER triggers are very useful for verifying business rules and then canceling the modification if the business rule is not met.

During the execution of an AFTER trigger, you have access to two virtual tables—one called Inserted and one called Deleted. The Deleted table holds a copy of the modified row or rows as they existed before a delete or update statement. The Inserted table has the same data as the base table has after an insert or update. This arrangement allows you to modify data in the base table while still having a reference to the data as it looked before and after the DML statement.

These special temporary tables are available only during the execution of the trigger code and only by the trigger's process. When creating AFTER triggers, you can have a single trigger fire on any combination of insert, update, or delete. In other words, one trigger can be set up to run on both insert and update, and a different trigger could be configured to run on delete. Additionally, you can have multiple triggers fire on the same statement; for example, two triggers can run on an update. If you have multiple triggers for a single statement type, the ordering of such triggers is limited. Using a system stored procedure, sp_settriggerorder, you can specify which trigger fires first and which trigger fires last. Otherwise, they are fired in the middle somewhere. In reality, this isn't a big problem. We have seen very few tables that had more than two triggers for any given DML statement.

INSTEAD OF triggers are a whole different animal. These triggers perform in the way you would expect: The code in an INSTEAD OF trigger fires in place of the DML statement that caused the trigger to fire. Unlike AFTER triggers, INSTEAD OF triggers can be defined on views as well as tables. Using them, you can overcome the limitation of views that have multiple base tables. As mentioned earlier, you can update a view only if you limit your update to affecting only a single base table. Using an INSTEAD OF trigger, you can update all the columns of a view and use the trigger to issue the appropriate update against the appropriate base table. You can also use INSTEAD OF triggers to implement advanced data integrity or business rules by completely changing the action of a DML statement.

You can also control trigger nesting and recursion behavior. With nested triggers turned on, one trigger firing can perform a DML and cause another trigger to fire. For example, inserting a row into TableA causes TableA's insert trigger to fire. TableA's insert trigger in turn updates a record in TableB, causing TableB's update trigger to fire. That is **trigger nesting**—one trigger causing another to fire—and this is the default behavior. With nested triggers turned on, SQL Server allows as many as 32 triggers to be nested. The INSTEAD OF trigger can nest regardless of the setting of the nested triggers option.

Server trigger recursion specifies whether or not a trigger can perform a DML statement that would cause the same trigger to fire again. For example, an update trigger on TableA issues an additional update on TableA. With recursive triggers turned on, it causes the same trigger to fire again. This setting affects only direct recursion; that is, a trigger directly causes itself to fire again. Even with recursion off, a trigger could cause another trigger to fire, which in turn could cause the original trigger to fire again. Be very careful when you use recursive triggers. They can run over and over again, causing a performance hit to your server.

CLR Integration

As of SQL Server 2005, we gained the ability to integrate with the .NET Framework Common Language Runtime (CLR). Simply put, CLR integration allows you to use .NET programming languages within SQL Server objects. You can create stored procedures, user-defined functions, triggers, and CLR user-defined types using the more advanced languages available in Microsoft .NET. This level of programming is beyond the scope of this book, but you need to be aware of SQL Server's ability to use CLR. You will likely run into developers who want to use CLR, or you may find yourself needing to implement a complex business rule that cannot easily be implemented using standard SQL Server objects and T-SQL. So if you are code savvy or have a code-savvy friend, you can create functions using CLR to enforce complex rules.

Implementing Supertypes and Subtypes

We discuss supertypes and subtypes in Chapter 2. These are entities that have several kinds of real-world objects being modeled. For example, we might have a supertype called phone with subtypes for corded and cordless phones. We separate objects into a subtype cluster because even though a phone is a phone, different types will require that we track different attributes. For example, on a cordless phone, you need to know the working range of the handset and the frequency on which it operates, and with a corded phone, you could track something like cord length. These differences are tracked in the subtypes, and all the common attributes of phones are held in the supertype.

How do you go about physically implementing a subtype cluster in SQL Server? You have three options. The first is to create a single table that represents the attributes of the supertype and also contains the attributes of *all* the subtypes. Your second option is to create tables for each of the subtypes, adding the supertype attributes to each of these subtype tables. Third, you can create the supertype table and the subtype tables, effectively implementing the subtype cluster in the same way it was logically modeled.

To determine which method is correct, you must look closely at the data being stored. We will walk through each of these options and look at the reasons you would use them, along with the pros and cons of each.

Supertype Table

You would choose this option when the subtypes contain few or no differences from the data stored in the supertype. For example, let's look at a cluster that stores employee data. While building a model, you discover that the company has salaried as well as hourly employees, and you decide to model this difference using subtypes and supertypes. After hashing out all the requirements, you determine that the only real difference between these types is that you store the annual salary for the salaried employees and you need to store the hourly rate and the number of hours for an hourly employee.

In this example, the subtypes contain very subtle differences, so you could build this subtype cluster by using only the supertype table. For this situation, you would likely create a single employee table that contains all the attributes for employees, including all three of the subtype attributes for salary, hourly rate, and hours. Whenever you insert an hourly employee, you would require that data be in the hourly rate and hour columns and that the salary column be left NULL. For salaried employees, you would do the exact opposite.

Implementing the types in this way makes it easy to find the employee data because all of it is in the same place. The only drawback is that you must implement some logic to look at the columns that are appropriate to the type of employee you are working with. This supertype-only implementation works well only because there are very few additional attributes from the subtype's entities. If there were a lot of differences, you would end up with many of the columns being NULL for any given row, and it would take a great deal of logic to pull the data together in a meaningful way.

Subtype Tables

When the data contained in the subtypes is dissimilar and the number of common attributes from the supertype is small, you would most likely implement the subtype tables by themselves. This is effectively the opposite data layout that would prompt you to use the supertype-only model.

Suppose you're creating a system for a retail store that sells camera equipment. You could build a subtype cluster for the products that the store sells, because the products fall into distinct categories. If you look only at cameras, lenses, and tripods, you have three very different types of product. For each one, you need to store the model number, stock number, and the product's availability, but that is where the similarities end. For cameras you need to know the maximum shutter speed, frames per second, viewfinder size, battery type, and so on. Lenses have a different set of attributes, such as the focal length, focus type, minimum distance to subject, and minimum aperture. And tripods offer a new host of data; you need to store the minimum and maximum height, the planes on which it can pivot, and the type of head. Anyone who has ever bought photography equipment knows that the differences listed here barely scratch the surface; you would need many other attributes on each type to accurately describe all the options.

The sheer number of attributes that are unique for each subtype, and the fact that they have only a few in common, will push you toward implementing only the subtype tables. When you do this, each subtype table will end up storing the common data on its own. In other words, the camera, lens, and tripod tables would have columns to store model numbers, SKU numbers, and availability. When you're querying for data implemented in this way, the logic needs to support looking at the appropriate table for the type of product you need to find.

Supertype and Subtype Tables

You have probably guessed this: When there are a good number of shared attributes and a good number of differences in the subtypes, you will probably implement both the supertype and the subtype tables. A good example is a subtype cluster that stores payment information for your customers. Whether your customer pays with an electronic check, credit card, gift certificate, or cash, you need to know a few things. For any payment, you need to know who made it, the time the payment was received, the amount, and the status of the payment. But each of these payment types also requires you to know the details of the payment. For credit cards, you need the card number, card type, security code, and expiration date. For an electronic check, you need the bank account number, routing number, check number, and maybe even a driver's license number. Gift cards are simple; you need only the card number and the balance. As for cash, you probably don't need to store any additional data.

This situation calls for implementing both the supertype and the subtype tables. A Payment table could contain all the high-level detail, and individually credit card, gift card, and check tables would hold the information pertinent to each payment type. We do not have a cash table, because we do not need to store any additional data on cash payments beyond what we have in the Payment table.

When implementing a subtype cluster in this way, you also need to store the subtype **discrimination,** usually a short code or a number that is stored as a column in the supertype table to designate the appropriate subtype table. We recommend using a single character when possible, because they are small and offer more meaning to a person than a number does. In this example, you would store CC for credit card, G for a gift card, E for electronic check, and C for cash. (Notice that we used CC for a credit card to distinguish it from cash.) When querying a payment, you can join to the appropriate payment type based on this discriminator.

If you need data only from either the supertype or the subtype, this method offers two benefits: you need go to only one table, and you don't retrieve extraneous data. However, the flip side is that you must determine which subtype table you need to query and then join both tables if you need data from both the supertype and a subtype table. Additionally, you may find yourself needing information from the supertype and multiple subtypes; this will add overhead to your queries because you must join multiple tables.

Supertypes and Subtypes: A Final Word

Implementing supertypes and subtypes can, at times, be tricky. If you take the time to fully understand the data and look at the implications of splitting the data into multiple tables versus keeping it tighter, you should be able to determine the best course of action. Don't be afraid to generate some test data and run various options through performance tests to make sure you make the correct choice. When we get to building the physical model, we look at using subtype clusters as well as other alternatives for especially complex situations.

Summary

In this chapter, we have looked at the available objects inside SQL Server that you will use when implementing your physical model. It's important to understand these objects for many reasons. You must keep all this in mind when you design your logical model so that you design with SQL Server in mind. This also plays a large part later when you build and implement your physical model. You will probably not use every object in SQL Server for every database you build, but you need to know your options. Later, we walk through creating your physical model, and at that time we go over the various ways you can use these physical objects to solve problems.

In the next chapter, we talk about normalization, and then we move on to the meat and potatoes of this book by getting into our sample project and digging into a lot of real-world issues.

CHAPTER 4

NORMALIZING A DATA MODEL

Data normalization is probably one of the most talked-about aspects of database modeling. Before building your data model, you must answer a few questions about normalization. These questions include whether or not to use the formal normalization forms, which of these forms to use, and when to denormalize.

To explain normalization, we share a little bit of history and outline the most commonly used normal forms. We don't dive very deeply into each normal form; there are plenty of other texts that describe and examine every detail of normalization. Instead, our purpose is to give you the tools necessary to identify the current state of your data, set your goals, and normalize (and denormalize) your data as needed.

What Is Normalization?

At its most basic level, **normalization** is the process of simplifying your data into its most efficient form by eliminating redundant data. Understanding the definition of the word *efficient* in relation to normalization is the key concept. **Efficiency,** in this case, refers to reducing complexity from a logical standpoint. Efficiency does not necessarily equal better performance, nor does it necessarily equate to efficient query processing. This may seem to contradict what you've heard about design, so first let's walk through the concepts in normalization, and then we'll talk about some of the performance considerations.

Normal Forms

E. F. Codd, who was the IBM researcher credited with the creation and evolution of the relational database, set forth a set of rules that define how data should be organized in a relational database. Initially, he proposed three sequential forms to classify data in a database: first normal form

(1NF), second normal form (2NF), and third normal form (3NF). After these initial normal forms were developed, research indicated that they could result in update anomalies, so three additional forms were developed to deal with these issues: fourth normal form (4NF), fifth normal form (5NF), and the Boyce-Codd normal form (BCNF). There has been research into a sixth normal form (6NF); this normal form has to do with temporal databases and is outside the scope of this book.

It's important to note that the normal forms are nested. For example, if a database meets 3NF, by definition it also meets 1NF and 2NF. Let's take a brief look at each of the normal forms and explain how to identify them.

First Normal Form (1NF)

In **first normal form,** every entity in the database has a primary key attribute (or set of attributes). Each attribute must have only one value, and not a set of values. For a database to be in 1NF it must not have any repeating groups. A **repeating group** is data in which a single instance may have multiple values for a given attribute.

For example, consider a recording studio that stores data about all its artists and their albums. Table 4.1 outlines an entity that stores some basic data about the artists signed to the recording studio.

Table 4.1 Artists and Albums: Repeating Groups of Data

Artist Name	Genre	Album Name	Album Release Date
The Awkward Stage	Rock	Home	10/01/2006
Girth	Metal	On the Sea	5/25/1997
Wasabi Peanuts	Adult Contemporary Rock	Spicy Legumes	11/12/2005
The Bobby Jenkins Band	R&B	Live!	7/27/1985
		Running the Game	10/30/1988
Juices of Brazil	Latin Jazz	Long Road	1/01/2003
		White	6/10/2005

Notice that for the first artist, there is only one album and therefore one release date. However, for the fourth and fifth artists, there are two albums and two release dates. In practice, we cannot guarantee which release date belongs to which album. Sure, it'd be easy to assume that the first release date belongs to the first album name, but how can we be sure that album names and dates are always entered in order and not changed afterward?

There are two ways to eliminate the problem of the repeating group. First, we could add new attributes to handle the additional albums, as in Table 4.2.

Table 4.2 Artists and Albums: Eliminate the Repeating Group, but at What Cost?

Artist Name	Genre	Album Name 1	Release Date 1	Album Name 2	Release Date 2
The Awkward Stage	Rock	Home	10/01/2006	NULL	NULL
Girth	Metal	On the Sea	5/25/1997	NULL	NULL
Wasabi Peanuts	Adult Contemporary Rock	Spicy Legumes	11/12/2005	NULL	NULL
The Bobby Jenkins Band	R&B	Running the Game	7/27/1985	Live!	10/30/1988
Juices of Brazil	Latin Jazz	Long Road	1/01/2003	White	6/10/2005

We've solved the problem of the repeating group, and because no attribute contains more than one value, this table is in 1NF. However, we've introduced a much bigger problem: what if an artist has more than two albums? Do we keep adding two attributes for each album that any artist releases? In addition to the obvious problem of adding attributes to the entity, in the physical implementation we are wasting a great deal of space for each artist who has only one album. Also, querying the resultant table for album names would require searching every album name column, something that is very inefficient.

If this is the wrong way, what's the right way? Take a look at Tables 4.3 and 4.4.

Table 4.3 The Artists

ArtistName	Genre
The Awkward Stage	Rock
Girth	Metal
Wasabi Peanuts	Adult Contemporary Rock
The Bobby Jenkins Band	R&B
Juices of Brazil	Latin Jazz

Table 4.4   The Albums

AlbumName	ReleaseDate	ArtistName
White	6/10/2005	Juices of Brazil
Home	10/01/2006	The Awkward Stage
On The Sea	5/25/1997	Girth
Spicy Legumes	11/12/2005	Wasabi Peanuts
Running the Game	7/27/1985	The Bobby Jenkins Band
Live!	10/30/1988	The Bobby Jenkins Band
Long Road	1/01/2003	Juices of Brazil

We've solved the problem by adding another entity that stores album names as well the attribute that represents the relationship to the artist entity. Neither of these entities has a repeating group, each attribute in both entities holds a single value, and all of the previously mentioned query problems have been eliminated. This database is now in 1NF and ready to be deployed, right? Considering there are several other normal forms, we think you know the answer.

Second Normal Form (2NF)

Second normal form (2NF) specifies that, in addition to meeting 1NF, all non-key attributes have a functional dependency on the entire primary key. A **functional dependency** is a one-way relationship between the primary key attribute (or attributes) and all other non-key attributes in the same entity. Referring again to Table 4.3, if ArtistName is the primary key, then all other attributes in the entity must be identified by ArtistName. So we can say, "ArtistName determines ReleaseDate" for each instance in the entity. Notice that the relationship does not necessarily hold in the reverse direction; any genre may appear multiple times throughout this entity. Nonetheless, for any given artist, there is one genre. But what if an artist crosses over to another genre?

To answer that question, let's compare 1NF to 2NF. In 1NF, we have no repeating groups, and all attributes have a single value. However, in 1NF, if we have a composite primary key, it is possible that there are attributes that rely on only one of the primary key attributes, and that can lead to strange data manipulation anomalies. Take a look at Table 4.5, in

Table 4.5 Artists: 1NF Is Met, but with Problems

PK—Artist Name	PK—Genre	Signed Date	Agent	Agent Primary Phone	Agent Secondary Phone
The Awkward Stage	Rock	9/01/2005	John Doe	(777)555-1234	NULL
Girth	Metal	10/31/1997	Sally Sixpack	(777)555-6789	(777)555-0000
Wasabi Peanuts	Adult Contempo-rary Rock	1/01/2005	John Doe	(777)555-1234	NULL
The Bobby Jenkins Band	R&B	3/15/1985	Johnny Jenkins	(444)555-1111	NULL
The Bobby Jenkins Band	Soul	3/15/1985	Johnny Jenkins	(444)555-1111	NULL
Juices of Brazil	Latin Jazz	6/01/2001	Jane Doe	(777)555-4321	(777)555-9999
Juices of Brazil	World Beat	6/01/2001	Jane Doe	(777)555-4321	(777)555-9999

which we have solved the multiple genre problem. But we have added new attributes, and that presents a new problem.

In this case, we have two attributes in the primary key: Artist Name and Genre. If the studio decides to sell the Juices of Brazil albums in multiple genres to increase the band's exposure, we end up with multiple instances of the group in the entity, because one of the primary key attributes has a different value. Also, we've started storing the name of each band's agent. The problem here is that the Agent attribute is an attribute of the artist but not of the genre. So the Agent attribute is only partially dependent on the entity's primary key. If we need to update the Agent attribute for a band that has multiple entries, we must update multiple records or else risk having two different agent names listed for the same band. This practice is inefficient and risky from a data integrity standpoint. It is this type of problem that 2NF eliminates.

Tables 4.6 and 4.7 show one possible solution to our problem. In this case, we can break the entity into two different entities. The original entity still contains only information about our artists; the new entity contains information about agents and the bands they represent. This technique removes the partial dependency of the Agent attribute from the original entity, and it lets us store more information that is specific to the agent.

Table 4.6 Artists: 2NF Version of This Entity

PK—Artist Name	PK—Genre	SignedDate
The Awkward Stage	Rock	9/01/2005
Girth	Metal	10/31/1997
Wasabi Peanuts	Adult Contemporary Rock	1/01/2005
The Bobby Jenkins Band	R&B	3/15/1985
The Bobby Jenkins Band	Soul	3/15/1985
Juices of Brazil	Latin Jazz	6/01/2001
Juices of Brazil	World Beat	6/01/2001

Table 4.7 Agents: An Additional Entity to Solve the Problem

PK—Agent Name	Artist Name	Agent PrimaryPhone	Agent SecondaryPhone
John Doe	The Awkward Stage	555-1234	NULL
Sally Sixpack	Girth	(777)555-6789	(777)555-0000
Johnny Jenkins	The Bobby Jenkins Band	(444)555-1111	NULL
Jane Doe	Juices of Brazil	555-4321	555-9999

Third Normal Form (3NF)

Third normal form is the form that most well-designed databases meet. 3NF extends 2NF to include the elimination of transitive dependencies. **Transitive dependencies** are dependencies that arise from a non-key attribute relying on another non-key attribute that relies on the primary key. In other words, if there is an attribute that doesn't rely on the primary key but does rely on another attribute, then the first attribute has a transitive dependency. As with 2NF, to resolve this issue we might simply move the offending attribute to a new entity. Coincidentally, in solving the 2NF problem in Table 4.7, we also created a 3NF entity. In this particular case, AgentPrimaryPhone and AgentSecondaryPhone are not actually attributes of an artist; they are attributes of an agent. Storing them in the Artists entity created a transitive dependency, violating 3NF.

The differences between 2NF and 3NF are very subtle. 2NF deals with partial dependency, and 3NF with transitive dependency. Basically, a

partial dependency means that attributes in the entity don't rely entirely on the primary key. Transitive dependency means that attributes in the entity don't rely on the primary key at all, but they do rely on another non-key attribute in the table. In either case, removing the offending attribute (and related attributes, in the 3NF case) to another entity solves the problem.

One of the simplest ways to remember the basics of 3NF is the popular phrase, "The key, the whole key, and nothing but the key." Because the normal forms are nested, the phrase means that 1NF is met because there is a primary key ("the key"), 2NF is met because all attributes in the table rely on all the attributes in the primary key ("the whole key"), and 3NF is met because none of the non-key attributes in the entity relies on any other non-key attributes ("nothing but the key"). Often, people append the phrase, "So help me Codd." Whatever helps you keep it straight.

Boyce-Codd Normal Form (BCNF)

In certain situations, you may discover that an entity has more than one potential, or candidate, primary key (single or composite). **Boyce-Codd normal form** simply adds a requirement, on top of 3NF, that states that if any entity has more than one possible primary key, then the entity should be split into multiple entities to separate the primary key attributes. For the vast majority of databases, solving the problem of 3NF actually solves this problem as well, because identifying the attribute that has a transitive dependency also tends to reveal the candidate key for the new entity being created. However, strictly speaking, the original 3NF definition did not specify this requirement, so BCNF was added to the list of normal forms to ensure that this was covered.

Fourth Normal Form (4NF) and Fifth Normal Form (5NF)

You've seen that 3NF generally solves most logical problems within databases. However, there are more-complicated relationships that often benefit from 4NF and 5NF. Consider Table 4.8, which describes an alternative, expanded version of the Agents entity.

Table 4.8 Agents: More Agent Information

PK—Agent Name	PK—Agency	PK—Artist Name	Agent PrimaryPhone	Agent SecondaryPhone
John Doe	AAA Talent	The Awkward Stage	(777)555-1234	NULL
Sally Sixpack	A Star Is Born Agency	Girth	(777)555-6789	(777)555-0000
John Doe	AAA Talent	Wasabi Peanuts	(777)555-1234	NULL
Johnny Jenkins	Johnny Jenkins Talent	The Bobby Jenkins Band	(444)555-1111	NULL
Jane Doe	BBB Talent	Juices of Brazil	(777)555-4321	(777)555-9999

Specifically, this entity stores information that creates redundancy, because there is a multivalued dependency within the primary key. A **multivalued dependency** is a relationship in which a primary key attribute, because of its relationship to another primary key attribute, creates multiple tuples within an entity. In this case, John Doe represents multiple artists. The primary key requires that the Agent Name, Agency, and Artist Name uniquely define an agent; if you don't know which agency an agent works for and if an agent quits or moves to another agency, updating this table will require multiple updates to the primary key attributes.

There's a secondary problem as well: we have no way of knowing whether the phone numbers are tied to the agent or tied to the agency. As with 2NF and 3NF, the solution here is to break Agency out into its own entity. 4NF specifies that there be no multivalued dependencies in an entity. Consider Tables 4.9 and 4.10, which show a 4NF of these entities.

TABLE 4.9 Agent-Only Information

PK—Agent Name	Agent PrimaryPhone	Agent SecondaryPhone	Artist Name
John Doe	(777)555-1234	NULL	The Awkward Stage
Sally Sixpack	(777)555-6789	(777)555-0000	Girth
John Doe	(777)555-1234	NULL	Wasabi Peanuts
Johnny Jenkins	(444)555-1111	NULL	The Bobby Jenkins Band
Jane Doe	(777)555-4321	(777)555-9999	Juices of Brazil

Table 4.10 Agency Information

PK—Agency	AgencyPrimaryPhone
AAA Talent	(777)555-1234
A Star Is Born Agency	(777)555-0000
AAA Talent	(777)555-4455
Johnny Jenkins Talent	(444)555-1100
BBB Talent	(777)555-9999

Now we have a pair of entities that have relevant, unique attributes that rely on their primary keys. We've also eliminated the confusion about the phone numbers.

Often, databases that are being normalized with the target of 3NF end up in 4NF, because this multivalued dependency problem is inherently obvious when you properly identify primary keys. However, the 3NF version of these entities would have worked, although it isn't necessarily the most efficient form.

Now that we have a number of 3NF and 4NF entities, we must relate these entities to one another. The final normal form that we discuss is **fifth normal form** (5NF). 5NF specifically deals with relationships among three or more entities, often referred to as **tertiary** relationships. In 5NF, the entities that have specified relationships must be able to stand alone as individual entities without dependence on the other relationships. However, because the entities relate to one another, 5NF usually requires a physical entity that acts as a resolution entity to relate the other entities to one another. This additional entity has three or more foreign keys (based on the number of entities in the relationship) that specify how the entities relate to one another. This is how many-to-many relationships (as defined in Chapter 2) are actually implemented. Thus, if a many-to-many relationship is properly implemented, the database is in 5NF.

Frequently, you can avoid the complexity of 5NF by properly implementing foreign keys in the entities that relate to one another, so 4NF plus these keys generally avoids the physical implementation of a 5NF data model. However, because this alternative is not always realistic, 5NF is defined to help formalize this scenario.

Determining Normal Forms

As designers and developers, we are often tasked with creating a fresh data model for use by a new application that is being developed for a specific project. However, in many cases we are asked to review an existing model or physical implementation to identify potential performance improvements. Additionally, we are occasionally asked to solve logic problems in the original design. Whether you are reviewing a current design you are working on or evaluating another design that has already been implemented, there are a few common steps that you must perform regardless of the project or environment. One of the very first steps is to determine the normal form of the existing database. This information helps you identify logical errors in the design as well as ways to improve performance.

To determine the normal form of an existing model, follow these steps.

1. Conduct requirements interviews.

   As with the interviews you conduct when starting a fresh design, it is important to talk with key stakeholders and end users who use the application being supported by the database. There are two key concepts to remember. First, do this work before reviewing the design in depth. Although this may seem counterintuitive, it helps prevent you from forming a prejudice regarding the existing design when speaking with the various individuals involved in the project. Second, generate as much documentation for this review as you would for a new project. Skipping steps in this process will lead to poor design decisions, just as it would during a new project.

2. Develop a basic model.

   Based on the requirements and information you gathered from the interviews, construct a basic logical model. You'll identify key entities and their relationships, further solidifying your understanding of the basic database design.

3. Find the normal form.

   Compare your model to the existing model or database. Where are the differences? Why do those differences exist? Remember not to disregard the design decisions in the legacy database. It's important to focus on those differences, because they may stem from specific denormalization steps taken during the initial design, or they may exist because of information not available to the original designer. Specifically, identify the key entities, foreign key relationships, and any entities and tables that exist only in the physical model that are purely for relationship support (such as many-to-many relationships). You can then review the key and non-key attributes of every entity, evaluating for each normal form. Ask yourself whether or not each entity and its attributes follow the "The key, the whole key, and nothing but the key" ideal. For each entity that seems to be in 3NF, evaluate for BCNF and 4NF. This analysis will help you understand to what depth the original design was originally done. If there are many-to-many relationships, ensure that 5NF is met unless there is a specific reason that 5NF is not necessary.

Identifying the normal form of each entity in a database should be fairly easy once you understand the normal forms. Make sure to consider every attribute: does it depend entirely on the primary key? Does it depend only on the primary key? Is there only one candidate primary key in the entity? Whenever you find that the answer to these questions is no, be sure to look at creating a separate entity from the existing entity. This practice helps reduce redundancy and moves data to each element that is specific only to the entity that contains it.

If you follow these basic steps, you'll understand what forms the database meets, and you can identify areas of improvement. This will help you complete a thorough review—understanding where the existing design came from, where it's going, and how to get it there. As always, document your work. After you have finished, future designers and developers will thank you for leaving them a scalable, logical design.

Denormalization

Generally, most **online transactional processing** (OLTP) systems will perform well if they've been normalized to either 3NF or BCNF. However, certain conditions may require that data be intentionally duplicated or that unrelated attributes be combined into single entities to expedite certain operations. Additionally, **online analytical processing** (OLAP) systems, because of the way they are used, quite often require that data be denormalized to increase performance. **Denormalization,** as the term implies, is the process of reversing the steps taken to achieve a normal form. Often, it becomes necessary to violate certain normalization rules to satisfy the real-world requirements of specific queries. Let's look at some examples.

In data models that have a completely normalized structure, there tend to be a great many entities and relationships. To retrieve logical sets of data, you often need a great many joins to retrieve all the pertinent information about a given object. Logically this is not a problem, but in the physical implementation of a database, joins tend to incur overhead in query processing time. For every table that is joined, there is usually a cost to scan the indexes on that table and then retrieve the matching data from each object, combine the resulting data, and deliver it to the end user (for more on indexes and query optimization, see Chapter 10).

When millions of rows are being scanned and tens or hundreds of rows are being returned, it is costly. In these situations, creating a denormalized entity may offer a performance benefit, at the cost of violating one of the normal forms. The trade-off is usually a matter of having redundant data, because you are storing an additional physical table that duplicates data being stored in other tables. To mitigate the storage effects of this technique, you can often store subsets of data in the duplicate table, clearing it out and repopulating it based on the queries you know are running against it. Additionally, this means that you have additional physical objects to maintain if there are schema changes in the original tables. In this case, accurate documentation and a managed change control process are the only practices that can ensure that all the relevant denormalized objects stay in sync.

Denormalization also can help when you're working on reporting applications. In larger environments, it is often necessary to generate reports based on application data. Reporting queries often return large historical data sets, and when you join various types of data in a single report it incurs a lot of overhead on standard OLTP systems. Running these queries on exactly the same databases that the applications are trying to use can result in an overloaded system, creating blocking situations and causing end users to wait an unacceptable amount of time for the data. Additionally, it means storing large amounts of historical data in the OLTP system, something that may have other adverse effects, both internally to the database management system and to the physical server resources.

Denormalizing the data in the database to a set of tables (or even to a different physical database) specifically used for reporting can alleviate the pressure on the primary OLTP system while ensuring that the reporting needs are being met. It allows you to customize the tables being used by the reporting system to combine the data sets, thereby satisfying the queries being run in the most efficient way possible. Again, this means incurring overhead to store data that is already being stored, but often the trade-off is worthwhile in terms of performance both on the OLTP system and the reporting system.

Now let's look at OLAP systems, which are used primarily for decision support and reporting. These types of systems are based on the concept of providing a **cube** of data, whereby the dimensions of the cube are based on fact tables provided by an OLTP system. These **fact tables** are derived from the OLTP versions of data being stored in the relational database. These tables are often denormalized versions, however, and they are optimized for the OLAP system to retrieve the data that eventually is loaded into the cube. Because OLAP is outside the scope of this book, it's enough for now to know that if you're working on a system in which OLAP will be used, you will probably go through the exercise of building fact tables that are, in some respects, denormalized versions of your normalized tables.

When identifying entities that should be denormalized, you should rely heavily on the actual queries that are being used to retrieve data from these entities. You should evaluate all the existing join conditions and search arguments, and you should look closely at the data retrieval needs of the end users. Only after performing adequate analysis on these queries will you be able to correctly identify the entities that need to be denormalized, as well as the attributes that will be combined into the new entities. You'll also want to be very aware of the overhead the system will incur when you denormalize these objects. Remember that you will have to store not only the rows of data but also (potentially) index data, and keep in mind that the size of the data being backed up will increase.

Overall, denormalization could be considered the final step of the normalization process. Some OLTP systems have denormalized entities to improve the performance of very specific queries, but more than likely you will be responsible for developing an additional data model outside the actual application, which may be used for reporting, or even OLAP. Either way, understanding the normal forms, denormalization, and their implications for data storage and manipulation will help you design an efficient, logical, and scalable data model.

Summary

Every relational database must be designed to meet data quality, performance, and scalability requirements. For a database to be efficient, the data it contains must be maintained in a consistent and logical state. Normalization helps reveal design requirements that remove potential data manipulation anomalies.

However, strict normalization must often be balanced against specialized query needs and must be tested for performance. It may be necessary to denormalize certain aspects of a database to ensure that queries return in an acceptable time while still maintaining data integrity. Every design you work on should include phases to identify normal forms and a phase to identify denormalization needs. This practice will ensure that you've removed data consistency flaws while preserving the elements of a high-performance system.

This completes Part I, which has laid the foundation for building an effective data model. Part II begins with Chapter 5, Requirements Gathering, which launches the overall business process of designing and deploying a data model.

BUSINESS REQUIREMENTS

REQUIREMENTS GATHERING

It's likely that you are reading this book either because you've been given a project that will make you responsible for building a data model, or you would like to have the skills necessary to get a job doing this type of work. (Or perhaps you are reading this book for its entertainment value, in which case you should seriously consider seeking some sort of therapy.)

To explain the importance of bringing your customers into the design process, we like to compare data model design to automobile engine design. Knowing how to design an automobile engine is not something that many people take up as a passing fancy; if you learn how to design them, it's a good bet that you plan to make a career of it. There is a great deal of focus on the technical details: how the engine must run, what parts are necessary, and how to optimize the performance of the engine to meet the demands that will be placed on it. However, there is no way to know what those demands will be without knowing the type of automobile in which the engine will be placed. This is also true of data models; although the logical model revolves around the needs of the business, the database will be largely dependent on the application (or applications) that will load, retrieve, and allow users to manipulate data.

When you're gathering requirements, you must keep both of these factors in mind. When you're building a new data model, the single most important thing to know is why, and for whom, you are designing the data model. This requires extensive research with the users of the application that will eventually be the interface to the database, as well as a review of any existing systems (whether they are manual processes or automated processes).

It's also important to effectively document the information you've gathered and turn it into a formal set of requirements for the data model. In turn, you'll need to present the information to the key project stakeholders so that everyone can agree on the purpose, scope, and key deliverables before design and development begin.

In this chapter, we discuss the key steps involved in gathering requirements for a project, as well as the kinds of data to look for and some samples of the kinds of documentation you can use. Then, in Chapter 6, we discuss the compilation and distillation of the required data into design requirements.

Requirements Gathering Overview

The key to effectively gathering requirements that lead to good design is to have a well-planned, detailed gathering process. You should be able to develop and follow a methodology that includes repeatable processes and standardized documents so that you can rely on the process no matter which project you are working on. This approach allows you to focus on the quality of the data being gathered while maintaining a high level of efficiency. No one wants to pay a consultant or designer to relearn this phase of design; you should be comfortable walking into any situation, knowing that this step of the process will be smooth sailing. Because you'll talk to a number of the key stakeholders during this phase, they need to get a sense of confidence in your process. This confidence will help them buy in to the design you eventually present.

The next several sections outline the kinds of data you need to gather, along with possible methods for gathering that data. We also present sample questions and forms that you can use to document the information you gather from the users you talk with. In the end, you should be able to choose many of these methods, forms, and questions to build your own process, one you can reuse for your design projects.

Gathering Requirements Step by Step

There are four basic ways to collect requirements for a project: conducting user and stakeholder interviews, observing users, examining existing processes, and building use cases. Each of these methods provides insight into what is actually needed in the data model.

Conducting Interviews

Arguably the most used information gathering technique is the interview. It's natural; when you want to know something, usually you go ask the person you think can answer the question. So, when designing a new application, developers usually start with the individuals who use the current application (or manual process). A developer can quickly gain valuable insight into the existing processes as well as existing problems that the new application may be able to solve. The same thing is true with data modeling; the only difference may be that you will likely develop the data model in conjunction with an application, meaning that you will need to accompany the application developers on interviews with business users. It's also very likely that you will need to conduct slightly more detailed technical interviews with the application developer to identify the application's needs for data storage, manipulation, and retrieval.

Interviews should be conducted after the initial kickoff of the project, before any design meetings take place. In fact, it's a good idea to begin gathering a list of the candidates to be interviewed at the project kickoff, because that meeting will have a number of high-level managers who can identify the people who can give you the necessary information.

Key Stakeholders

Often the process of selecting individuals to be interviewed is equal parts political and technical. It's important to identify the people who can have the most insightful information on existing business processes, such as frontline employees and first-level managers. Usually, these are the end users of the application being built, and the primary source and destination of the data from a usage standpoint.

Additionally, it's a good idea to include other resources, such as vendors, customers, or business analysts. These people can provide input on how data is used by all facets of the business (incoming and outgoing) and offer a perspective on the challenges faced by the business and the goals being set for the proposed application.

Including people from all these groups will also help ensure that as many types of users as possible have input into the design process, something that increases the likelihood that they will buy in to the application design. Omitting any individual or group that is responsible for a significant portion of the business can lead to objections being raised late in the design process. This can have a derailing effect on the project, leaving everyone feeling that the project is in trouble.

When you select a list of potential interviewees, be aware that your initial list will likely be missing key people. As part of the interviewing process, it's very likely that you'll discover the other people who should be interviewed to gain deeper insight into specific processes. Be prepared to conduct multiple rounds of interviews to cover as much of the business as possible.

Sample Questions and Forms

Every project varies in size, scope, requirements, and deliverables. For small or medium-size projects, there may be four or five business users to interview. In some situations, however, you may have an application that has numerous facets or numerous phases, or you may need to design various data models to support related applications. In this situation, there may be dozens of people to interview, so it may be more efficient to draft a series of questionnaires that can help you gather a large portion of the data you'll need. You can then sort the responses, looking for individuals whom you may need to schedule in-person interviews with, to seek clarification or to determine whether there is more information to be shared.

Whether you use a questionnaire or conduct good old-fashioned in-person interviews, you'll need to build a list of questions to work from. To get an idea of the type of questions that should be asked, look at Table 5.1.

Table 5.1 Sample Questions for Requirements Gathering Interviews and Questionnaires

Question	Purpose	Candidate Type
What is your job role?	Identify the perspective of the candidate.	All
How many orders do you process daily/weekly/monthly?	Gain an idea of the workload.	Data entry personnel
How do customers place orders?	Understand how data is input into the system.	Customer service personnel
What information do you need that the current system does not provide?	Understand any information users are missing or may be gathering outside the existing process.	Fulfillment employees
What works well in the current system? What could be improved?	Gain insight into work-flow enhancements.	Employees, managers
Please explain your data entry process.	Understand the existing process.	Employees
How do you distribute the workload?	Understand ancillary data needs.	Managers

Notice that these questions tend to fall into one of two categories: open-ended questions and closed-ended questions. **Open-ended ques-**

tions, such as, "What works well in the current system?" give the interviewee room to provide all relevant information. Conversely, **closed-ended questions** tend to provide process-oriented information. Both types of questions provide relevant data. Both types should be included in in-person interviews as well as questionnaires. However, there's one thing to remember when using a questionnaire: Interviewees have no one to ask for clarification when filling out a questionnaire. Make your questions clear and concise; this often means that you include more closed-ended questions. It may be necessary to revisit the respondents to ask the open-ended questions and to obtain clarification on the questionnaires.

As interviews are conducted and questionnaires are returned, you need to document and store the information for later use. You may be gathering information from various types of sources (interviews, questionnaires, notes, etc.), so even if you don't use a questionnaire, consider typing up a document that lists the questions you'll be asking. This will help ensure that you ask the same (or similar) questions of each interviewee. It also means that when you start analyzing the responses, you'll be able to quickly evaluate each sheet for the pertinent information (in Chapter 6 we discuss how to recognize the key data points). The benefit of this practice is that if you need to switch from doing in-person interviews to using questionnaires, you'll already have a standard format for the questions and answers.

When you're working in conjunction with application developers (unless of course you are the application developer), they will ask most of these questions. However, as the data modeler you should be a part of this process in order to gain an understanding of how the data will be used and to have a better sense of what the underlying logical structure should look like. If you aren't conducting interviews (or if they've already taken place), ask for copies of the original responses or notes. Then work with the application developers to extract the information specific to the data model.

Observation

In addition to interviewing, observing the current system or processes may be one of the most important requirements gathering activities. For anyone involved in designing an application, it's vital to understand the work that must be accomplished and recognize how the organization is currently doing that work (and whether or not workers are doing it efficiently). It's easy for members of an application design team to let their own ideas of how the work "should" be done affect their ability to develop a useful application. Observing the workers actually doing their work will give you the necessary perspective on what must be done and how to improve the lives of the employees, compared with using the coolest new technology or technique simply because it's available.

Often, observation can be included in the interview time; this helps minimize disruption and gives workers the opportunity to step through their processes, something that may lead to more thorough information in the interview. However, it's a good idea to conduct interviews before observation, because observation is a good way to evaluate the validity of the information gathered during the interviews, and it may also clear up any confusion you may have about a given process. Either way, there are a few key questions you'll need to answer for yourself during observation to help ensure that you haven't missed anything that is important to the design of the data model.

- What data is being collected or input?
- Is there duplication of data? Are workers inputting the same data multiple times in different fields?
- Is any data being moved from one system to another (other than manual input to an application)? For example, are workers copying data from one application to another via cut and paste?

Each of these questions will help you gain insight into what the current work flow is and where problems may exist in the process. For example, if users frequently copy data from one application (or spreadsheet) to another, there may be an opportunity to consolidate data sources. Or, in the case of an existing database, there may be issues with relationships that require a single piece of data be put into multiple locations. This kind of observation will give you hints of aspects of the process that need more investigation or ideas for designing a new process (supported by your data model) that will reduce the workload on employees.

Finally, you should observe multiple users who have the same job function. People tend to behave differently when they are being watched than when they are going about their business unsupervised. People tend to develop shortcuts or work around certain business rules because they feel it is more effective to do so. Understanding these shortcuts will help you understand what is wrong in the current process.

When you conduct an observation, interrupt as little as possible; it may even be best to note any questions you have and do a post-observation interview for clarification. In any case, be conscious that what you see may not be what you get; if you find that observation data and interview data conflict, more analysis and investigation are necessary.

Previous Processes and Systems

Frequently, when a developer has been engaged to create an application, it is because either an existing manual process needs some degree of automation or an existing application no longer meets the needs of the business. This means that in addition to the techniques we've talked about so far, you need to evaluate the existing process to truly understand the direction the new application should take. For the data modeler, it's important to see how the company's data is being generated, used, and stored. Additionally, you'll want to understand the quality of the data and develop ways to improve it.

Manual Systems

In a manual process or system (no computer applications being used), the first order of business is to acquire copies of any and all business process documents that may have been created. These include flowcharts, instruction sheets, and spreadsheets—any document that outlines how the manual processes are conducted. Additionally, you need sample copies of all forms, reports, invoices, and any other documents being used. You need to analyze these forms to determine the kind of data they are collecting and the ways they are being used. In addition to blank copies, it is helpful to acquire copies of forms that contain actual data. Together, these documents should give you a comprehensive view of how the employees conduct business on a daily basis, at least on paper.

You should also work with employees and management during the interview process to understand how the documents are generated, updated, and stored. This practice will give you insight into which data is considered long term and which is considered short term. You then need to compare the documents against the information you received during interviews and observation. If you find discrepancies between the forms and their use, you'll know that there is an opportunity to improve the work flow, and not only automate it. Also, you may identify documents that are rarely (or never) used, or documents that have information written in (because the form contains no relevant data field); these are also clear indications of problems with the existing process that you can solve in the new system.

Existing Applications

In many ways, redesigning (or replacing) an existing application can be more difficult than building a new application to replace a manual process. This is because there is an existing work flow built around the application, not to mention the data that has already been stored. Often, the new system will need to mimic certain behaviors of the existing system while changing the actual work under the hood. Also, you need to understand the data being stored and figure out a way to migrate the existing data to the new system.

In addition to formal applications, you should take this time to look for spreadsheets or end user database solutions, such as Microsoft Access, that may exist in the organization. Often, data stored on users' computers is just as important as something that makes it into an enterprise solution. These "islands of information" exist in the users' domain of control, and typically this kind of information is hard to pry away from them without management intervention.

To analyze and understand the existing application from a data modeling standpoint, you should acquire copies of any process flow documents, data models, data dictionaries, and application documentation (everything from the original requirements documents to training documents). If nothing else, generate (or ask for) schema definitions for all existing physical databases, including all tables, views, stored procedures, functions, and so on. Try to gather screen captures of any application windows that require user data input, as well as screens that output data to the user. Also, you'll need the actual code being used by the application as it pertains to data access. All these documents will help you understand how the application is manipulating data; in some cases, there may be specific logic embedded in the application that can be handled in the database. Knowing this ahead of time will help prevent confusion during application design.

In addition, you need to look at the application from a functionality standpoint. Does it do what the customer wants it to do, or are there gaps in its feature set? This review can be helpful in determining the processes that you want to carry forward to the new system, processes that should be dropped, and processes that may be missing from the current system and need to be added. These existing applications may also provide you with other system requirements that will be implemented outside the data model, such as

- Access control and security requirements
- Data retention requirements
- Process work flow

You also need to compare the interview and observation notes against the use of the existing application. Are there manual processes that support the application? In other words, do users have to take extra steps to make the application function or to add or change data already stored in the application? Certain user actions—such as formatting phone numbers in a field that contains a series of numbers with no format—indicate problems in the existing system that could be fixed in the database itself.

Use Cases

If you're familiar with common software engineering theory, you know the concept of use cases. **Use cases** describe various scenarios that convey how users (or other systems) will interact with the system that is being designed to achieve specific goals or business functions. Generally, use cases avoid highly technical language in favor of natural language explanations of the various parts of the system in each scenario. This allows business analysts, management, and other nontechnical stakeholders to understand what the system is doing and how it helps the business succeed.

From a design standpoint, the process of building use cases provides deeper insight into what is required of the system. Use cases are logical models in that they are concerned only with tasks that need to be completed and the order in which they must be done, without describing how they are implemented in the system. To build effective use cases, it is essential to work with various end users who will be interacting with the system once it is built. They will help provide, via the techniques we've talked about so far, low-level detail on the actual work that needs to be accomplished, without being distracted by technical implementation details.

To effectively present a new design, you often need to develop at least two kinds of use cases: one for the existing process, and one for the new process. This practice helps nontechnical stakeholders understand the differences and reassures them that the value from the current system will be carried forward to the new system.

A number of references are available that can give you detailed information on developing use cases; for our purposes, we present a template that covers most aspects of use case description, along with a simple use case diagram. Feel free to use these in your project work.

Now let's take a look at building a sample use case.

Use Case Descriptions

A **use case description** is the basic document that outlines, at a high level, the process that the use case describes. From the description you can build a **use case diagram** that lays out the entire process (or set of processes) associated with a system. The use case description generally consists of all the information needed to build the use case diagram, but in a text-based format. See Figure 5.1 for a sample use case description of a process involving an operator booking a conference call for a customer.

This document contains several types of information. Let's break it down into sections, field by field.

- Overview information
  The first six boxes describe what the use case documents, as well as general administrative overhead for the document itself.
  - Use case name
    This is the name of the specific use case being described. The name should be the same on both the description document and the use case diagram (which we discuss a bit later).
  - ID
    This is a field that can be used to help correlate documents during the design process.
  - Priority
    In some scenarios, it may be necessary to prioritize use cases (and their corresponding processes) to help determine the importance of certain processes over others.
  - Principal
    This is usually the trigger of the use case; it's generally a customer (internal or external), another process, or a business-driven decision. This is the thing that causes the process documented by this use case to be executed. (In some references, the principal is called an **actor**.)
  - Use case type
    There are two types of use cases and two levels of use cases. **Overview** use cases contain very high-level, basic information about a process. In contrast, **detailed** use cases contain as much information as possible about the process. You can also classify use cases by the type of information they contain. **Essential** use cases contain information about the general steps executed within the process, and **real** use cases describe the specific implementation

Use case name: Make reservation		ID: 11	Priority: High
Principal: Customer		Use case type: Detailed, Essential	
Stakeholders: Customer - Wants to make a reservation, or change an existing reservation Reservationist - Wants to provide customer with service.			
Description: This use case describes how the business makes a reservation for a conference call, as well as describing how the business makes changes to an existing reservation.			
Trigger: Customer calls into the reservations line and asks to make a reservation or change an existing reservation. Type: External			

Relationships:
 	
   Include: Manage Bridge Lines
 	
   Extend: Create Customer Record
 	
   Generalization: Base use case			

Flow of Events:
1. Customer calls the reservations line.
2. Customer uses interactive voice response system to choose "Make or Change Reservation."
3. Customer provides Reservationist with name, address, company name, and ID number.
   a. If no ID number, then Reservationist executes Create Customer Record use case.
4. Reservationist asks if Customer would like to make a new reservation, change an existing reservation, or cancel a reservation.
   a. If Customer wants to make a new reservation, then S-1; new reservation subflow is performed.
   b. If Customer wants to make a change to a reservation, then S-2; modify reservation subflow is performed.
   c. If Customer wants to cancel a reservation, then S-3; cancel reservation subflow is performed.
5. Reservationist provides confirmation of reservation or change to Customer.			

Subflows:
S-1: New Reservation
   1. Reservationist asks for desired date, time, and number of participants for conference call.
   2. Reservationist executes Manage Bridge Lines use case. If no lines available found, suggest alternate availability.
   3. Reservationist books conference call after reaching agreement with Customer; gives Conference Call Number.
S-2: Modify Reservation
   1. Reservationist asks for Conference Call Number.
   2. Reservationist locates existing reservation.
   3. Reservationist performs S-1 if changing time; S-3 if canceling.
S-3: Cancel Reservation
   1. Reservationist asks for Conference Call Number.
   2. Reservationist locates existing reservation.
   3. Reservationist cancels conference using Manage Bridge Lines use case.			

FIGURE 5.1   Use case description

details of each step. For example, an essential use case might document that a rental car company employee "matches available cars to a customer"; the corresponding real use case documents that the employee "uses a third-party application to review available inventory by model to determine the best available vehicle based on the customer's request."

- Stakeholders
  These are the individuals who have a tangible, immediate interest in the process. In our example, a customer wants to reserve a conference call, and a reservationist assists customers. In this context, stakeholders are not those individuals who benefit from the process in an ancillary way (such as the employees' manager). This list always includes the principal.

- Description
  The purpose of the process documented in the use case is to meet the needs of the principal; the brief description is usually a single statement that describes the process and how it meets that need.

- Trigger
  The trigger is simply a statement describing what it is that sets this process in motion.

- Type
  A trigger can be an **external** trigger, meaning it is set in motion by an external event, such a customer call. Or a trigger can be **temporal,** meaning it is enacted because of a timed event or because of the passage of time, such as an overdue movie rental.

- Relationships
  The relationships explain how this use case is related to other use cases, as well as users. There are three basic types of relationships for use cases: include, extend, and generalization.

  - **Include**
    This relationship describes which other use cases must be executed in order for this use case to complete. Using this relationship, it is possible to break down complex systems into individual, related use cases. After design begins, this relationship makes it easy to break the workload into smaller pieces, enabling multiple teams to work on a single system simultaneously.

■ **Extend**

Most processes have optional behavior that is outside the "normal" course of events for that process. In our example, creating a customer record is a process that only occasionally needs to execute within the context of making or modifying a reservation. So the use case "Create Customer Record" is listed as an extension of the current use case.

■ **Generalization**

In some cases, certain use cases inherit properties of other use cases, or are **child** use cases. Whenever there is a more general use case whose children inherit properties, there is a *generalization* relationship between the use cases. In our example, the use case is the parent use case. We look at a sample child use case a little later.

■ Flow of Events

This section deals with the actual events that occur in the process—the meat and potatoes. Be sure to document the majority of the steps necessary to complete the process.

■ Subflows

Here's where you document any branches in the process, to account for various actions that need to take place. Depending on the level of detail you are putting into the use case, this section may become quite lengthy. Be careful to note any use cases whose Subflows section becomes too long; this indicates that you may need separate use cases to break down the process.

You can choose to add other types of information, from the execution time of the process to lists of prerequisites for the use case to be activated. It may also be worthwhile, in the case of detailed use cases, to document the data inputs and outputs. This will be particularly important to you as a data modeler so that you can associate data movement with the processes that will be built on top of the database.

Use Case Diagrams

Now that you have documented the process as a use case, you have the building blocks necessary to create a use case diagram. A **use case diagram** is a visual representation of how a system functions. Each process, or use case, is shown in the diagram in relation to all the other use cases that make up the system. Additionally, the diagram shows every person (principal) and trigger to show how each use case is initiated.

Remember that a use case (and a use case diagram) is a very basic documentation of a system and its processes. As such, a use case diagram is a general-use document and can seem almost overly simplified in comparison with the actual system. Its usefulness comes from relating the processes to one another and from giving nontechnical as well as technical personnel a way to communicate about the system.

To expand on our use case description example, take a look at Figure 5.2, which describes the conference call system. Note that this diagram conforms to the Unified Modeling Language (UML) specifications for use case diagrams.

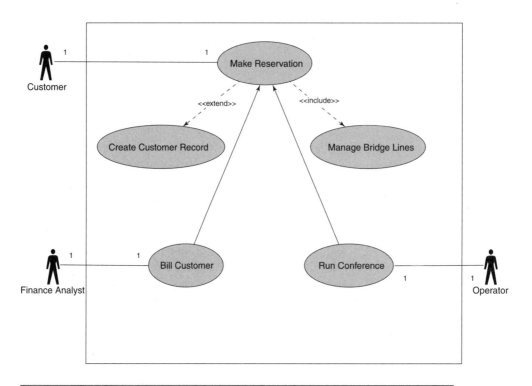

FIGURE 5.2 Use case diagram for conference call system

Unified Modeling Language

UML is a standards specification established and maintained by the Object Management Group (OMG). UML establishes a common language that can be used to build a blueprint for software systems. More information can be found at the OMG Web site at www.omg.org.

This diagram lays out the individual relationships between each use case in the conference call system. The use case we documented, "Make Reservation," is a base use case that includes the "Manage Bridge Lines" use case, and it is extended by the functionality in the "Create Customer Record" use case. Additionally, you can see that both the "Run Conference" and "Bill Customer" use cases inherit properties from the "Make Reservation" use case. And finally, you can see the principals (or actors) that trigger the use cases. This diagram, when combined with the use case descriptions for each use case, can help everyone involved in the project talk through the entire system with a common reference in place.

Remember that most projects have a great many of these diagrams. As a data modeler, you're responsible for understanding most these diagrams, because most of them either input data into the system or retrieve and update data already in the system. Thus, it is important to attend the use case modeling meetings and to make sure to include your input into how each system interacts with the company's data.

Business Needs

In case it hasn't been said enough in this book so far, now is a good time to remind you: Applications, and their databases, exist only to meet the needs of an enterprise, whether it's a business, a school, or a nonprofit venture. This means that one of the most important aspects of application design, and the design of the application's supporting database, is to develop a strong understanding of the organization's needs and to figure out how your design will meet those needs.

To identify the business needs, you usually meet with the key stakeholders. Usually, the organization has already identified a business need (or needs) before initiating a development project. It is your job, however, to identify the specific needs that are being addressed by the application that your data model will support, and to determine how your data model helps meet those needs. During the initial round of project meetings, as well as during interviews, listen for key words such as *response time, reporting, improve work flow, cut costs,* and so on. These words and phrases are key indicators that you are talking about the needs to be addressed by the project. From a data modeling perspective, you may be responsible for implementing the business logic enforcing certain rules about the data, or you may be responsible for helping to determine supporting data (and objects) that may not be immediately evident.

It's critical that all your design decisions align with the end goal of the project. Often, this means knowing the limitations of your technology and understanding how that technology relates to the business.

Balancing Technical Limitations with Business Needs

Now that you've identified all the areas where your design can help the organization, it's time to temper ambition with a touch of pragmatism. As information technology and information systems specialists, we tend to follow the latest and greatest in hardware, software, and design and development techniques. A large part of our careers is based on our ability to learn new technology, and we like to incorporate everything we've learned into our projects. Similarly, businesspeople (owners, analysts, users) want their applications to do everything, be everything, and solve every problem, without ever throwing an error. Unfortunately, the temptation to use everything we know to meet the highest expectations can lead to almost uncontrollable scope creep in a design project.

To balance what can be done against what needs to be done, you need to engage in a little bit of prioritization. Once you have the list of requirements, the data from the interviews, and so on, you need to decide which tasks are central to the project and determine the priority of each task.

Gathering Usage Data

Now it's time to look at the performance-related data you need in order to successfully design a functional, scalable data model. Although it's not technically a part of the core data model design, it's worthwhile to begin collecting and understanding information that relates to how a database, in its physical implementation, will perform. Initially, you should note any information gathered during the observation, interview, and use case phases to determine how much data will be created and manipulated and how that data will be stored. Additionally, if you are replacing an existing online system, you'll get an idea of how the current system performs and how that will translate into the new system.

Reads versus Writes

When you are conducting user interviews and observations, be sure to note the kinds of data manipulation taking place. Are users primarily inputting data, or are they retrieving and updating existing data? How many times does the same record get touched? Knowing the answers to questions like these can help you get an idea of how the eventual application will handle the data in your database.

For example, consider a project to redesign a work-flow application for high school teachers who need to track attendance and grades. During multiple observations with the teachers and administrators, you see teachers inputting attendance for each student every day, but they may enter grades only once a week. In addition to gathering information about what data is collected and how users enter that data (in terms of data types and so on), you note that they update attendance records often but update grades less often.

In another observation, you see a school administrator running reports on student attendance based on multiple criteria: daily, monthly, per student, per department, and so on. However, they've told you they access grades only on a quarterly basis (semester quarters—every eight weeks—and not calendar quarters). Similarly, you've noted that the grades call for a moderate number of writes in the database (on a weekly basis) and an even lower number of reads. You now know that the attendance records have a high number of writes but a lower number of reads. Again, this information may not necessarily affect design, but it helps you leverage certain specific features of SQL Server 2008 in the physical implementation phase. In Chapters 9 and 10 we go into detail; for now, it's enough to know that gathering this information during the requirements gathering phase of design is important for future use.

Data Storage Requirements

As with gathering read and write data, compiling some data storage requirements early in design will help smooth the physical implementation. Even during the design phase, knowing ahead of time how much data you'll be storing can affect some design decisions.

Let's go back to the work-flow application for those high school teachers. Table 5.2 shows the sample data being input for those attendance records; we'll call this the Attendance entity.

Table 5.2 Sample Data Being Input for Attendance Records

Field Name	Data Type	Description
StudentID	Int	Student identifier
Date	Datetime	Date for attendance record
Class	char(20)	Name of the class attended (or not)
TeacherID	Int	Teacher identifier
Note	char(200)	Notes about the entry (e.g., "tardy due to weather")

Obviously, there are some assumptions being made here concerning StudentID and TeacherID (being foreign keys to other entities). For now, let's focus on the data types that were chosen. As discussed in Chapter 3, we know the amount of bytes each record in the physical table will occupy. Here, we have 8 bytes of int data, 220 bytes of char data, and 8 bytes from the datetime field. Altogether, we have 236 bytes per record. If we have 1,200 students in the school, for each date we have about 283,200 bytes, or 276.56K. The average school year is about 180 days; this is roughly 48MB of data for a school year. What does this mean to us? The attendance data, in and of itself, is not likely to be a storage concern. Now, apply this exercise quickly to every entity that you are working on, and you'll find roughly how much data you'll be storing.

Although this knowledge has huge value during implementation, you may wonder why we're talking about it now. Suppose that, during the design phase, you are given a last-minute requirement to change the identity fields because the new student identifiers require a much longer field. Now the stakeholders want an alphanumeric ID (for now, we ignore the merits of such a decision). Suddenly, we're storing a 12-character char field for both of those two int fields. Substituting the new values, we end up with 52MB of data for the same entity and time period. Although in this case the difference is negligible, in other entities it could have a huge impact. Knowing what the impact will be on those larger entities may drive you to review the decision to change a data type before committing to it, because it could have a significant effect in the physical implementation.

Again, most of this information will be more useful later in the project. Remembering to gather the data (and compile and recompile it during initial design) is the important thing for now.

Transaction Requirements

This might be the most important type of performance-related data to obtain during requirements gathering. You need to forecast the kind of transaction load your data model will need to support. Although the pure logical design will be completely independent of SQL Server's performance, it's likely that you will be responsible for developing and implementing the physical database as well (or at least asked to provide guidance to the development team). And as we discussed in Chapter 4, the degree of normalization, and the number of entities, can lead to bulky physical databases, resulting in poor query performance.

As with the other types of data being gathered, you glean this information primarily from interviews, observations, and review of the existing system. Generally, to start identifying the transaction load on your model, you must identify pieces of information that relate to both transaction speed and transaction load. For example, whenever there is a process in place that requires a user to wait for the retrieval of data—such as a customer service operator bringing up a customer record—you'll need to understand the overall goal for the expediency of that record retrieval. Is there a hard-and-fast business rule in place? For example, a web application might need to reduce the amount of time a web user must wait for a page to return with data, and therefore it would restrict how much time a database query can take. Similarly, you'll want to take notes on how many users are expected to hit the database built from your model at any given time. Will there be internal and external users? How many on average, and how many during peak times? What is the expected number of users a year from now? The answers to these questions will give you insight into performance expectations.

Again, consider the example of our teacher work-flow application. What if, instead of being designed for one school, the school board decides that this application should span all schools in the district so that it could centralize reporting and maintenance? Suddenly, the model you were developing for 200 users at a school with 1,200 students may need to support 1,200 users managing records for 7,200 students. Before, the response times were based on application servers in a school interacting with database servers in the same room. Now, there may be application servers all over, or possibly at the central administration offices, and there may be only one database server to support them all. However, the organization still expects the same response time even though the application (and database) will have to handle an increased load and latency. You will need to compile and review this information during design to ensure that your model will scale well. Do you need any additional entities or relationships? Are there new attributes to existing entities? And, when physically implemented, will your data model support the new requirements?

Summary

Gathering requirements is daunting and sometimes tedious, but it is a crucial step in the design phase of a functional data model. The key is to gather as much data as possible; documents, screen captures, code, spreadsheets, interviews, observations, and use cases are all things you can use to figure out exactly what the new design will be. Here we've presented some techniques for gathering data. In the next chapter, we look at how to take the volumes of data we've gathered and turn it into requirements that will guide the design and development process for our fictitious company, Mountain View Music.

CHAPTER 6

INTERPRETING REQUIREMENTS

In Chapter 5, we looked at gathering the requirements of the business. This process is similar to the process you go through whether you are building a house, developing an application, or trying to plan a birthday party. Much of what we look at is theory and can be applied in any of these scenarios. Sure, we looked at a few topics specific to database design, but the overall process is generic.

In this chapter, we get at the heart of database design; we look at how you begin to shape the business requirements into a database model, and eventually a physical database. We also get into the specifics of our make-believe customer, Mountain View Music, by taking a look at its requirements and exploring how to turn them into a model.

Mountain View Music

Before we go further, let's get an overview of Mountain View Music. It is important that you understand the company we will be working with and know how it is laid out; it will help you better understand the requirements as we talk about them. Again, this is a company that we made up out of thin air.

We've tried to keep the numbers and the details as realistic as possible. In fact, at one point we both sat down and actually discussed the company's warehousing operation in detail. We figured out the likely busy times and came up with a staffing schedule that would make sense to cover the shipment demand. We wanted to figure out how big the company is to help us determine the transaction load to expect on the database. The scenario is as real as we can make it; don't be surprised if we go into the Internet musical equipment business after this book is complete.

Mountain View Music was founded in 1991 in Manitou Springs, Colorado. The founder, Bill Robertson, is a passionate music lover with a keen business sense. All through high school and college he participated in music programs. Not only was he a musician, but also he provided leadership help where he could. Eventually, Bill ended up with an MBA from Colorado University, thus cementing his career as a music entrepreneur.

After it opened, it didn't take long for Mountain View Music to become popular with the locals. Customers from Manitou Springs, Colorado Springs, and the surrounding areas loved the small shop's atmosphere, and they all got along with Bill.

Mountain View offered competitive prices, and the company had a line on some hard-to-find items. Because of this, Mountain View received several calls a day from customers who wanted to order products and have them shipped to other parts of the state. In 1995, Bill decided to expand the business to include mail orders. This move required a substantial investment in new employees, along with a warehouse from which to ship products. The warehouse is located near downtown Colorado Springs. Just as hoped, the mail order arm of Mountain View music took off, and soon the company was processing about 500 orders per week. This may not sound like a lot, but considering the average order was about $350, the mail order arm was pulling in a little more than $170,000 per week.

The next logical step for a successful mail order company in the late nineties was the big move to e-commerce. Mountain View played with designing its own Web site and started working with a small development company to achieve a more professional look. By 1999, the site was in full swing, serving 600 to 700 orders per week. Much to the disappointment of the local music community, the storefront in Manitou Springs was shut down in 2000 because it was not as profitable as the online music store.

Despite some bumps in the road after the dot-com bubble burst, Mountain View Music came through and is still running. At this point, Mountain View Music has the typical problem you will see in formerly small companies: a disjointed use of IT. Because the company started as a small retail location, it started with everything on pen and paper. Since its beginnings, a few computers have been brought in, and some of the company's information has slowly migrated to spreadsheets and a few third-party applications. Much of this information is redundant, and keeping everything straight has become a bit daunting.

This is where we come into the picture. Mountain View has brought in an outside consulting firm to help it redesign its systems. We are that firm's database designers. The project is a complete redesign of the current order management systems. Mountain View wants a single application with a single database that can manage its business. Because all the financial and accounting work is done by a third-party company, the new system will not need to handle any financials beyond the details of the orders and purchases the company makes. For the rest of this book, we focus on the process of building and implementing this new database. Along the way we look at some application integration points, but our focus is on the database design.

Compiling Requirements Data

The first thing you must do after you have all the requirements is to compile them into a usable set of information. Step 1 is to determine which of the data you've received is useful and which isn't. This can be tricky, and often it depends on the scope of the project. If you're building a new database and designing a new application for your customer, you may find a lot more data that is useful, but not to the database design. For example, customers may tell you that the current system needs more fields from which data can be cut and pasted. Although this is helpful data, it's something that the application architects and developers need to know about, and not something that concerns a database designer.

Hopefully, on joint projects, everyone with a role in the project can get together and sort through the requirements together and separate the good from the bad and the ugly. We focus on the information that you, as the database designer, really need to do your job. The rest of the data can be set aside or possibly given to a different team.

Identifying Useful Information

What makes information useful to a database designer? In short, it's anything and everything that tells you about data, how data relates to other data, or how data is used. This may sound a little oversimplified, but it is often overlooked. You need to consider any piece of data that could end up in the database. This means that you can leave no stone unturned. Also, you may end up with additional requirements from application developers, or even your own requirements, such as those that will ensure referential integrity. These too are important pieces of information that you will receive.

Here are examples of useful information you may receive:

- Interview descriptions of processes
- Diagrams of current systems or databases
- Notes taken during observation sessions
- Lists that describe data that is required to meet a regulation
- Business reports
- Number estimates, such as sales per day or shipments per hour
- Use case diagrams

This list certainly isn't exhaustive, but it gives you a good idea of what to look for in the requirements. Keep in mind that some information that you need to keep may not directly affect the database design, but instead will be useful for the database implementation. For example, you need information about data usage, such as how many orders the company handles per day, or how many customers the company has. This type of information probably won't influence your design, but it will greatly affect how you pick indexes and plan for data storage.

Also, be on the lookout for irrelevant information; for example, some information gathered during user interviews doesn't offer any real value. Not all users provide helpful details when they are asked. To illustrate this point, here is a funny anecdote courtesy of one of our tech editors. While working on redesigning an application for a small college, he kept asking, "How long can a name be?" The reply he received was, "An address label is four inches wide." This answer is not wrong, of course, but it's not very useful. Be very clear with your customers, and guide them toward the answer you need; in this case, ask them how many letters a name can have.

One last note: Keep your eyes open for conflicting data. If you ask three people about the ordering process and you get three different answers, you may have stumbled upon a process that users do not fully understand. When this happens, you may need to sit down with the users, their supervisors, or even upper management and have them decide how the process should work.

Identifying Superfluous Information

Superfluous information is, by definition, extra or redundant information. We won't go as far as to call it useless, because it may be useful to other groups or during other phases of design. Here, you are looking for anything that doesn't help to further define the data requirements. Anything that has nothing to do with data, its usage, or relationships can probably be ignored. Don't destroy this data, but set it aside and do not use it as one of your main sources of information.

Here are a few examples of superfluous information you may receive from your customers:

- Application usage reports
- Employee staffing numbers
- Diagrams of office layout
- Company history
- Organization charts

Much of this type of data may help you in your endeavors, but it isn't really linked to data. However, some of these items may provide you with information you will need when implementing the database. For example, an org chart may be handy when you're figuring out security. Remember that the focus here is to find the data you need in order to design the database model. Also, keep in mind that requirements gathering is an iterative process, so don't be afraid to go back to users for clarification. A piece of information that seems to be useless could prove to be invaluable with a little more detail.

Determining Model Requirements

After you have sorted through the requirements, you can start to put together your conceptual model. The **conceptual model** is a very high-level look at the entities, their attributes, and the relationships between the entities. The most important components here are the entities and their attributes. You still aren't thinking in terms of tables; you just need to look at entities. Although you will start to look at the attributes that are required for each entity, it isn't crucial at this point to have every attribute nailed down. Later, when you finish the conceptual model, you can go back to the company and make sure you have all the attributes you need in order to store the required data.

Interpreting User Interviews and Statements

The first thing you need to do is make a high-level list of the entities that you think the data model needs. The two main places you will look are the user interviews and any current system documentation you have available.

Keep in mind that you can interview users or have them write an overview of the process. In some cases you may do both, or you may come back after the fact and interview a user about an unclear statement.

The following statement comes from the write-up that Bill Robertson, Mountain View Music owner and CEO, gave us regarding the company's overall business process.

> Customers log on to our Web site and place an order, or call an employee who places the order on the customers' behalf. All orders contain the customer information, the order detail, which has information about the products, the quantities that the customer purchased, and the payment method. When we receive the order into the system, the customer information has already been checked and crucial bits, such as the customer's address, have been verified by the site. The first thing we do is process the order items. We make sure that the products being purchased are in stock and we place a hold on those products. If a product is not in stock, we place that item or the entire order on back order, depending on the customer's preference. Products that are in stock have a hold placed on them. Once the products are on hold, we process the payment for the order. By law, once we accept payment, we must ship within 30 days. This is why we make sure the product is on hold before we process the payment. For payment, we take credit cards, gift cards, and direct bank draft via an electronic check. After the payment has been cleared, we send the order to the warehouse where is it picked, packed, and shipped by our employees. We do this for about 1,000 orders per week.

This very brief overview gives us a lot of details about the type of data that the company needs to store as well as how it uses that data. From this we can start to develop an entity list for our conceptual model. Notice that this is a pretty typical explanation that a user might give regarding a process. What we like to see are clear and concise explanations without a lot of fluff. That is exactly what the CEO has provided us here.

Modeling Key Words

Certain words that you see in the information provided you by your customers will help you figure out the kinds of objects you should include in the data model. There are four things to look for when examining key words: entities, attributes, relationships, and usage detail (if any). Let's look at the kinds of key words that would lead us to find the data diamonds in the rough.

Entities Key Words

We look for nouns to help us find entities. Nouns are people, places, and things. Most entities represent a collection of things, specifically physical things that we work with. It is for this reason that nouns are a great identifier of entities. Let's say a user tells you that the company has several sites and each site has at least ten employees. You can use the nouns to start an entity list; in this case, the nouns are *site* and *employees.* You have now determined that you will need a Site and an Employee entity in the data model.

Attribute Key Words

Like entities, attributes are described as nouns, but the key difference is that an attribute does not describe more than a single piece of data. For example, if a customer describes a vehicle, you will likely want to know more about the information he needs about the vehicle. When a customer describes the vehicle identification number (VIN) for a vehicle, there isn't much more detail to be had. Vehicle is an entity, and VIN is an attribute.

When we look for attributes, we also need to look for applied ownership of information. Words like *own, have, contain,* or *belong* are your biggest clues that you might have a few attributes being described. Ownership can describe a relationship when it's ownership between two entities, so make sure you don't turn entities into attributes and vice versa. Phrases like "Students have a unique student ID number" indicate that students own student IDs, and hence a student ID is one attribute of a student. You also need to look for phrases like, "For customers we track x, y, and z." Tracking something about an entity is often a flag that the something is an attribute.

Relationship Key Words

The same kinds of key words you looked for to determine attributes can also apply to relationships. The key difference is that relationships show ownership of other relationships. How do you tell the difference between an attribute and a relationship? That is where a little experience and trial and error play a big role. If I say, "An order *has* an order date and order details," I am implying that an order owns both an order date and order details. In other words, the order date is a single piece of information, whereas order details present more questions about the data required for the details; but both are part of an order.

Additionally, verbs can describe relationships between entities. Saying that an employee *processes* an order describes a relationship between your employee and your order entity.

Key Words in Practice

Using these key word rules, let's look again at the statement given us by Mountain View's CEO. We start by highlighting the nouns that will help us establish our entity list. Before you read further, go back to the original statement and come up with an entity list of your own; later you can compare it to the list we came up with.

> *Customers* log on to our Web site and place an *order*, or call an *employee* who places the *order* on the *customers'* behalf. All *orders* contain the customer information, the *order detail*, which has information about the *products* and quantities that the *customer* purchased, and the *payment* method. When we receive the *order* into the system, the customer information has already been checked and crucial bits, such as the customer's address, have been verified by the site. The first thing we do is process the *order items*. We make sure that the *products* being purchased are in stock and we place a hold on those *products*. If a *product* is not in stock, we place that item or the entire *order* on back order, depending on the *customer's* preference. *Products* that are in stock have a hold placed on them. Once the *products* are on hold, we process the *payment* for the order. By law, once we accept *payment*, we must ship within 30 days. This is why we make sure the *product* is on hold before we process the *payment*. For *payment*, we take credit cards, gift cards, and direct bank draft via an electronic check. After the *payment* has been cleared, we send the *order* to the warehouse where is it picked, packed, and shipped by our *employees*. We do this for about 1,000 orders per week.

You'll notice that we highlighted the possible entity nouns each time they occurred. This helps us determine the overall criticality of each possible entity. Here is the complete list of possible entities from the statement:

- Customer
- Order
- Order Detail, Order Item
- Product
- Payment
- Employee

Each of the entities in this list describes something that the business works with and needs to store data about. Most of them are obvious, but payment was a little harder to pick out. Initially when going through the statement, it may look as though a payment is simply an attribute of the order, but that interpretation is mistaken. Later when the various payment methods are described, we see that there is much more to payment methods than meets the eye. For this reason, we listed it as an entity, something that may change as we gather more data. Also watch out for words or phrases that could change the meaning of the data, such as *usually, most of the time,* or *almost always.* If the customer says that orders are usually paid for with one form of payment, you will want to clarify to make sure that the database can handle the "usually" as well as the "rest of the time."

Next, let's go over the same statement for key words that may describe attributes. At this early point, we wouldn't expect to find all or even most of our attributes. Once we have a complete list of entities we will return to the organization and hammer out a complete list of the required attributes that will be stored for each entity. Just the same, if you run through the statement again, you should find a few attributes. Following is a new entity list with the attributes we can glean from the statement:

- Customer
  Address
- Order
- Order Detail, Order Item
  Quantity
- Product
- Payment
  Credit Cards
  Gift Cards
  Electronic Check
- Employee

We now know that we must track the customer's address and the quantity ordered for an order item. It's not much, but it's a start. We could probably expand Address into its component parts, such as city, state, ZIP, and so on, but we need a little more detail before we make any assumptions. Again, payment offers a bit more complexity. The only further details we have about payment are the three payment methods mentioned: credit cards, gift cards, and electronic checks. Each of these seems to have more detail that we are missing, but we are reluctant to split them into separate entities; it's bad modeling design to have multiple entities that contain the same data, or nearly the same type. Later we talk more about the difficulty surrounding payments.

Last but not least, we need to determine the relationships that exist between our entities. Once more, we need to go through the statement to look for ownership or action key words as they relate to entities. This time, we create a list that describes the relationship in a natural language (in our case, English), and later we translate it to an actual modeling relationship. This step can be a bit trickier than determining entities and attributes, and you have to do a little inferring to find all the detail about the relationships. The following list shows all the relationships we can infer from the data; in each case the suspected parent of the relationship is shown in italics.

- *Customers* place Orders
- *Employees* place Orders
- *Orders* contain Order Details
- Order Details have some quantity of *Products*
- *Orders* contain Payments

Once we have the initial list, we can translate these relationships into modeling terms. Then we will be ready to put together a high-level **entity relationship diagram** (ERD). Much of the data you need is right here in the CEO's statement, but you may have to go back and ask some clarifying questions to get everything correct.

Let's look at the first relationship: Customers place Orders. In this case, the Customer and the Order entity are related, because Mountain View Music's customers place orders via the Web or the phone. We can assume that customers are allowed to have multiple orders and that each order was placed by a single customer. This means that there exists a one-to-many relationship between the Customer and Order entities.

Using this same logic, we can establish our relationship list using modeling terms. The relationships as they exist so far are shown in the following list:

- Customer–1:M–Order
- Employee–0:M–Order
- Order–1:M–Order Detail
- Products–1:M–Order Detail
- Payments–1:M–Order

We have almost everything we need in order to turn the information into an ERD, but we have one last thing we need to talk about. We need to develop our interpretation of payments and explore how they will be modeled. We were told that Orders have Payments, and there are several types of payments we can accept. To get our heads around this, we probably need to talk with the customer and find out what kind of data each payment method requires. Further discussion with the customer reveals that each payment type has specific data that needs to be stored for that type, as well as a small collection of data that is common to all the payment methods.

When we listed our attributes, we listed credit card, gift card, and electronic check as attributes of the Payment entity. If you take a closer look, you will see that these aren't attributes; instead, they seem to be entities. This is a common problem; orders need to be related to payment, but a payment could be one of three types, each one slightly different from the others. This is a situation that calls for the use of a subtype cluster. We will model a supertype called Payment that has three subtypes, one for each payment method.

Interpreting Flowcharts

During the requirements gathering phase, you may have used flowcharts to help gather information about the processes the users follow. For Mountain View Music, we created a flowchart to gain a better understanding of the warehouse processes. Sitting down with the warehouse manager, Tim Jackson, after observing the warehouse employees for a day, we came up with the flowchart shown in Figure 6.1.

Let's walk through the life cycle of a product as determined by the flowchart in Figure 6.1. First, an employee from the purchasing department places a purchase order for products from one of Mountain View's suppliers or vendors. The vendor then ships the product to Mountain View, where the warehouse employees receive the product. The product is then placed into inventory, where it is available for purchase by a customer. When a customer places an order, a packing slip is generated and automatically printed for the warehouse. An employee picks and packs the products that were ordered based on the detail on the packing slip. Packed products are then shipped out the door by one of the carriers that Mountain View uses for shipping.

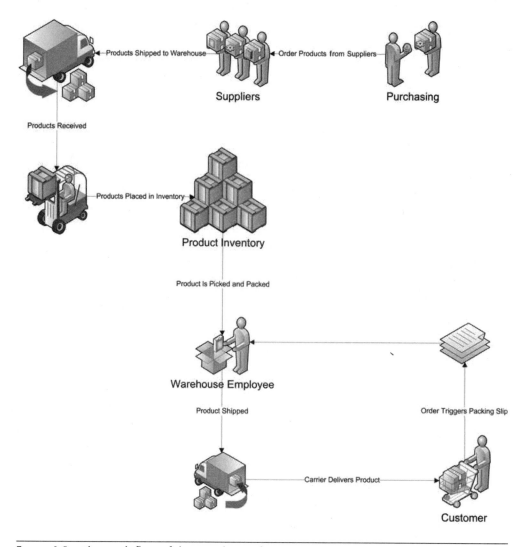

Figure 6.1 The work flow of the warehouse for Mountain View Music

In a nutshell, that is all there is to the warehouse. However, we are lacking a few details—specifically, how the product is physically stored and accounted for in the system. Going back to our warehouse manager, we receive the following explanation.

When product is received, it is counted and verified against the original purchase order. Before the product is placed into inventory, it is left in a staging area in the warehouse. The staging area is nothing more than a space where product can be stacked until there is time to move it to the shelves. The shelves in the warehouse are divided into *bins,* which specify the row, column, and shelf on which the product is stored. Each bin is given a unique identifying number that makes it easy for the warehouse employees to locate. Additionally, a large bin may be made up of several smaller bins to store small products.

Product is accounted for in one of two ways. First, generic products, such as guitar picks or strings, are simply counted and that total is recorded. Each time a generic, or nonserialized, part is sold, the system simply needs to deduct one from inventory. Some larger, usually high-dollar items are stored by serial number. These serialized parts must be tracked individually. This means that if we receive 300 serialized flutes, we need to know where all 300 are and which one we actually sold to a customer.

Using what we have in the flowchart and what we got from the warehouse manager, we can again make some conclusions about entities, attributes, and relationships. The process is much the same as before; you comb the information for clues. The following is the entity list that we can deduce from the given information about the warehouse:

- Nonserialized Products
- Serialized Products
- Employee
- Customer
- Purchase Order
- Purchase Order Detail
- Bins
- Vendors

This list contains some of the same entities that were in our first list: products, employees, and customers. For now this isn't a problem, but you want to make sure you consolidate the list before you proceed to the modeling phase. Also, we assumed an entity called purchase order detail, making a purchase order similar to a customer order. We do not get very much about attributes from the warehouse manager, but we can flesh it out later. As far as relationships go, we can determine a few more things from the data we now have. The following list shows the relationships we can determine:

- *Employee* places Purchase Order
- *Purchase Orders* are placed with Vendors
- *Purchase Orders* have Purchase Order Details
- Purchase Orders Details have *Products*
- Products are stored in *Bins*

Expressed in modeling terms, these relationships look like this:

- Employee–1:M–Purchase Orders
- Vendors–1:M–Purchase Orders
- Purchase Orders–1:M–Purchase Order Details
- Products–1:M–Purchase Order Details
- Bins–1:M–Products

Interpreting Legacy Systems

When looking at previous systems, you should have tried to determine not only the type of data stored (the data model) but also that system's inputs and outputs. Comparing the data that was stored in the new model is straightforward. If your customer has kept track of all its products before, it stands to reason that it will want to do so in the new system. This type of data can be verified and mapped to the new model. What can be trickier are the inputs and outputs.

When looking at the previous system, you may find forms or computer screens that the Mountain View employees or customers were exposed to during normal business. When you analyze this document, these forms will offer you critical insight into the types of information that needs to be stored and to business rules that need to be in place. Take a look at Figure 6.2, which shows the form that warehouse employees fill out when they are performing an inventory count.

Looking at this form, we learn a few key pieces of information about the Product entity. Some of this information agrees with what we found out earlier from the warehouse manager. First, all products have an SKU number and a model number. The SKU number is an internal number that Mountain View uses to keep track of products, and the model number is unique to the product manufacturer.

Next, we see the format of the BIN Number where products are stored. When building our model, we now know that the BIN Number contains both letters and numbers, so we will want to store this data in a varchar field. Finally, we see again that the products are tracked by serial

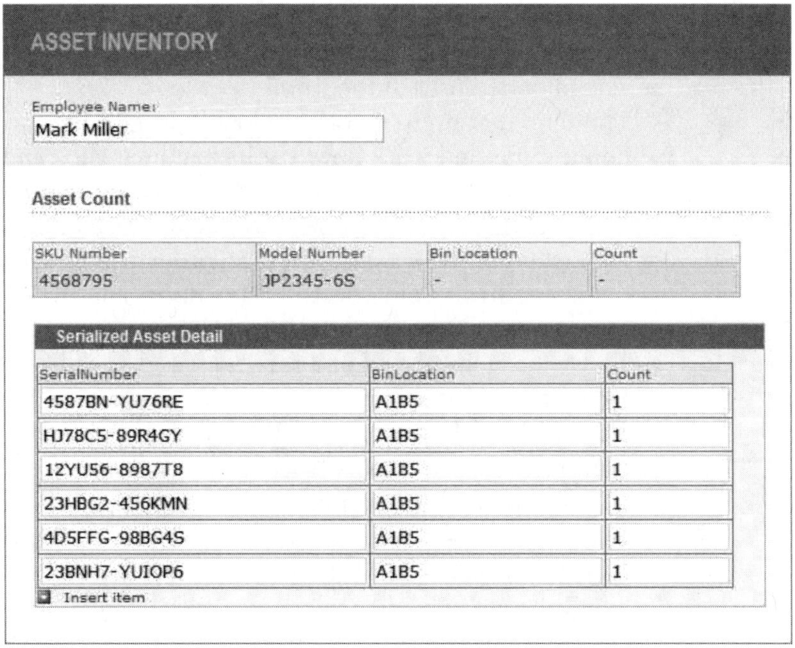
ASSET INVENTORY

Employee Name:

Mark Miller

Asset Count

SKU Number	Model Number	Bin Location	Count
4568795	JP2345-6S	-	-

Serialized Asset Detail

SerialNumber	BinLocation	Count
4587BN-YU76RE	A1B5	1
HJ78C5-89R4GY	A1B5	1
12YU56-8987T8	A1B5	1
23HBG2-456KMN	A1B5	1
4D5FFG-98BG4S	A1B5	1
23BNH7-YUIOP6	A1B5	1

Insert item

FIGURE 6.2 A form that is filled out during inventory to ensure an accurate count of the product on hand

number when needed. One such product is guitars; this means that each guitar, in this case, will need to be stored as a distinct entry in our product table. We were told that some products are not stored by serial number. In this case, we simply need to store a single row for that product with a count on hand. Because it's not a good practice to break up similar data in a model, we need to ensure that our model accounts for each of these possible scenarios.

Each form you look at should be examined for several things, because each can provide you insight about the data and its uses. The following list shows what you should look for and the types of information you can garner from each.

- The data that the form contains
  The data contained on the form gives you clues about what needs to be stored. You can determine the data type, the format, and maybe the length of the data to be stored. Seeing mixed alphanumeric data

would lead you to store the data in a varchar column. An SKU number that is solely numerals may point you toward an int.

- The intended user of the form
  The intended user can offer valuable insight into possible security implications and work flow. Understanding who can place an order will help you later when you need to add security to the database so that only the appropriate people can see certain data. Additionally, understanding how a user places an order or how an inventory count is recorded can help you to better understand the work flow and help you to design the model accordingly.

- The restrictions placed on users
  Restrictions that a form places on its user can be clues to data requirements or business rules. If the customer information form asks for three phone numbers (such as home, work, and mobile) but requires only that one be filled in, you may have a business rule that needs to be implemented. Additionally, a form may limit the customer's last name to 50 letters; this probably means that you can limit the data type of last name to 50 characters.

Interpreting Use Cases

As we discussed in Chapter 5, use cases help define a process without all the technical language of the process or system getting in the way. Because you should have a basic understanding of use cases at this point, we next talk about how you go about pulling data modeling requirements from a use case. Take a look at the use case diagram in Figure 6.3 and the use case documentation in Figure 6.4.

Let's look at this use case in detail and extract the modeling requirement. We will look at the two principals in the use case: warehouse employees and customers. In terms of our data model, we already have an employee and a customer entity, so it looks as if we have all the principals in our model. Next, we look at the actual use cases, of which there are five:

- Add Items to Web Site Cart
- Checkout on Web Site
- Print Packing Slip
- Pack Order
- Ship Order

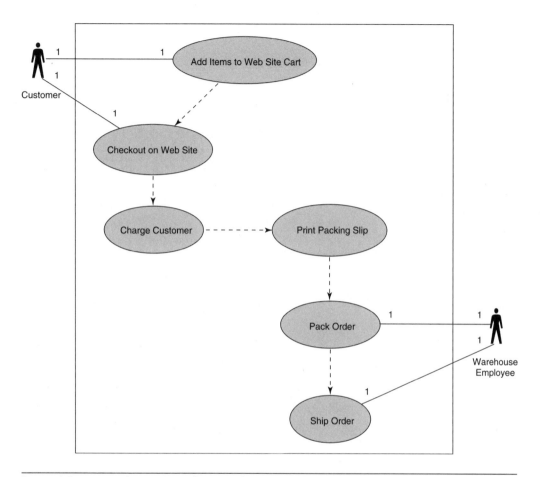

FIGURE 6.3 A simple use case diagram for a customer placing an order on the Web site

All but two of these cases have been covered in previous requirements, but it's good to see that things are in agreement with what we have already discovered. The two new items deal with adding items to a shopping cart and checking out via the company Web site. We don't know much yet, except that we have this new object, a shopping cart, so we are going to have to talk to a few people. In talking with the project manager, we discover that most of the shopping cart logic will be handled by the application's middle tier, but the application will require a place to store the shopping cart if the user leaves the site and returns at a later date. To handle this, we will need a shopping cart entity with a relationship to products. Additionally,

Use case name: Place Order on Web Site	ID: 15	Priority: High
Principal: Customer	Use case type: Detailed, Essential	

Stakeholders: Customer - Wants to purchase products via the company Web Site
Warehouse Employee: - Wants to pick, pack, and ship customer orders.

Description: This use case describes how customers go about adding products to the cart, checkout, and how the order is prepared for and shipped to the customer.

Trigger: Customer places products into shopping cart and checks out, thus completing an order.

Type: External

Relationships:

   Include: Checkout on Web Site, Charge Customer, Print Packing Slip, Pack Order, & Ship Order

Flow of Events:
1. Customer places products in shopping cart.
2. Customer chooses to check out and provides payment information.
3. The system charges the customer.
4. The system prints the packing slip to the warehouse.
5. A Warehouse Employee picks up the packing slips and uses them to find and pack the customer's order.
6. A Warehouse Employee ships the order to the customer.

Subflows:

FIGURE 6.4   Use case documentation for a customer placing an order on the Web site

the cart will need to track the quantity and the status of these products. The status of the product in the cart will help provide the functionality to save an item in the cart and check out with other items. Based on this we can update our entity list to contain a Shopping Cart entity.

This section only touches on interpreting use cases; there are volumes of books dedicated to the topic if you want to learn more. The important thing here is to look at the principals, the use cases, and the relationship between the use cases for clues to help you build your data model.

Determining Attributes

After you have gone over all the documented requirements that were gathered from the users, your data will likely still have a lot of gaps. The sketchiest will be the attributes of the entities. People tend to explain things at very high levels, except for the grandmother of one of your authors, who explains things in excruciating detail. If she were our customer, we can guarantee we would have all we need at this point, but she is not, so we will have to do some digging.

What do we mean by detail? Most people would explain a process in a generic way, such as, "Customers place orders for products." They do not say, "Customers, who have first names, last names, e-mail addresses, and phone numbers, place orders for products based on height, SKU, weight, color, and length." It is this descriptive detail about each entity that we need in order to build our logical model. At this point, if you don't have what you need, get in a room with your customers and ask them to help you fill in the gaps.

Bring a complete list of entities to the meeting, and make sure you also have the list of attributes you have so far for each entity; see Table 6.1 for our final entity list.

You will notice that we have added an entity description to the list. This tells us what the entity is for and helps us constrain the type of data that will be stored in the entity.

Once this list is complete, you need to go through each and every entity and ask the users what detailed data they need to store for that particular entity. Where applicable, you should try to ask about the possible lengths of the data to be stored. For example, if you're told that the database needs to store a product description, ask them to specify the length of the longest, average, and shortest description they might need. Take some time to verify the attributes you identified from the requirements.

Table 6.1   A Complete Entity List for Mountain View Music

Entity Name	Description
Bins	A representation of a physical location in the warehouse where products are stored.
Customers	Stores all information pertaining to a customer. In this case a customer is anyone who has purchased or will purchase a product from Mountain View Music.
Employees	Contains all information for any employee who works for Mountain View Music.
Orders	All data pertaining to a customer's order.
Order Details	Contains information pertaining to the product, number of the product, and other product detail specific to the order.
Payments	Contains all the information about a customer's payment method. This is being implemented as a subtype cluster containing three additional entities: credit cards, gift cards, and electronic checks.
Credit Cards	All data about a customer's credit card so that it can be charged for orders.
Gift Cards	Stores all the data pertaining to a customer's gift card.
Electronic Checks	Holds all the required data in order to draft an electronic check from a customer's bank account.
Products	This entity contains all the information about the various products the company sells.
Purchases	Information related to purchases that have been made from vendors.
Purchase Details	Contains the information about the specific products and quantities that were purchased from vendors.
Shipments	Detail about the shipments of products to fulfill customer orders.
Shipping Carriers	A list of each of the shipping carriers that Mountain Views uses: FedEx, UPS, USPS, etc.
Shipping Methods	The methods for shipping available from the carriers: ground, overnight, two-day, etc.
Shopping Cart	An entity used to store a customer's shopping cart on the Web site; this allows them to leave the site and return later.
Vendors	Companies that Mountain View orders products from for sale on the Web site.

Let's look at the process we would follow to fill in the entities for the Customer entity. From our earlier data, we already know that the customer entity will contain address data. To seek further clarification, we talk with Bill, the CEO, and Robyn Miller, the customer service manager. There is no one method you must follow in these conversations; you usually begin by simply asking what kind of information needs to be tracked. As the discussion progresses, your job is to write down what is said—on a whiteboard or easel if possible—and ask clarifying questions about anything you are unsure about. Remember, you are solving the customer's problem, so your job is to help people tell you what they know, and not to plant thoughts in their heads or steer them.

Robyn tells us that when Mountain View tracks an address, it needs to know the street address, city, state, and ZIP code. Occasionally, shipments go to Canada, so it's decided to track region instead of state. This decision gives the system the flexibility to store data about countries that do not have states. Additionally, we now need to track the country in which the customer lives.

There are also a few other obvious pieces of data that we need to track. First and last name, e-mail address, an internal customer ID, and the user's password for the site are the remaining attributes that Mountain View tracks for its customers. You should also find out which pieces of data are required and which could be left out. This will tell you whether the attribute can allow null data.

Table 6.2 shows the complete list of attributes for the customer entity, the data type, nullability, and a description of the attribute.

Table 6.2 A Complete List of Attributes for the Customer Entity

Attribute	Data Type	Nullability	Description
CustomerID	INT	NOT NULL	An internal number that is generated for each customer for tracking purposes
EmailAddress	VARCHAR(50)	NULL	The customer's e-mail address
FirstName	VARCHAR(15)	NOT NULL	The customer's first name
LastName	VARCHAR(50)	NOT NULL	The customer's last name
HomePhone	VARCHAR(15)	NULL	The customer's home phone number
WorkPhone	VARCHAR(15)	NULL	The customer's work phone number
MobilePhone	VARCHAR(15)	NULL	The customer's cell phone number
AddressLine1	VARCHAR(50)	NOT NULL	Used to store the street address
AddressLine2	VARCHAR(50)	NULL	For extended address information such as apartment or suite
City	VARCHAR(30)	NOT NULL	The city the customer lives in
Region	CHAR(2)	NOT NULL	The state, province, etc. of the customer; used to accommodate countries outside the United States
Country	VARCHAR(30)	NOT NULL	The country the customer lives in
ZipCode	VARCHAR(10)	NOT NULL	The customer's postal code
WebLogonPassword	VARCHAR(16)	NULL	For customers with a Web site account, a field to hold the encrypted password

You will need to go through this clarification process for all the entities you have determined up to this point. This information will be used in the next phase, creating the logical model. There is no hard science behind this process; you just keep working with the relevant people in the organization until you all agree on what they need.

Determining Business Rules

We hear business rules talked about in IT circles all the time. What are they? In short, business rules are requirements of the business that must be adhered to in order for the business to function properly. For example, a company might say that its customers need to provide it with a valid e-mail address or that their bill is due on the first of each month.

These rules are often implemented in different places in an IT system. They can be as simple as limiting the customers' last names to 50 letters when they enter them on a Web site, or as complex as a middle tier that calculates the order total and searches for special discounts the customer may be entitled to based on this or past purchases.

A debate rages in IT about the correct place to implement business rules. Some people say it should be done by the front-end application, others say everything should be passed to middleware, and still others claim that the business rules should be handled by the database management system. Because we don't want a slew of nasty e-mails, we won't say which of these methods is correct. We will tell you, however, that your database must implement any business rules that have to do with data integrity.

How do we determine which business rules need to be implemented, and how do we enforce these rules in our model? This calls for a little black magic, some pixie dust, and a bit of luck. Some rules are straightforward and easy to implement, but others will leave you scratching your head and writing a little T-SQL code. In this section we look at how to spot business rules and the methods you can use to enforce them.

Determining the Business Rules

As we stated earlier, you need to enforce any business rules that have to do with data integrity inside the database system. Some of these rules are inherently enforced in the logical model, and others require the advanced features of SQL Server 2008. In either case, you should determine and document all these rules when you are interpreting the business requirements. Table 6.3 provides some of the types of business rules that you should enforce and shows the method you will likely use to enforce them using SQL Server.

Table 6.3 Business Rules You Should Enforce in Your Data Model or in SQL Server

Business Rule	Enforcement	Example
Data must be a certain type.	Data Type	Product SKU numbers are always whole integers.
Information cannot exceed a given length.	Data Type–Length	Due to display limitations on the Web site, a product description can contain no more than 500 characters.
Data must follow a specific format.	Constraint	An e-mail address must follow the convention XXXX@XXXX.YYY, where X is some piece of string data and YYY is a domain type such as .COM, .NET, .GOV, etc.
Some items can exist only as part of or when owned by another item.	Primary Key–Foreign Key Relationship	An order must be owned by customer. An order detail item must be part of an order.
Information must contain some number of characters.	Constraint	For an address to be valid, it should contain at least five characters. If it contains fewer than five, the data is likely to be incomplete or incorrect.
Given a set of similar data, no one piece of information is required, but at least one of the set is required.	Constraint	When collecting a customer's home, work, and cell phone number, it is not required that they provide all phone numbers but it is required that they provide at least one of the phone numbers.

By no means does Table 6.3 provide a comprehensive list of the types of rules you are likely to encounter, but it gives you an idea of what you can and should do in your database. You will notice that several scenarios can be handled in your data model only. It's easy to handle data types, lengths, and relationships when you build your logical model. Other business rules are a bit more complex and need to be handled later when you implement your physical model on SQL Server.

For now, as you are interpreting your requirements, be sure to use the appropriate entity to document any rules that come along. Whenever you are told that something needs to work a certain way or be stored a certain way, write it down. Later you will use this information to build your logical, and ultimately your physical, model.

Cardinality

As we discussed in Chapter 2, cardinality further defines a relationship. When looking at the requirements you have gathered, you should keep a keen eye out for anything that indicates cardinality. When talking with the CEO, we were told the following:

> Customers log on to our Web site and place an order, or call an employee who places the order on the customers' behalf.

You will recall that this helped us to define a 1:M relationship between Customer and Order and a 0:M relationship between Order and Employee. We didn't talk about it in much detail at the time, but these relationships also contain the implied cardinality from the CEO's statement. We can see that each Order must be owned by a customer; either the customer placed the order, or an employee did. Therefore, each Order must have one customer, no more and no less, but a customer can have many orders. Now let's look at the 0:M cardinality of Employee to Order. An order does not have to be placed by an employee, but an employee can place multiple orders. The cardinality helps to further refine the relationship.

Implementing cardinality in our model can be simple or complex. In the example, the order table will contain a mandatory foreign key that points to the PK in the customer table. Each time an order is entered, it must be tied to a customer. Additionally, an optional foreign key will be created in the order table pointing to the employee PK. Each order can have an employee, but it is not required that there be one. You can implement more-complex cardinality, such as limiting an order to no more than five detail items, by using constraints and triggers.

Data Requirements

Although not technically a modeling concern, data storage and data retention requirements are crucial to your physical implementation. Where feasible, try to pull this information from the requirements you gather. These pieces of information will aid you in determining the initial database size and future growth trends. Without such information, you will be at best taking a wild guess. Whenever you are given a number, such as orders taken per day or the total number of customers the company has, write it down. Later you can use formulas to figure out table size, and ultimately database size, based on the type of data stored.

Additionally, don't be afraid to ask about retention of each of the entities. For example, how long do you keep order information or customer data? If the company intends to purge all information older than seven years, you can expect the database to grow for seven years and then level off a bit. If the company intends to keep data forever, then you may need to build some sort of archive to prevent the database from suffering performance hits later in its life. In either case, the time to start probing for this information is during the requirements phase. If, when you are interpreting the requirements, you don't find any or all of this type of data, go back to the customer and ask. If nothing else, this practice gets people thinking about it and there are no surprises later when the database administrators ask about data purging.

Requirements Documentation

Once you have completed the requirements evaluation, you should have several pieces of documentation that you will need in the next phase, the creation of the logical model. In this chapter we've talked about most of this documentation, but we want to take this opportunity to review the documents you should now have. The following is a list of each piece of documentation you should have at this point.

Entity List

You should have a list of the entities that the requirements have dictated. This list won't likely be complete at this point; however, all the entities that the business cares about should be on the list. Later you may find that you will need other entities to support extended relationships or to hold application-specific data. This list should include the following:

- The name of the entity
- A description of the entity
- From which requirement the entity was discovered (e.g., interview with CEO)

Attribute List

Each item on your entity list should have a corresponding attribute list. Again, this may not be a complete list because you may still discover new information or need to rearrange things as you implement your model. This list should contain these items:

- The name of the attribute
- The attribute's data type and the data type length, precision, and scale when applicable
- The nullability of the attribute
- A description of the data that will be stored in the attribute

Relationship List

You should also produce a relationship list that documents all the relationships between all your entities. This list should include the following information:

- The parent entity of the relationship
- The child entity of the relationship
- The type of relationship (1:1, 1:M, M:M, etc.)
- Any special cardinality rules
- A description of the relationship

Business Rules List

Finally, you should include a list of the business rules you have determined up to this point. As we discussed earlier, many of the business rules will be implemented in the model, and some will be physically implemented only in SQL Server 2008. This list should contain some notation as to whether the business rule is a "modeling" rule. The list should contain these items:

- The purpose of the business rule (e.g., encrypt credit card numbers)
- A description of how the business rule will be implemented
- An example of the business rule in practice
- A flag as to whether the rule can be implemented in the model

Looking Ahead: The Business Review

In addition to generating all the documentation you need to build your data model, remember that you'll need to present your data model, along with supporting documentation, to all the stakeholders of the project. Let's look at some of the documentation you'll need.

Design Documentation

Undoubtedly, one of the most tedious tasks for designers and developers is generating documentation. Often, we have an extremely clear idea of what we have done (or what we are doing), and generating documentation, particularly high-level overview documentation, can seem to take time away from actual work. However, almost everyone who has ever had to design anything has learned that without appropriate documentation, stakeholders will be confused and you will likely experience delays in the project.

Even though there are a myriad of ways to document a data model, there are a few key principles to keep in mind that will help you write clear, concise documentation that can be read by a wide, nontechnical audience.

First, remember that not everyone understands the terms you use. You need to generate a list of highly technical terms and their basic definitions, up and including terms like *entity, attribute,* and *record.* Also, as we all know, there are a lot of acronyms in the IT and IS industry. Try to avoid using those acronyms in your documentation, or if you use them, be sure to define them.

Second, create a data dictionary. A **data dictionary** is a document that lists all the pieces of data held in a database, what they are, and how they relate to the business. Recently it has become customary to label this information *meta data,* but *data dictionary* is the most familiar term.

Finally, make sure to work with application developers to create a comprehensive list of all the systems involved in the current project, and describe how this data model or database will relate to them. If your new project will work with existing systems, it is often helpful to describe the new project in terms of how it relates to the applications users are already familiar with. This kind of document is helpful for technical and nontechnical people alike.

Using Appropriate Diagrams

Most people, including technical people such as programmers and system administrators, find it easier to conceptualize complex topics if you use a visual aid. How many times have you been having a discussion with someone and said, "I wish I had a whiteboard"? This is because we are often talking about numerous systems, and we are also talking about data movement through a given system. This is particularly true of data models and databases; we need to visualize how data enters the system, what is done to it, where it is stored, and how we can retrieve it.

To this end, it is often helpful to create a number of diagrams that look at the data model you have created. Initially, if you used a modeling tool, you can actually export an image file (jpeg, BMP, etc.) of the actual model. You can create views of the model that show only the entities, or the entities and their attributes, or even all the entities, their attributes, and relationships. You can usually generate an image of the physical model or database as well. Because of its portable format, this kind of file can be useful when you're posting documentation to a document management tool or even a Web site. Unfortunately, without a technical person to explain the data model, most nontechnical users can get very little actual information out of the visual representation of the model.

For nontechnical folks, flowcharts are often the best way to represent what is happening with the data. You can label the names of the entities as objects inside the flowchart.

Using Report Examples

When you are discussing the proposed data model with various individuals, one of the most helpful things you can do is deliver samples of what they will actually see after the model is built. Often this means building mockups of deliverables, such as application windows or reports. Reporting examples, in particular, provide a quick way for end users to understand the kind of data that they will see in the end product. Because this is what they are most concerned about, spend some quality time developing sample reports to present when you meet with the nontechnical stakeholders.

Converting Tech to Business

Imagine, for a moment, that you have to take your car to a mechanic because it has a problem whose cause you cannot determine. All you know is that the car makes a sound it hasn't made before, and you know it can't be good. When you go the mechanic, he'll ask you a series of questions, writing down your answers as you talk. Then he takes that information and physically inspects your vehicle, documenting the findings. Finally, if he discovers the problem, he documents it and then researches and documents the solution. Before he implements the solution, he'll want to talk to you to explain the details of the work that needs to be completed, as well as the cost. Generally, he tells you what the problem is, and its solution, in the simplest terms possible. He uses simple language in an attempt to convey the technical knowledge to you in a manner you'll understand, because he cannot assume that you have any knowledge about the inner workings of an automobile.

When you are meeting with stakeholders, you are the mechanic. Just like a mechanic, you'll have to simplify the terms you're using, while avoiding making someone feel as though you are talking down to him. Most importantly, you need to frame your entire explanation of the data model in terms of the larger system, and in terms of the business. You need to relate your entities, attributes, and relationships to familiar terms such as customers and order processes. This practice not only helps the stakeholders understand the model but also helps them see the value in the model as it relates to their business.

Summary

This chapter has walked you through extracting useful information from the business requirements you've gathered. We also discussed documentation that you should be generating along the way in order to help you gain business buy in later in the project. You will use all this information as we move forward with building our logical, and ultimately our physical, model. Next up, in Chapter 7, we put the information we've gathered to use and build Mountain View Music's logical model.

CREATING THE LOGICAL MODEL

CREATING THE LOGICAL MODEL

Everything you've read until now has been laying the foundation for building a data model. In this chapter, we finally start to use the concepts introduced in the first six chapters. We begin by taking a look at the modeling semantics, or notation standards, and discussing the features you'll need in a modeling tool. Then we work through the process of turning requirements into organized pieces of data, such as entity lists. Finally, after we have created all the objects that our model needs, we build the model, deriving its form and content from all the pieces of information we've gathered. So let's dig in.

Diagramming a Data Model

Obviously, most of the concepts we've covered are just that—conceptualized information about what a data model is and what it contains. Now we need to put into practice some guidelines and standards about how the model is built. We need to put names to entities, outline what those entities look like on paper (well, not necessarily paper, but you know what we mean), determine how to name all the objects relating to those entities, and finally, decide which tool we'll use to create the model.

Suggested Naming Guidelines

If you've spent any time developing software, in any system, you've come to understand that consistent naming standards throughout a system are a must. How much time does a developer waste fixing broken code because of a case-sensitive reference that uses a lowercase letter instead of an uppercase letter? In database systems, how much time do developers waste searching through the list of objects in a database manually because the objects aren't named according to type? Although the names you use in your logical model don't affect physical development, it's just as important to have a consistent naming convention. When you name your entity that contains employee information, do you name it Employee or Employees? What about sales info—Sale or Sales? Keeping a consistent naming convention can help avoid confusion as well as ensure readability for future design reviews.

We address physical naming conventions in Chapter 9, but at this point you should understand that it is important to designate your naming convention for the data model now, and ensure that it is not a mapping of the physical naming convention. Because the physical implementation of a data model usually requires that you create objects that don't exist in the data model, naming your tables exactly the same as your entities may create confusion, because there will be tables that don't map to entities. Remember that the data model is the logical expression of the data that will be stored.

The emphasis here is that you have a standard—any standard, as long as it is consistent. Here, we offer the set of guidelines that we used to develop the data model for Mountain View Music. Figure 7.1 shows each type of object in the data model. We'll talk about each object, how it's named, and why.

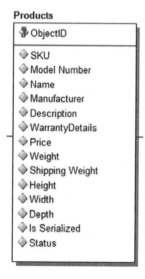

FIGURE 7.1 The Products entity from the Mountain View Music data model

Entities

In Figure 7.1, you can see the Products entity. Notice that it is plural (Products), and not singular (Product). Why? It is because the entity represents the kind of information that is being stored. It is a collection of products—the description of information stored about our company's products. As a naming standard, we prefer to use plural entity names to reflect that the given entity describes all the attributes stored for a given subject: Employees, Customers, Orders.

It's likely that your model will contain entities whose sole purpose is to describe a complicated relationship and cardinality. We discuss these types of entities in Chapter 2: subtypes and supertypes, along with many-to-many relationships, where additional attributes are associated with the joining entity. In the case of subtypes, the entity will still be named according to the data being stored. When it comes to naming entities that help model many-to-many relationships, the entity name describes what is being modeled. For example, in Figure 7.2, you can see the entity we've used to model the relationship between Products and Vendors.

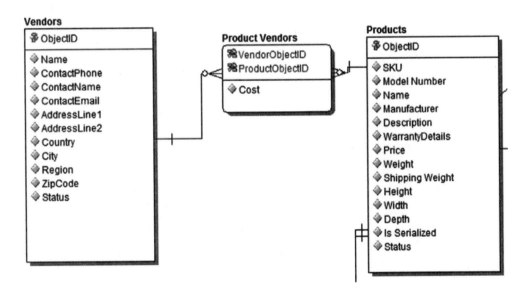

FIGURE 7.2 The Product Vendors entity from the Mountain View Music data model, showing a M:M relationship

Notice that the entity name is simply a readable concatenation of the names of the two entities being referenced. This is descriptive—allowing us to know exactly what the purpose is—without being overly long.

Always keep in mind that your data model will be viewed by technical and nontechnical personnel. That doesn't mean you should sacrifice design to make the data model accessible to those who aren't IT or IS professionals, but using common English names for entities will make it easier to explain the model. Most people know what Product Vendors means, but ProdVend may not make sense without explanation. Also, because case sensitivity is not an issue in a logical model, using mixed-case names makes perfect sense. In addition to being easier, it seems more professional to business analysts, managers, and executives.

Attributes

In the Products entity, you can see the list of attributes. Because an attribute is a single data point for the given entity, it is singular in nature. The names of attributes can actually mean multiple instances of a given type of data when used in plain English, so it is important to be specific about the plurality of the attribute in a data model. For example, we could store multiple addresses for an employee in an Employees entity. But because we can't actually model multiple addresses stored by a single attribute, naming the attribute Addresses would be incorrect; it is simply Address. We would use additional attributes to store multiple addresses, such as Home Address versus Mailing Address.

Another aspect of naming attributes is the need to deal with fields that designate identification of records. For example, in Figure 7.1 you can see the ObjectID attribute. This attribute is simply intended to provide a surrogate unique identifier for each record. For each product, we might say that SKU, Name, and Model Number will uniquely identify a product; however, we may run into problems if a new product with the same name replaces an older product but uses a different SKU. Or the vendor might change the model number of an existing product. To avoid having to update key fields, and possibly lose historical visibility, we prefer to use an object identifier. When deciding how to name this attribute, we know that because it is an attribute of a specific entity, we simply name it ObjectID, without being redundant and naming it *Entity*ObjectID. By following this standard throughout our model, we always know what the substitute unique identifier is of any given entity; it is ObjectID.

As with entity naming, you should be as conscious as possible of the fact that nontechnical personnel will read through this design at least once. Attribute names should be concise and unambiguous. And as with entity naming, it's good to use mixed-case attribute names unless there is a specific reason not to.

Notations Standards

Naming conventions used in your data model are based strictly on your personal preference, or at least your professional preference, but there are industry-standard specifications that outline how a data model should be notated, or described. Although there is plenty of history surrounding the various notation methods, we cover the notation method that is most popular and offer a basic history of where it came from and why to use it. So get out your notebooks, spit out your gum, and pay attention. There will be a quiz later.

IDEF

In the mid-1970s, the U.S. Air Force was in the midst of an initiative to define and update its computing infrastructure, specifically as related to manufacturing. As part of that project, an initiative was launched called Integrated Computer-Aided Manufacturing, or ICAM. Dennis E. Wisnosky and Dan L. Shunk, who were running the project, eventually concluded that manufacturing was in fact an integrated process, with several components describing the whole. They needed to develop tools, processes, and techniques to deal with all the various components; in addition, they understood inherently the data-centric nature of manufacturing and the need to analyze and document which data existed and how it moved from system to system.

Eventually, the two men created a standard for modeling data and showing how it relates to itself and other systems, as well as modeling process and business flow. These standards were initially known as the ICAM definitions, or IDEFs. To this day, ICAM continues to refine and define new standards based on the original IDEF, with an eye toward continuing to improve information technology and understanding how it relates to real-world systems.

Here are the most commonly used IDEFs:

- IDEF0: Function modeling
- IDEF1: Information modeling

- IDEF1X: Data modeling
- IDEF2: Simulation model design
- IDEF3: Process description capture
- IDEF4: Object-Oriented design
- IDEF5: Ontology description capture

Feel free to explore the Internet for more information on each of these specifications as they pertain to you in your professional life. For our purposes, we are concerned primarily with IDEF1X. After all, it was designed specifically for data modeling. However, our data model for Mountain View Music is not notated using IDEF1X. We are using another standard that is gaining ground specifically among users of proprietary data modeling tools: Information Engineering (IE) Crow's Feet notation.

Figure 7.3 shows our Products and Vendors entities and relationships notated using the IDEF1X standard.

The relationships are notated with a single solid line, and, in this case, the child entity is notated with a solid circle at the connection point. The solid circle indicates that this is the "many" side of a one-or-more-to-many relationship. In IDEF1X, the solid circle can appear on either end of the

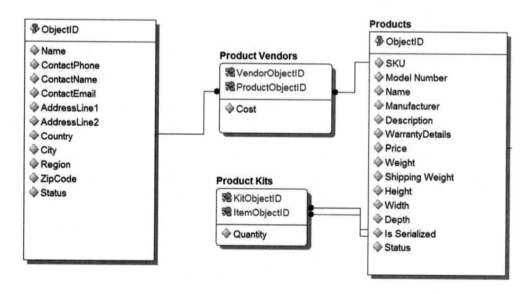

FIGURE 7.3 The Product Vendors entity and its related entities, in the IDEF1X notation

connection, and that is how the cardinality is described; in the case of a one-to- or zero-to- relationship, a text label "1" or "Z" is added. Additionally, there is usually a text label on the connection that is a verb that describes the relationship.

Now, Figure 7.4 shows the same objects using the Crow's Feet notation.

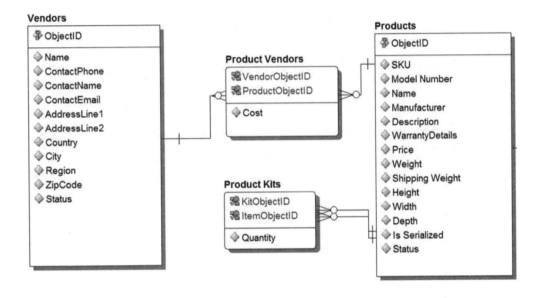

FIGURE 7.4   The Product Vendors entity and its related entities, in the IE Crow's Feet notation

In this version, at the child entity connection you see a set of three lines breaking from the main line. This denotes the cardinality of the relationship and also happens to look like a caveman drawing of a bird's claw (hence the name of the standard). In this notation, zero, one, and many connections are labeled with "0," "1," or a crow's foot, respectively. If there is a zero-or-one-to- type of relationship, there will be a "01" on the line at the appropriate end of the connection. Often, the zeros and ones look like circles and lines and less like an actual numeral; this often depends on the modeling tool being used.

Both the IE and the IDEF1X notation styles can be used for data modeling, and both are descriptive enough for all modeling purposes. Which one you choose is almost irrelevant; it's more important to choose and consistently use a notation standard, no matter which one you actually use. In our case, the IE standard sufficed and, for us, was a quicker and easier-to-read notation standard. Most data modeling tools allow you to switch between notation standards, so once you have some entities and relationships defined, you can try out different notations and see which ones you like. No matter what you use, be sure that you understand how to read it and, more importantly, how to describe the notation to others. More on this later in this chapter.

Modeling Tool

Many data modeling tools are available, everything from industry-standard tools (such as ERwin Data Modeler from Computer Associates or ER/Studio from Embarcadero Technologies) to freeware tools. The features and functionality you need in a modeling tool extend beyond which notation it supports. Although it's not necessarily a part of the overall design process for a data model, choosing a data modeling tool can determine your level of success—and frustration—when it comes to creating a model. Here, we present a list of features that you should keep an eye out for when choosing a modeling tool. It is not meant to be an exhaustive list; rather, it is the list of must-haves for any data modeler to get the job done.

Notation

This is a core requirement. All modeling tools have at least one notational standard. Ideally, your choice will have more than one, because in some projects you may find that specific notation standards have already been implemented. In that case, if your chosen tool offers that standard, you won't need to purchase another tool. Also, be sure that the tool you choose has at least IDEF1X, because it is an industry standard and is likely to be used most often in existing models.

Import/Export

Unfortunately, most modeling tools use a proprietary format. However, the tool you use should be able to export your models to images and, ideally, to XML documents. This capability will make the tool interoperable with a wide range of modeling software and will help you share your model with other users. Finally, the tool should be able to export its metadata to as many formats as possible, particularly those used by UML tools.

It is also ideal to be able to import flat files, such as SQL scripts, to generate (reverse-engineer) databases. Although you won't use this feature a lot to generate new models, it can be helpful to start with an existing physical model in order to generate a new logical data model. If your tool can import the schema of a physical database, it can be a real time-saver.

Physical Modeling

Several of the available data modeling tools can not only help you generate the logical data model but also help create a physical model for use in the SQL Server 2008 database you are deploying to. This feature can also be a huge time-saver during the development phase and, when used with proper change management and source code management, can even assist in deploying databases and managing versions of databases that are deployed. In our opinion, this capability is high on the list, particularly for larger environments.

Most data modeling tools, particularly those that advertise themselves as enterprise class, will offer far more features than these. However, these are the primary pieces of functionality that any data modeling tool should offer. To make sure it meets the needs of your project or job, be sure to thoroughly review any modeling software before buying.

Using Requirements to Build the Model

So far, this book has been about setting the groundwork for building a data model for a realistic scenario. We've covered everything from the basic definition of a data model to the details of each type of data a company may need to store. We now have all the tools necessary to begin building a data model for Mountain View Music (we abbreviate the company name as MVM throughout the remainder of this chapter). First, we lay out how our various data points from the requirements gathering phase will map to the objects we'll create in a data model. We also discuss implementing business rules in a data model.

Entity List

When the user interviews and surveys were conducted in the requirements gathering phase, we made sure to take notes regarding certain key words, usually nouns, which represented the types of data that the new model (and its eventual database) would have to support. We now need to narrow that list to a final list of the most likely suspects.

For example, Table 7.1 shows the list of nouns gathered during requirements gathering, along with a brief description of what the noun refers to. You'll recognize this is almost the same list from Chapter 6; however, we've added some entities, as we discuss in a moment.

This list of entities accounts for some specific issues that arise when you try to relate these entities to one another, as well as issues created by moving to an online system. Because the other entities have been discussed in detail, we'll review the new ones and explain why they exist.

- **Lists and List Items**

  These entities account for a type of information that exists only to support the system and is not accounted for in traditional requirements gathering. In this case, we realized that we would need to track the status of shipments, and because items in a single order can be shipped in separate shipments, we need to relate the status of all order items and the shipment they are part of. Additionally, we need a flexible list of status codes, because that kind of data can change based on business rules. Finally, we realized that this subset of information is not the only lookup-style information we might need. In the future, there may be needs to create lists of information based on status, product type, and so on. So we built a flexible solution by creating these generic Lists and List Items entities. Lists represents any list of information we might need—for example, the status of an order. List Items is simply a lookup table of potential items for the list—in this case, the status codes. With this solution, we can add any type of list in the future without adding other entities.

- **Product Attributes**

  When addressing the existence of a product, you must account for where that product comes from and how it is packaged and sold. Additionally, for a company like MVM, it is necessary to deal with the fact that different products have different kinds of attributes. For example, a guitar does not have all the same physical attributes as a saxophone (although there are some attributes in common). To model this scenario correctly, it became necessary to create a Product Attributes entity that represents various types of attributes a product can have. So instead of including every possible attribute for all products in the Product entity, we've essentially created an

Table 7.1   A New Entity List for Mountain View Music

Entity Name	Description
Bank Accounts	Holds all the required data to draft an electronic check from a customer's bank account.
Bins	A representation of a physical location in the warehouse where products are stored.
Credit Cards	All data about a customer's credit card so that it can be charged for orders.
Customers	Stores all information pertaining to a customer. In this case a customer is anyone who has purchased or will purchase a product from Mountain View Music.
Employees	Contains all information for any employee who works for Mountain View Music.
Gift Cards	Stores all the data pertaining to a customer's gift card.
List Items°	(See text.)
Lists°	(See text.)
Order Details	Contains information pertaining to the product, number of the product, and other product details specific to the order.
Orders	All data pertaining to a customer's order.
Payments	Contains all the information about a customer's payment method. This is being implemented as a subtype cluster containing three additional entities: Credit Cards, Gift Cards, and Bank Accounts.
Product Attributes°	This entity contains attributes specific to products that are not stored in the Products entity.
Product Instance°	This is an entity that facilitates a M:M relationship with the Products and Bins entities.
Product Kits°	Represents collections of products sold as a single product.
Product Vendors°	Facilitates a M:M relationship with the Products and Vendors entities.
Products	This entity contains all the basic information about the various products the company sells.
Purchase Details	Contains the information about the specific products and quantities that were purchased from vendors.
Purchases	Information related to purchases that have been made from vendors.
Shipments	Details about the shipments of products to fulfill customer orders.
Shipping Carriers	A list of each of the shipping carriers that Mountain Views uses: FedEx, UPS, USPS, etc.
Shipping Methods	The methods for shipping available from the carriers: ground, overnight, two-day, etc.
Shopping Cart	An entity used to store a customer's shopping cart on the Web site; this allows them to leave the site and return later.
Vendors	Companies that Mountain View orders products from for sale on the Web site.

°New entity

entity that represents the attributes that are specific to any product. We then have a relationship between Products and Product Attributes that is a one-to-zero-or-more relationship (because a product doesn't necessarily have one of these custom attributes).

- **Product Instance**

  Another problem with products is that they must be stored somewhere. Because we have bins (represented by the Bins entity) that hold products, we need to have a relationship between Bins and Products. The problem is that some products are so small that they are mixed within a bin, meaning that a single bin can hold different types of products. Other products are large enough that they require dedicated bins, but a given bin may hold several packages containing that product type. And in some cases a single product takes an entire bin (for example, a large piano-style keyboard). Finally, we may have a product, such as a drum set, that is composed of several pieces, and the components may be stored in multiple bins. So we have, in effect, a many-to-many relationship. To resolve this, we created a Product Instance entity that allows us to relate multiple products to multiple bins as needed.

- **Product Kits**

  This entity addresses situations in which we have a product for sale that is a grouping of products. For example, MVM may occasionally run promotions to sell a guitar with an amplifier and an instrument cable to connect them. Normally, these are individual products. We could simply automatically generate an order that adds each item; however, that creates problems with pricing differences (because the point is to reduce the customer's price) between the promotional price and the standard price. Additionally, if we add each item separately, we don't have as much historical visibility into how many of each item was sold as part of the promotion versus those sold through a standard order. Although there are other possible solutions, we chose to handle this through a separate entity that effectively creates a new product composed of the promotional items.

- **Product Vendors**

  This entity solves a similar problem as Product Instance does. Because MVM may purchase multiple products from a specific vendor, or it may buy the same product from different vendors, we have a many-to-many relationship; this entity facilitates that relationship.

These new entities help us relate the important pieces of data to one another. After the basic entity list is in place, it is a matter of analyzing the existing entities and their relationships to evaluate where there are holes in the logical flow and storage of data. When you're trying to discover these entities, it's helpful to ask yourself the following questions.

1. For every entity, are there attributes that apply sometimes, but not always, to that entity?

   The answer to this question will help you discover situations where an entity's attributes are either too far reaching, or where you may need to create a separate place to store the list of attributes that may only occasionally apply to specific instances of the first entity.

2. For every entity, is there another entity that might have multiple relationships to the entity being reviewed?

   Obviously, this question helps you uncover many-to-many relationships.

3. For every entity, is there another type of data that should be stored that isn't listed as a current entity?

   This is more of a process or commonsense question. For example, with MVM, it was obvious that we needed to store Shipments. However, when we started thinking about attributes of a shipment, it occurred to us that MVM uses multiple shipment methods and multiple carriers, even though no one explicitly mentioned that in the interviews. So while we were accounting for shipments, we hadn't correctly identified all possible information relevant to that process until we were reviewing our entity list.

We now have the complete list of entities for the MVM data model. Next, we need to fill out the detailed information for each entity.

Attribute List

We now need to associate a list of attributes with every entity we've created in order to define the data points that are being represented. This includes every attribute for all entities, with the exception of those that define relationships; we cover those shortly.

As with the identification of the entities themselves, you extract the attributes of each entity from the information you obtained during requirements gathering. You need to make sure that you have the definitive list of attributes for each entity, as described in Chapter 6; when you build the model, you'll enter each of these attributes—with its data types (including precision and scale, when applicable) and nullability—into the entity object in the model.

When compiling attribute lists for an entity, you need to conduct one specific bit of analysis. You need to compare attribute lists between related entities to be sure that any attributes being stored as a specific data type and length are consistent with attributes of other entities storing the same type of information. This is the perfect use of domains in your data model. For example, if you define a first_name domain and use it everywhere you need a first name, you will ensure that the types and lengths are consistent. Here's another example: If you are storing mobile phone numbers for vendors and for customers, make sure you use the same format.

Although these two attributes are unrelated, it's a good idea to be consistent. In that way, when development of the physical model starts, as well as application development, no one has to remember that the mobile phone number format is different from table to table. Because the data types used in the tables are based on the data types used in the data model, it is the modeler's responsibility to be as consistent as possible.

Relationships Documentation

Now that you know the entities you have created and their specific attributes, it's time to start listing the relationships between them. You need to list the relationships for each entity; in this way, as you create the model you are simply typing in the relationship parameters, without trying to discover and define relationships on the fly.

First, start with obvious relationships—Customers to Orders, Orders to Order Details, and so on. For each relationship, note the parent/child, the cardinality, and whether or not it is mandatory or identifying. After those are defined, start working through defining relationships between subtypes and supertypes, and many-to-many relationships using tertiary entities.

Although listing every relationship between every entity in the MVM model would be wasteful (you'll find the complete model in Appendix B), it's important to give a sample. Table 7.2 outlines the relationship information that you should document and list.

Table 7.2 A Sample of the Relationship List for Mountain View Music

Parent Entity	Child Entity	Type	Cardinality
Bank Accounts	None	N/A	N/A
Bins	Product Instances	M, I	One to zero or more
Credit Cards	None	N/A	N/A
Customers	Orders	M	One to zero or more
	Shopping Cart	M, I	One to zero or more
Employees	Orders	M	One to zero or more
	Purchases	M	One to zero or more
Gift Cards	None	N/A	N/A
Payments	Bank Accounts	S	Exclusive
	Credit Cards	S	Exclusive
	Gift Cards	S	Exclusive

Type: M = Mandatory, I=Identifying, S=Subtype

Remember that this is a short list of relationships. The total list will be large, because there will be an entry in the Parent Entity column for every entity in the model. This comprehensive list serves as a single source of information as you work through building your model in the modeling software.

Business Rules

Business rules, as discussed in Chapter 6, can be implemented in various ways throughout an IT system. Not all business rules will be implemented in the data model and ultimately the physical database. Because we're not inviting debate on exactly where all business rules should go, we focus on those that belong in the data model, usually because they specifically relate to data integrity.

Types of Rules Implemented in a Logical Model

In general, all the relationships that dictate whether or not data can be added, updated, or deleted from a database are types of business rules. For example, if a company requires that a valid phone number be stored for a customer—whether it is a cell phone, a home phone, or a work phone—you can create a constraint to prevent the customer record from being saved without at least one of those fields containing data.

Two types of business rules are usually enforced in the data model.

- Data format
  This includes any requirements that a given type of data have a specific length, type of character, and specific order of characters. Examples include date and time formats, user name and password fields, and alphanumeric value constraints (e.g., no letters in a Social Security Number field).
- Data relationships and integrity
  Relationships that require the association of data from one entity with another are business rules in a data model. For example, all orders must be associated with a customer, or all outgoing shipments must have shipping details. Another example is the requirement that multiple records be updated if a single piece of information is changed—for example, updating the ship date of a shipment automatically updates similar fields in order summary tables.

Other business rules can be implemented in the database, but that is usually discussed on a per project basis and is always subject to the capabilities of SQL Server. For our purposes, simple data integrity rules are being implemented in MVM via relationships based on primary keys and foreign keys.

Building the Model

At this point in the design process, we've evaluated existing systems, interviewed employees, and compiled documentation on all the data relevant to the system we are modeling. We've even generated lists of potential entities and their attributes, as well as the relationships between them. Now it's time to begin assembling the data model.

In this section, we start placing entities and their attributes in our diagram and identifying and labeling our keys and relationships. We also review the cardinality of those relationships and ensure that we've correctly labeled them. We also document and label our domains and ensure that our model is readable and accurate based on our requirements.

Entities

In Chapter 6, we laid out all the entities that were derived from the information we obtained during requirements gathering. At this point, we can open our data modeling tool and begin adding entities. Figure 7.5 shows the entire list of entities for MVM, entered as basic entities with no attributes.

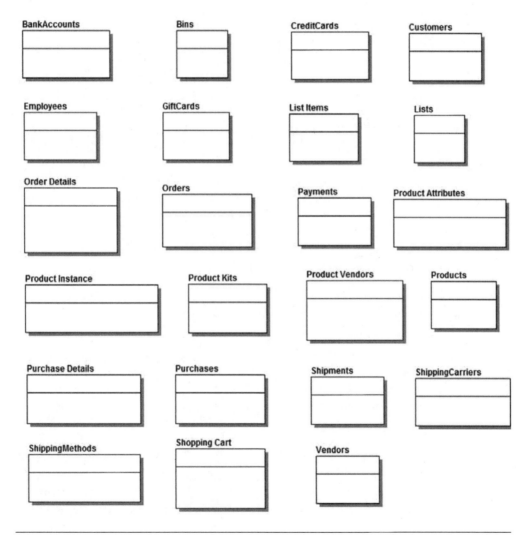

FIGURE 7.5 The entities for Mountain View Music, in alphabetical order from left to right, top to bottom, with no detail

It's not very exciting at this point. However, as we add each layer of information in the following sections, it will get significantly more complicated very quickly.

Primary Keys

Now that we have entities in the model, the very next thing that needs to be added are the primary keys for every entity. This is because relationships are based on the primary keys, so we can't add the relationships until all the primary keys are in place. Additionally, when you start creating relationships between entities, you will add the parent's attribute to the child's attribute list (most software does this for you when you add the relationship).

For most entities in the MVM model, we are using a surrogate primary key to represent the uniqueness of a record. In some cases, there is a composite primary key in order to ensure data integrity; some entities have no key except for the composite foreign key relationship between two other entities in a many-to-many relationship. Figure 7.6 shows the entities with their native primary keys, including the few that have no primary key.

This is slightly more interesting, although all we can see are the ObjectID fields. However, that gives us enough structure to start adding the relationships.

Relationships

At this point, we can start adding relationships based on our relationship list. There is not necessarily a preferred order for adding relationships to the model, but it's safe to say that adding the simple, zero-or-one-to-many relationships first will speed things up greatly.

Once you have added the easier, simpler relationships, you can begin working with more-complicated relationships, such as the many-to-many relationships and any subtype clusters you may have. Speaking of subtype clusters, if you review Figure 7.7, you'll see that MVM required one.

Notice that the attributes that previously had no primary key now do; these keys are composite keys made up of the relationships to keys in the related parent tables. At this point, we now have primary keys in every entity in the model. Additionally, after you've added all the relationships, you'll have a nearly complete picture of the data model. However, we need to ensure that our relationships visually annotate the desired cardinality.

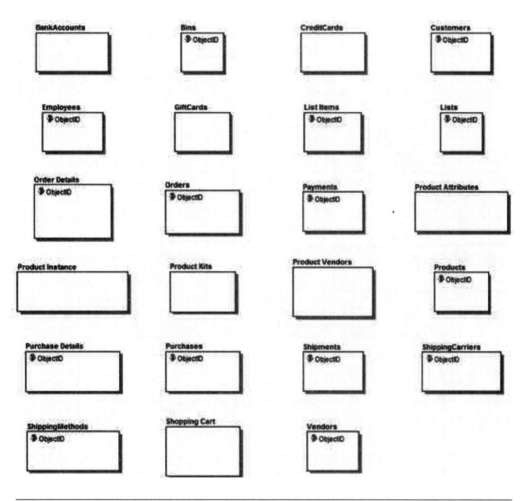

FIGURE 7.6 The entities for Mountain View Music, with primary keys

Modeling Cardinality

Recall that in Chapter 2 we discussed the cardinality of relationships. We explained the differences between one-to-many and zero-or-one-to-many relationships. As you add the relationships to your data model, you need to specify exactly which cardinality each relationship has at a granular level. In particular, you need to evaluate each relationship to determine its cardinality and notate it in the modeling software. If you omit the granular-level definition, the software usually chooses a default for you, which, in

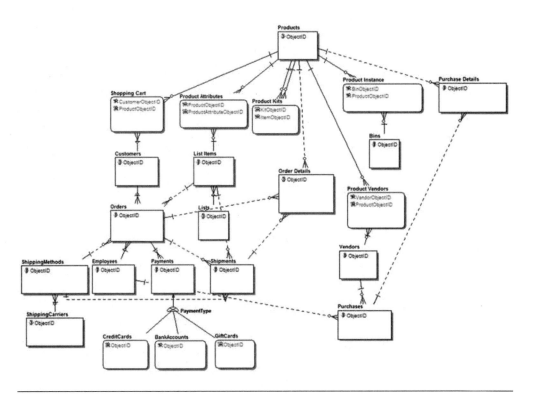

FIGURE 7.7 The entities for Mountain View Music, with primary keys and relationships added

the case of applications that can generate physical models from the logical model, may result in incorrect schema.

Domains

Now that our model has entities, primary keys, and relationships, it's a good time to review the domains we're using. In truth, this is a review phase that will help facilitate the addition of the full list of attributes for each entity. But it also serves to facilitate the process of adding the attributes.

As described in earlier chapters, domains are definitions of attributes that are universal to the model. For example, the system may require that all employee identification numbers (EINs) be nine digits long, regardless of leading zeros. Thus, we have chosen to model this using the char data type, which will have a length of nine characters. The EIN may be an attribute of several entities. In this case, we should add the EIN domain to the data model, specifying its name, its data type, and its length. Then, as we begin adding attributes, we can usually drag and drop the domain onto the attribute, and it will automatically configure the attribute appropriately.

Even if you aren't using a data modeling tool that can store and add domains with the click of a mouse, documenting your domains is important. It will help when you're adding attributes to multiple entities; you'll already know what the specifications are, and you'll have somewhere to look for them if you forget.

Attributes

Finally, we are ready to add the list of attributes to the entities. We've already added several attributes when we added primary keys and then relationships. Now we are adding the attributes that are specific to each entity.

When adding attributes, you may need to be picky about the order in which you enter them. For readability, it is important to order the attributes in a way that makes sense for the entity. One common example is the Employees entity, as shown in Figure 7.8.

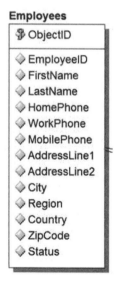

FIGURE 7.8 The Employees entity for Mountain View Music, with primary keys and all attributes added

You can see that the attributes are ordered in what we might consider a common order: name, phone, address, and status. We could easily order these in any way, but this order is closer to what most people think of as information about a person. It's certainly not set in stone, nor is there a hard-and-fast rule about attribute ordering. Just remember that you'll be explaining this model to nontechnical personnel, and they'll be looking at these attributes as simply labels of information. Ordering them can make it easier to explain and easier for users to review on their own if necessary. In any case, most modeling software allows you to rearrange the order of attributes after they have been added, so you should be able to rearrange these if the need arises.

As you add attributes, be sure to constantly review your domain list to make sure you haven't either (1) missed a domain that should have been created or (2) missed using a domain in an entity. This is sometimes an iterative process, and you are likely to make changes here (as well as in the rest of the model) when you review the model with the business stakeholders.

We have completed our first version of the MVM data model. If all the previous steps have been done correctly, then building the model is the easiest step, because all we're doing is creating a logical, visual representation of the information obtained and analyzed during requirements gathering.

Summary

In this chapter, we've finally built our model by using techniques described throughout the rest of the book. We've addressed specific issues regarding entity lists, attribute lists, and the hows and whys of relationship modeling in logical models. Next, in Chapter 8, we look at the various generic pitfalls that most modelers run into and explore ways to avoid them.

COMMON DATA MODELING PROBLEMS

Perfecting a data model is no easy task. To do it correctly, you must balance the physical limitations of SQL Server 2008 and simultaneously meet the requirements of your customer's business. Along the way, there are several pitfalls you may encounter. Many of the problems you will face are quite common, and you can avoid them by understanding them. In this chapter, we discuss some of the more common modeling problems and explain how to identify them, how to fix them if they occur, and how to avoid them altogether.

Entity Problems

Data models are built around entities, so that is where we start when looking for problems. Some entity problems are obvious, and others are a little harder to pick up on and fix. We focus on problems surrounding the number of entities and attributes, and problems that can arise when you don't pair attributes with an appropriate entity.

Too Few Entities

In the name of a clean, simple, easy-to-use data model, many modelers create fewer entities than are required. This practice can often lead to a model that's inflexible and difficult to use.

If you suspect that your model has too few entities, the first thing to look for is having similar data in the same entity. For example, look at the original Customers entity for Mountain View's logical model, as shown in Figure 8.1.

Customers

🔑 ObjectID	INTEGER
◆ EmailAddress	VARCHAR(50)
◆ CustomerID	CHAR(10)
◆ FirstName	VARCHAR(50)
◆ LastName	VARCHAR(50)
◆ HomePhone	VARCHAR(15)
◆ WorkPhone	VARCHAR(15)
◆ MobilePhone	VARCHAR(15)
◆ HomeAddressLine1	VARCHAR(50)
◆ WorkAddressLine1	VARCHAR(50)
◆ HomeAddressLine2	VARCHAR(50)
◆ WorkAddressLine2	VARCHAR(50)
◆ HomeCity	VARCHAR(30)
◆ WorkCity	VARCHAR(30)
◆ HomeRegion	CHAR(2)
◆ WorkRegion	CHAR(2)
◆ HomeCountry	VARCHAR(50)
◆ WorkCountry	VARCHAR(50)
◆ HomeZipCode	VARCHAR(10)
◆ WorkZipCode	VARCHAR(10)
◆ WebLogonPassword	VARCHAR(16)

FIGURE 8.1 The original Customers entity for Mountain View Music

Notice the seemingly duplicate address data. In the strictest sense of the word this data isn't really duplicate data—it contains work information versus home information—but the type of data is redundant. We were told during requirements gathering that Mountain View needed to store at least two addresses for each customer and that the home and the work addresses were the most common addresses on file. Storing the data in the way that we have in Figure 8.1 presents a few problems. The first problem is that the model is not flexible. If we need to store additional addresses later, we would not be able to do so without first modifying the entity to add columns. Second, the data is difficult to retrieve in this state. Applications would need to be written to understand the complexity and pull data from the correct columns. This problem is compounded by the changes that would need to be made to the application if we later add a third address.

This is a clear example of having too few entities, and we can tell that by the duplication of information. The fix here is to give the duplicate data its own entity and establish a relationship with the original entity. In Figure 8.2 we have split the address data into its own entity.

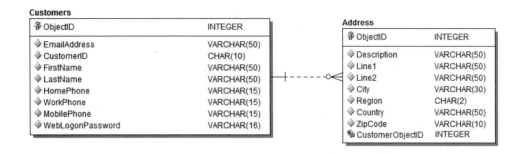

FIGURE 8.2   The Customers entity with the address data correctly split out

As you can see, the new entity has each address attribute only once, and we have added a new attribute called Description. The description allows Mountain View to identify the address at the time of entry. Splitting the address data out of the customer entity in this way allows for more flexibility and eliminates the need to change the application or the data model later. With this model, the company is no longer limited to only a home and a work address; it can now enter as many as it likes. Maybe the customer has two houses or wants to ship something as a gift. Either way, our new model allows it.

This kind of thing can happen often when you are building a model. You mistake what should be a second entity for attributes of the entity you are building. This error isn't limited to things like addresses, which are attributes of customers. It can also happen with two completely different items that end up in the same entity. For example, suppose we're storing data about classes at a local college. If we create a Class entity, we need to track the professor for each class. The quick—and might we say, sloppy—way is to add a few attributes to the Class entity to track the information about the professor, as shown in Figure 8.3.

Class	
ObjectID	INTEGER
Name	VARCHAR(50)
Days	VARCHAR(25)
Time	DATETIME
ProfessorName	VARCHAR(50)
ProfessorEMail	VARCHAR(50)
ProfessorPhone	VARCHAR(15)

FIGURE 8.3   A Class entity that also contains Professor information

By adding attributes for the professor's name, phone number, and e-mail address, we meet the requirements of the Class entity; that is, we are tracking the class's professor. However, if you look below the surface, you should see some glaring problems. The biggest problem is that this setup violates the rules of first normal form and all that goes with it. We have not successfully separated our entities into distinct groups of information. We are storing both class and professor data in the same entity. In these situations, you need to split the entity along 1NF guidelines. Figure 8.4 shows the appropriate way to store this information.

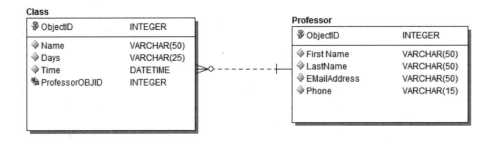

FIGURE 8.4   The Class entity with the professor information moved to a new Professor entity

As you are building models or reviewing existing models, keep an eye out for these types of situations. We all want our data models to be simple and easy to understand, but don't oversimplify. Remember that the things you are modeling have some level of complexity, and as a rule your model should not be less complex than real life. Having a lot of entities doesn't necessarily lead to a confusing model, so don't be afraid to include all the entities you need to build an accurate representation of real life.

Too Many Entities

As you might expect, if having too few entities can be a problem, then having too many entities can also cause headaches. The usual trap here is trying to overnormalize a database. Although normalization is a good thing, overnormalization can cause performance problems and limit the model's flexibility. Adding extra entities in places that aren't obvious can sometimes be a good thing, but you must fully understand the data and its usage be-

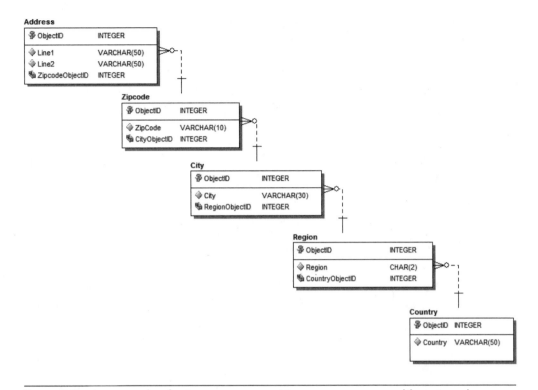

Address

ObjectID	INTEGER
Line1	VARCHAR(50)
Line2	VARCHAR(50)
ZipcodeObjectID	INTEGER

Zipcode

ObjectID	INTEGER
ZipCode	VARCHAR(10)
CityObjectID	INTEGER

City

ObjectID	INTEGER
City	VARCHAR(30)
RegionObjectID	INTEGER

Region

ObjectID	INTEGER
Region	CHAR(2)
CountryObjectID	INTEGER

Country

ObjectID	INTEGER
Country	VARCHAR(50)

FIGURE 8.5 An example of using too many entities to represent an address in a data model

fore you go over the top. Figure 8.5 shows an example of what is, in our opinion, a model using too many entities.

Now, this is, in most cases, a perfect example of using too many entities. We have indeed followed normalization rules—each entity pertains to only one grouping of data—but the performance implications of stitching this data back together are enormous. Unless you have a compelling reason to do something like this, such as building a data model for the post office, then we recommend that you avoid this tactic. That said, we have worked with an application that implemented a version of this, but it was only two tables. Street address information was stored in the Address entity, and that contained a foreign key to an entity called ZipDetail. The ZipDetail entity held the ZIP code, city, state, and country information. This particular application stored a lot of address data, and breaking out the street address from the rest of the detail provided a space savings because that information wasn't ever repeated.

Having too many entities can slow the performance of the database after it's implemented. As good data modelers, not only should we care about normalization and clever data storage, but also we need to be cognizant of the performance implications of our decisions in the model.

Attribute Problems

The biggest hurdle you will encounter when working with attributes is making sure that they are appropriate and store the correct data. Too often, we put unneeded attributes in entities or we misuse the attributes that are there. Remember your normalization rules: Each attribute should hold only one kind of data. It is tempting to go the easy route and create columns called attribute1 and attribute2, but that is a trap you want to avoid. Let's look at other common attribute problems so that you can avoid them in your model.

Single Attributes Contain Different Data

When we say a single attribute with different data, we are referring to a scenario in which you create attributes named attribute1, attribute2, attribute3, and so on. That is, you add several columns with similar names and data types in order to hold some nonspecific information. Mountain View needs to store information about its products—musical instruments and their related accoutrements. This presents a bit of a modeling problem. The products need to be stored in a Products table so that they can be tied to orders and inventory can be tracked, but different types of instruments are very different. Clarinets do not have strings, and guitars don't have mouthpieces. This scenario leads us to create a products table having the generic attribute columns shown in Figure 8.6.

This table was built this way so that each instrument could have attributes that are unique to it. For example, a guitar needs to store the type of wood for the neck, the type of wood for the body, the tuner style, the number of strings, the metal the frets are constructed from, and the finish. In contrast, for a saxophone we need to store the type of metal, the horn's key, the type of material used for the pads, the width of the bell, and the type of finger pads.

Products

🔑 ObjectID	INTEGER
◆ SKU	INTEGER
◆ Model Number	VARCHAR(25)
◆ Name	VARCHAR(100)
◆ Manufacturer	VARCHAR(25)
◆ Description	VARCHAR(255)
◆ WarrantyDetails	VARCHAR(500)
◆ Price	MONEY(10,0)
◆ Weight	DECIMAL(5,2)
◆ Shipping Weight	DECIMAL(5,2)
◆ Height	DECIMAL(4,2)
◆ Width	DECIMAL(4,2)
◆ Depth	DECIMAL(4,2)
◆ Is Serialized	BIT
◆ Status	TINYINT
◆ ProductAttribute1	VARCHAR(80)
◆ ProductAttribute2	VARCHAR(80)
◆ ProductAttribute3	VARCHAR(80)
◆ ProductAttribute4	VARCHAR(80)
◆ ProductAttribute5	VARCHAR(80)

FIGURE 8.6 A poor product entity design, supporting different attributes for different products

How do you store the different attributes of the instruments without making your database look like an overgrown Excel spreadsheet? There are a few options. You could make a different entity for each type of instrument, but this solution would be very inflexible. If the company decides to carry a new type of instrument, you would need to add new entities; if it decides to track something else about an instrument, you would need to add attributes to an entity. To solve this problem for Mountain View, we add another entity called Product Attributes, as shown in Figure 8.7.

Setting up a two-table solution builds flexibility into the design and allows for a more optimal use of storage. In this example, all the product attributes are records of the Product Attributes entity, and anything that is common to all products is stored in the Products entity. Using this model, we can add products and product entities at will. However, more important than the added flexibility, we got rid of that repeating attribute monstrosity.

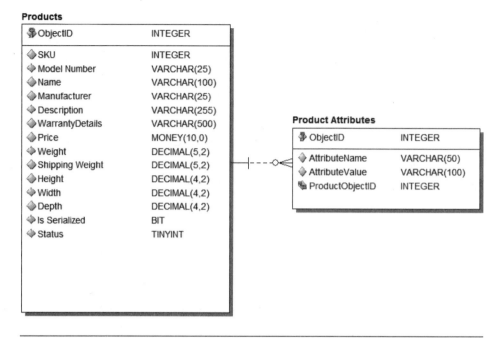

FIGURE 8.7 A two-table solution for storing product attributes

Remember that everything comes with a cost; in this case, gaining flexibility causes us to lose the structure offered by specifying the attributes in columns. This could make it harder to compare two similar products. Each situation is different, and there is no right or wrong answer here. You must do what makes sense in your situation.

Incorrect Data Types

Choosing incorrect data types, either because you are being lazy or because of bad requirements gathering, can be a serious problem when it comes time to implement. The most common thing we have run into is creating entities that have a ton of varchar columns and nothing else. The varchar columns can store everything from strings to numbers to dates and are often also the PK or an FK.

Why is this bad? Shall we list the reasons?

- Extra unneeded storage overhead
- No data integrity constraints
- The need to convert the data to and from varchar
- Slow join performance

Let's take a closer look at each of these problems.

Extra Unneeded Storage Overhead

Depending on the type of data being stored, using the wrong data type can add extra storage overhead. If you are holding phone numbers in the form of 1235557890, it means that you save 10 characters each time a phone number is stored. You have a few good data type choices when storing phone numbers in this way; you could use a varchar, a char, or a bigint. Recall from Chapter 3 that a bigint requires 8 bytes of storage, and the storage for the char and varchar data types depends on the data being stored. In this case, the 10-digit phone number would require 10 bytes of storage if you use the char, and 12 bytes of storage if you use the varchar.

So just looking at the storage requirements dictates that we use a bigint. There are other considerations, such as the possible length of the formatted number. If you want to store numbers in a different format, such as (123) 555-7890, then you would need one of the string data types. Additionally, if you might store international numbers, which tend to be longer than 10 digits, you might consider using varchar. In that way, the shorter number takes up less space on disk and you can still accommodate longer numbers.

There are other things to consider, and each situation is unique. All we want to illustrate here is the extra storage overhead you would incur by using the string types.

A word of caution: Don't go too far when streamlining your storage. Although it is a good practice to avoid unneeded storage overhead, you don't want to repeat the mistake that made Y2K such a big deal. Rather than store all four digits of the year when recording date information, programmers stored only the last two digits to conserve space. That worked when the first two digits were always 19, but when the calendar pointed to the need for four digits (2000), we all know what happened (in addition to COBOL programmers getting rich): A lot of code had to be rewritten to expand year storage. In the end, we are saying that you should eliminate unneeded storage overhead, but don't go to extremes.

No Data Integrity Constraints

If we use varchar for attributes without considering the actual data, we could have data integrity problems. The main reason we use data types is to enforce data integrity. If we are storing a date, the datetime data type ensures that the entered information is a valid date. Storing a date in a varchar could lead to problems. For example, what if the application code has a glitch that omits the first "/" and writes the date as "35/2007"? You might say, "So what? We can fix that with a script," but can you really fix it? Take the date January 13, 2005, as an example. If that gets stored as 113/2005, you have a problem. It could be converted to 1/13/2005 or 11/3/2005. Had we used the datetime data type from the start, we would have received an error when the application wrote 113/2005, and the problem could have been found and fixed. There are literally hundreds of examples, but we think you get the point: Use the correct data type, and you are on your way to having solid data integrity.

The Need to Convert Data

Data stored in varchar attributes is, not surprisingly, stored as a string. This means that it is stored, referred to, sorted, and grouped as a string. Why is this an issue? Let's look at the problem you encounter when sorting. When you sort strings, they sort alphabetically, and numbers sort numerically. This can lead to very different results. To illustrate this, we created a table called SortTest using the following code in SQL Server.

```
CREATE TABLE SortTest(
StringDate varchar(50),
RealDate datetime)
```

As you can see, we have two columns: one varchar and one datetime. Now we insert all the dates for January 2007 in the format "1/1/2007" into this table. Here are the insert statements we use.

```
INSERT INTO SortTest VALUES('1/1/2007' , '1/1/2007')
INSERT INTO SortTest VALUES('1/2/2007' , '1/2/2007')
INSERT INTO SortTest VALUES('1/3/2007' , '1/3/2007')
INSERT INTO SortTest VALUES('1/4/2007' , '1/4/2007')
...
INSERT INTO SortTest VALUES('1/31/2007' , '1/31/2007')
```

Now let's get down to the problem. We will select the data from the table and sort the select by each of these columns. When we sort by the RealDate column, we get 31 records, all in perfect date order from January 1 to January 31—no big surprise. Now let's see what happens when we sort by the StringDate column; the results of the select are shown in Table 8.1.

Table 8.1 The Results of Sorting by a Date Stored in a String Column

StringData	RealDate
1/1/2007	2007-01-01 00:00:00.000
1/10/2007	2007-01-10 00:00:00.000
1/11/2007	2007-01-11 00:00:00.000
1/12/2007	2007-01-12 00:00:00.000
1/13/2007	2007-01-13 00:00:00.000
1/14/2007	2007-01-14 00:00:00.000
1/15/2007	2007-01-15 00:00:00.000
1/16/2007	2007-01-16 00:00:00.000
1/17/2007	2007-01-17 00:00:00.000
1/18/2007	2007-01-18 00:00:00.000
1/19/2007	2007-01-19 00:00:00.000
1/2/2007	2007-01-02 00:00:00.000
1/20/2007	2007-01-20 00:00:00.000
1/21/2007	2007-01-21 00:00:00.000
1/22/2007	2007-01-22 00:00:00.000
1/23/2007	2007-01-23 00:00:00.000
1/24/2007	2007-01-24 00:00:00.000
1/25/2007	2007-01-25 00:00:00.000
1/26/2007	2007-01-26 00:00:00.000
1/27/2007	2007-01-27 00:00:00.000
1/28/2007	2007-01-28 00:00:00.000
1/29/2007	2007-01-29 00:00:00.000
1/3/2007	2007-01-03 00:00:00.000
1/30/2007	2007-01-30 00:00:00.000
1/31/2007	2007-01-31 00:00:00.000
1/4/2007	2007-01-04 00:00:00.000
1/5/2007	2007-01-05 00:00:00.000
1/6/2007	2007-01-06 00:00:00.000
1/7/2007	2007-01-07 00:00:00.000
1/8/2007	2007-01-08 00:00:00.000
1/9/2007	2007-01-09 00:00:00.000

When you sort strings, the first letter is examined and sorted, then the second letter, and then the third, and so on. This causes our date data to get out of whack. After 1/1/2007, the next number in the alphanumeric sort is 1/10/2007. This makes for an ugly result set.

To get around this problem now, you must convert the StringDate column during your select operation. We won't go into the details of the query engine, but suffice it to say, the conversion of a string into a date adds overhead to the select query. Paraphrasing a saying from a wise, uh, man, "Overhead leads to higher CPU utilization, higher CPU utilization leads to poor performance, poor performance leads to suffering." Again, had we used the correct data type, we could have avoided the problem of needing to convert the string and avoided the eventual suffering.

Slow Join Performance

When you need to join your foreign key tables to your primary key tables, the slowest joins occur when you use strings. This is a generalization, but it usually holds true. That being said, you want to avoid using strings as key fields when possible. So using nothing but strings would obviously violate this guideline. If you use the appropriate data types, you will reduce the possibility of having a string in your key field.

Relationship Problems

One of the trickiest parts of building a data model is getting all your relationships correct. Assuming that you have created all the appropriate entities, you still have to build relationships between them. This quandary is compounded by a couple of tricky relationship types, specifically one-to-one and many-to-many relationships.

One-to-One Relationships

Although 1:1 relationships have their place, they often split an entity in two that should in fact remain a single entity. A good 1:1 relationship is something like presidents to countries. Each country has only one president, and each president is president of only one country. In this case, each of these entities is different, but the relationship needs to be constrained to 1:1.

Now let's look at a bad 1:1 that would probably mean you have too many entities. In this example, we have a data model that stores information about a small nonprofit organization consisting of only a board of directors and no other employees. You could model the board members as shown in Figure 8.8.

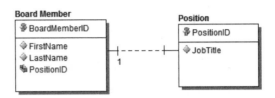

FIGURE 8.8   Board of directors model for a small nonprofit organization

In this model, we have two entities—one for the board members and one for the board members' positions—and the relationship between them is 1:1. We have to ask ourselves, "What does this buy us? Is there any value in splitting this data into two entities versus adding a position attribute to the employee table?" If the answer is that we are not adding value, then we should collapse these two entities into one table. If the second table were holding a lot of extra detail about the position and not every board member had an assigned position, then we would be more willing to let the entities exist as two. In our case, we would opt to combine the entities.

When examining 1:1 relationships you should ask yourself a couple of questions.

1. Are the two entities truly distinct?
2. Are the values in one of the entities only attributes of the other entities?

If you look at each 1:1 in this way, you will avoid potential problems that can crop up later.

That said, if you have an entity and quite a few attributes are needed only for a small minority of your records, you might consider splitting them off with a one-to-one relationship. This is a rare case, but it can help keep your model cleaner and simpler to use. For example, suppose you have an entity that will contain as many as 10 million records, and it has 100 attributes. You find out that only 100,000 of the records will use attributes 20 through 100. In this case, 99 percent of the records will use only 20 percent of the attributes, and the other 1 percent of the records will have all the attributes. This might be a good time to split the entity to prevent having a table that is mostly empty. It will also speed the retrieval of the records that do use all the data, because you will have all that information in a single, smaller table. As we said, this is a rare case, but you may run into it when creating a model.

Many-to-Many Relationships

The next stop on our journey though the world of data modeling problems is the big, bad many-to-many relationship. Once you have a handle on how to physically implement a many-to-many relationship, working with them isn't very difficult.

What problems are there that you should be aware of when using many-to-many relationships? Often, the fact that you have implemented a pure many-to-many relationship is, in and of itself, the problem. When we say "a pure many-to-many relationship," we mean one in which the join table is made up only of the foreign keys that point to the other tables. For example, look at the many-to-many relationship shown in Figure 8.9.

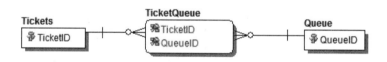

FIGURE 8.9   A "pure" many-to-many relationship

In this example, we have two tables—Tickets and Queue—with a many-to-many relationship between them, implemented here using TicketQueue as a join table. Not shown are the other attributes of these three tables. Both Tickets and Queue contain other elements in addition to their primary keys. In this case, the join table, TicketQueue, exists only to define the relationship; it does not add any further information about tickets or queues.

At first glance, you might think this relationship is just fine, but let's take a moment and think about what we are modeling. We are trying to model a relationship whereby tickets are placed into work queues. Each queue can have multiple tickets, and each ticket can be in multiple queues; so far, our many-to-many is looking OK. What you have to ask yourself in this situation is, "Are there any other attributes we should have in the join table to complete the picture of what we are modeling?" In this example, there indeed are other helpful attributes that we could add. For example, we might add an InsertedTime column to the TicketQueue table to track when the ticket was placed on the queue.

There are perfectly valid uses for many-to-many relationships, but if you look closely at your model, you will find that there are other attributes that you can add to the join tables. Don't get us wrong; we are not saying that many-to-many relationships are bad, but they do add the extra overhead of having to bring a third table into a relationship. We are big fans of reducing the number of tables to increase performance. Properly evaluating your many-to-many relationships is a big step toward a clean, well-performing database model.

Summary

In this short chapter, we've covered some of the common problems that you may run into when building your data model. By making yourself aware of these issues you should be able to plan accordingly and avoid these mistakes. Once a data model has been completed—physically implemented—and you start using the database in a production environment, making changes is often difficult at best. We always want to build good, sound models, but sometimes we fall into these simple traps. Hopefully, you now have the tools you need to build models without building in these little headaches.

PART IV

CREATING THE PHYSICAL MODEL

CHAPTER 9

CREATING THE PHYSICAL MODEL WITH SQL SERVER

We have come a long way since we started our discussion about data modeling, but now we are on the downhill slide. You have done all the hard work—gathering requirements, transforming them into a logical model, and acquiring customer approval of that model. Throughout this process you had to make sure to avoid common problems and keep everything normalized to a reasonable level.

Now it's time to use the logical model and the business requirements to come up with your physical model. This physical model will become your actual database in SQL Server. This chapter first covers the naming guidelines we suggest for SQL Server objects, and then we talk about creating your physical model. So without further ado, let's get right into creating our physical model in Microsoft SQL Server.

Naming Guidelines

Naming guidelines are extremely important when you create your physical model. There are literally hundreds of naming standards out there, and each has its pros and cons. At the end of the day, it doesn't matter which standard you use, as long as you use a standard.

Why is a naming standard so important? First, it provides a quick indicator of the type of object you are working with. If all tables start with the same prefix, such as "table" or "tbl," and if all views start with "vw" or "view," then you will be able to tell at a glance where data is coming from. This practice can save a lot of time and is especially helpful if you find yourself looking at T-SQL code that is not performing well. Also, when performance tuning, you will have different considerations for views than you do for tables, so it's helpful to know quickly which type of object you are accessing.

Second, naming standards can prevent problems that can arise because of your SQL Server configuration. This comes into play most often in case sensitivity. If you name your objects in a standardized way, then your code can be written in the same way. This match of code to object name is crucial if you are going to host your database on a case-sensitive server. If you refer to a table in code as Employee and the table is actually named employee, a case-sensitive server will tell you the table doesn't exist.

"OK," you might be saying, "I'll just set up my SQL Server to be case insensitive." But what if that decision is taken away from you, now or five years from now? There is nothing worse than going back over old code to make sure that the case matches the table because your customer decided it needed case sensitivity. Using good naming standards now prevents you from having to do more work later.

Finally, naming standards can help force good standards on the database developers. We have worked with some extremely talented developers, but talent in C# does not always translate to talent in T-SQL. Developing for databases is a whole different animal, so anything you can do to enforce better standards will be a big help.

As we said, there is no right or wrong method for your database naming standards. No matter which standard you implement, the point is that you have one. To see whether your standard is a good one, ask yourself a few questions.

- Does the naming standard make sense to you?
  You need to make sure that the standard makes sense to you and that you will be able to follow it during your design. If the standard contains hard-to-use or hard-to-remember elements, then you will likely forget about them and end up deviating from your own standard.
- Will others understand the standard?
  Your standard must also make sense to others. If it doesn't make sense to the other people who will be using it, then they too may forget parts of the standard. Make sure you run your thinking by a colleague before the standard gets etched in stone.
- Does the standard lend itself to consistency?
  Can you implement your standard the same way over and over again? As we mentioned earlier, complex elements make for a difficult-to-implement standard. Just remember to keep it simple.

Now let's look at the naming standard we are using in the model for this book. Again, this standard is not the only way, and your standard may be very different, but we want you to understand our thinking before we get into building the physical model. If, however, you like the standard laid out here, we highly recommend its use because we have had great success with it.

General Naming Guidelines

Whether you are naming tables, stored procedures, columns, or any other SQL Server object, there are a few rules that you should plan to follow. These rules ensure that the names you use will not cause problems and will prevent you from having to add extra code when referencing these objects. We look at the general rules now and get into the object-specific rules a little later. Again, these are not hard-and-fast rules, but they are good guidelines.

Never Use Spaces in Object Names

Although SQL Server will happily allow you to enter names that contain spaces, don't do it. A view name like "Orders by Customer" may seem like a good idea (after all, it is descriptive), but you should avoid it at all costs. Some applications are completely unable to deal with the space in an object name, and your T-SQL code can deal with this name only if you enclose it in square brackets, such as [Orders by Customer].

Never Use Hyphens in Object Names

Using hyphens (-), also commonly known as dashes, can cause a problem similar to the one caused by using spaces. A hyphen in T-SQL is, among other things, the minus operator. Using a hyphen in an object name not only will confuse the compiler but also can lead to unexpected results. Although a hyphen won't cause as many problems as a space, it is still wise to avoid its use.

Do Not Name Objects Using SQL Server Keywords

This one can be a real pain. Naming an object with a keyword can lead to all kinds of problems. The list of SQL Server keywords is too long to include here, but you will know it's a keyword if it turns blue in the SQL

Server tools or in a T-SQL query or script. Keywords include, but are not limited to, the following:

- SELECT
- INSERT
- UPDATE
- DELETE
- DISK
- BEGIN
- END

There is really no good way to know all the keywords, although there are some references on the Internet, so your best bet is to use the compiler and a little common sense. If you have been around SQL Server for any length of time, you will recognize many keywords. Just remember that if it's a command that can be used to do something in SQL Server, then it's probably a keyword. Additionally, you can find a complete list of in Appendix C, "SQL Server 2008 Reserved Words."

What's the big deal? Why can't you use keywords for object names? First of all, it can confuse other people who are trying to read a script that was written against the database. Second, and more importantly, it confuses the T-SQL compiler. When SQL Server encounters a script like the one that follows, it can't make heads or tails of the syntax and throws an error.

```
SELECT where, and, name, date
FROM INSERT
WHERE and = 1
AND where = 'Omaha'
```

This is an extreme example, but you can see how SQL Server would have no idea you have a table named INSERT with columns named "where," "and," "name," and "date." You would receive a syntax error when compiling this code, and you would need to surround all the keywords with square brackets, as follows. This fixes the syntax problems but doesn't make it any easier for a person to read.

```
SELECT [where], [and], name, date
FROM [INSERT]
WHERE [and] = 1
AND [where] = 'Omaha'
```

Keep the Names Short

In our opinion, too many people abuse the ability to give things longer names these days. This isn't limited to databases by any stretch. In Windows, files can have extremely long names, and SQL Server is no different. A short but descriptive name is always a better alternative to a long, more human-readable name. Long names don't cause syntax problems, but they cause frustration and can cause developers to write some ugly-looking code. Imagine a database where stored procedures have names such as proc_select_all_customer_data_by_company_grouped_by_month. Although this doesn't break any of our other rules—no spaces or dashes, and no keywords—it is a little long to deal with. Imagine trying to type that in each script you write. It would be time consuming, not to mention causing great difficulty in locating a typo if one should occur. Now imagine a whole script filled with table and view names similar to this one. It is always best to keep it short. In this case, a name like proc_monthly _custdata_by_company, though still a little long, would be a much better alternative.

In addition to being short, the name should be descriptive. Don't go too far to the other extreme and start calling views something like mtcusdat. This name could mean almost anything. Make sure you follow both aspects of this rule: short and simple, but long enough to have meaning.

Using Case in Your Names

Here is where we receive the fan mail and the hate mail all in one section of the book. When it comes to using case, we feel that the best option is to keep *everything* in your database in lowercase. This means it is more difficult to separate two words in an object, so we use underscore characters between them.

Now, we agree that a name like TblActiveCustomers is a lot nicer to look at than tbl_active_customers, but there is a specific reason we prefer the latter. It all goes back to case sensitivity, as we mentioned earlier. If you are enforcing good standards in your database and in your code, all references to database objects should match the case of the object name. The problem is that so many SQL Servers are set up to be case insensitive that it makes it easy to get lazy. With a name like TblActiveCustomer, it's too easy to reference it in the code as tblActiveCustomer or tblactivecustomer. This is all fine and good on a case-insensitive box, but if the database is placed on a case-sensitive server then all the code will need to be fixed. If everything is always in lowercase, it's a lot easier to remember the standard.

Remember that these are guidelines. You can implement however you want, but in the long run, having everything in lowercase will cause you fewer headaches.

Naming Tables

When we name our tables, we use a convention of prefacing the table with "tbl_" followed by a meaningful name. We do this so that you can quickly identify a table when looking at objects or queries. Some people would argue that it is obvious which objects are tables, because they are listed as tables in the SQL Server tools and they are always referenced in the same places in T-SQL statements. We agree with the first argument, but as for the second, it forgets about views. Views and tables are referenced in the same way, and it is often helpful to be able to quickly identify whether a view or table is being used when you're looking at a T-SQL statement. Additionally, you might need to look at documentation, such as a data dictionary, offline. It is again helpful to be able to quickly identify your tables.

As for the actual name, we make sure it's meaningful and we separate words with underscore characters. One other important note: We never pluralize the names of our tables. The table is named for the data it holds, as in tbl_customer; even though it holds multiple customers, we do not name the table tbl_customers. Here are some of the tables you will see in the Mountain View Music database:

- tbl_order
- tbl_customer
- tbl_product
- tbl_employee

That convention handles 80 percent of the tables we will encounter in our database, but there is always the other 20 percent to deal with. Some tables serve a special purpose, such as join tables in many-to-many relationships. You may decide that you need to set up a M:M relationship between a customer table and an address table. If you think about it, this makes sense; a customer can have many addresses, and more than one customer can share an address. As we discussed in Chapter 3, you need to create a third join table to set up this M:M relationship. In this case, we start the table name with "tbl_" and then we use both of the other table names in this new name. In the example of customers and addresses, we would call the join table tbl_customer_address.

Additionally, for lookup tables, some people like to add a prefix, such as "lkup," after "tbl_ ." This would give a table containing status codes a name like tbl_lkup_status_code. Although we don't think this is a bad idea, it is not something we implement. The main reason we avoid this strategy is that whoever ends being up the DBA for this database shouldn't care whether the table contains lookup data. To the DBA it is just another table that the applications need to read, and possibly write to.

Naming Columns

Columns are not given prefixes, and they are the lone exception to our prefix rules. When naming a column, just make sure you give it a descriptive name. If you need a column to hold a customer's first name, a column called first_name or even firstname is just fine. Try to be consistent where you place your underscores. Don't name one column first_name and another lastname; it will lead to confusion. Also, be extra careful with reserved words in column names.

One last convention that has always been an area of debate is using the table name in the column name as a prefix—for example, giving the column that contains your customer's phone number a name like customer_phone. Although this does help to avoid ambiguous column references in T-SQL, it can also add a lot of extra code that you just don't need in order to figure out which column you are talking about. Because you use periods (.) to separate the portions of the object's name in SQL Server, you can reference the customer's phone number as tbl_customer.phone, which is less messy than the alternative tbl_customer.customer_phone. You wouldn't include the name of the database in the name of a table, so don't do it with columns.

Naming Views

Views are similar to tables, so their naming convention is similar. We preface them with "vw_" and then add a descriptive name. Views tend to have slightly longer names than tables do, because views often pull together data from multiple tables. A view that pulls together data from two tables—tbl_address and tbl_customer—might be given a name like vw_customer_addresses. In this case, we have tossed out the rule about avoiding a plural name. That's because for a view that contains multiple addresses for each customer, it is more appropriate to call it vw_customer _addresses instead of vw_customer_address.

Naming Stored Procedures

Naming stored procedures is simple; we preface them with "prc_" followed by a descriptive name. Stored procedures can often update many tables in one shot, so again be careful not to let the name get too long. One tip: If you don't like our prefix "prc_" and you would rather use your own, that is fine, but we caution against using "sp_." That is the prefix that Microsoft uses in SQL Server for system stored procedures, and using "sp_" can lead to confusion.

Naming User-Defined Functions

User-defined functions are named in the same manner as stored procedures. The prefix we use for UDFs is "udf_." SQL Server has several built-in functions that use "fn_" as the prefix, so you should avoid that as an alternative.

Naming Triggers

Triggers present an interesting problem when it comes to naming. We still use a prefix, in this case "trg_," but triggers are also attached to a specific table and tie to a specific statement or statements that run against that table. Triggers can be configured to run *after* an insert, update, or delete or *instead of* an insert, update or delete. You can even define a single trigger to run on multiple conditions such as after an insert *and* after an update on the same table. Although it would be nice to use a descriptive name such as trg_upd_tbl_customer, it can get a little messy if the trigger runs in response to more than one condition. Imagine the name for a trigger that fires on delete, insert, and update on a table name that contains customer history; it would be something like trg_ins_upd_del_tbl_customer_history. That is just ridiculous.

How do we solve this problem? We name triggers in the same way we name stored procedures: a "trg_" prefix followed by a descriptive name. Beyond that, we are OK with looking up the detail on triggers when we are working with them.

Naming Indexes

Indexes are named in a similar manner as the other objects. We start with the prefix "idx_" and follow with a description of the index. For example, an index on the customer table's first_name and last_name columns could be called idx_customer_name. The idea is to provide enough detail about the purpose of the index without the name getting out of hand. It is simple enough to use tools or queries to look up which columns are in the index.

Naming User-Defined Data Types

User-defined data types (UDTs) can be quite useful when you're trying to enforce consistency in similar data across multiple objects. If you choose to use UDTs, we suggest you name them in a way that makes sense to you— no special prefix, only a good descriptive name. For example, you may have multiple tables that contain an order number column. If you want to ensure that all of those columns have exactly the same format and type, you could create a UDT called ordernum to enforce the required data type.

Naming Primary Keys and Foreign Keys

When we name our primary keys, we simply start with "PK_" and end with the table name. For example, your customer table called tbl_customer would contain a primary key called PK_tbl_customer. We keep the "tbl" prefix in the name to avoid confusion.

Foreign keys are a little trickier because they commonly exist in one table and reference another. As you may have guessed, we start foreign keys with an "FK_" prefix. After that, the name has two parts: the first is the referencing table, and the second is the referenced table. For example, suppose we want to name the foreign key on the order detail table named tbl_order_detail that references the order table tbl_order. We would name it FK_tbl_order_detail_tbl_order. We again leave the "tbl_" prefixes in the name of the foreign key. This helps to avoid confusion by offering a clear separator for the referencing and the referenced table.

Naming Constraints

Defaults and constraints are straightforward. Defaults are named with a "DF_" prefix followed by the table and then the column on which the default exists. For example, if the customer table has a column named status with a default value, we name our default constraint DF_tbl_customer _status. For check constraints, we start with a "CK_" prefix and follow with a meaningful name. If you want to ensure that an entity contains at least one phone number, you might write a check constraint. The name for this check constraint would be something like CK_ phone_number. Finally, for unique constraints we use the prefix "UNQ_."

Deriving the Physical Model

Until now, we have done a lot of work with entities and our logical model. Now we walk through the process of building the physical model based on the logical model. This process is often a matter of deciding what to call your tables and creating one table per entity. On the other hand, it can be a lot trickier. In some cases, you need more than one table to represent an entity, and other times you use a single table to represent multiple entities. Remember that entities are meant to model real-world objects, such as customers or employees. When you create tables, they also need to model real-world objects, but the other concern here is storing the data in a way that makes sense in terms of a relational database. This is the reason we don't always see a one-to-one mapping of entities to tables.

To build our physical model, we start by creating one table per entity and then split or combine tables on a case-by-case basis. Some people like to do the splitting and combining in a second pass, and others do it as they go through the model the first time. Ours is a hybrid method. We go through once, putting things where they make the most sense, and then we come back and look at what we have done to make sure it looks correct.

Using Entities to Model Tables

At this point in the process you should have a complete logical model set up and documented in a data modeling tool. Depending on the tool, you may have the ability to translate what you have in the logical model into a physical model.

If your tool doesn't have this option, you need to find another way to document your physical model. You can model it directly in SQL Server by using a database diagram, which would actually create the tables and other objects, or you can set up another "logical" model but this time follow your rules for physical modeling.

In our case, the tool supports both a physical and a logical model. When we created our logical model, we used the tool to separate the entities into logical groupings called **submodels.** Submodels simplify working with large data models, because they allow you to view a subset of entities instead of 300 entities at once. The submodels we created are as follows.

- Products
  This final submodel contains all the details about the products sold
  and the product vendors.
- Inventory
  This submodel contains all the details about the company's physical
  inventory.
- Orders
  All entities related to orders, payments, and customers exist in this
  submodel.
- Web Session
  These entities allow us to implement a Web shopping cart to save
  orders in progress.
- Lists
  This small submodel contains the two entities used to implement a
  lookup list.

As you can see in Figures 9.1 and 9.2, showing the complete logical
model versus a submodel, the smaller submodel makes it easier to view
and work with the entities.

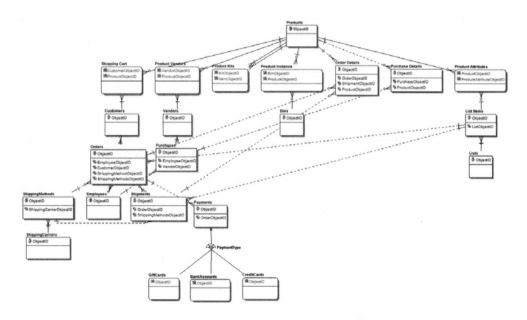

FIGURE 9.1 The complete Mountain View Music logical model

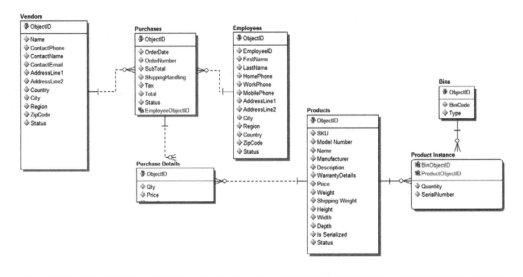

FIGURE 9.2 The Inventory submodel from the Mountain View Music logical model

As we work toward our physical model, we will go through each of our submodels one at a time. In this way, we can take small sections and build the physical model in a logical manner rather than try to look at the entire model at the same time.

In addition, as we go through, we will see that certain entities, such as Employees, exist in multiple submodels. We will deal with these entities in the model that they truly belong to. In other words, entities such as List Items appear for lookup purposes in many of our submodels; however, because there is an entire submodel dedicated to lists, we will ignore the List Items entity until we get to the Lists submodel. For this first pass, we concern ourselves only with getting entities from our logical model and finding a place for them in our physical model; we deal with columns and relationships in the next section.

Products Submodel

The first submodel we need to work with for our physical database contains the entities relating to the company's products. This submodel is shown in Figure 9.3, and the entities we will be working with are as follows:

- Products
- Vendors
- List Items
- Product Vendors
- Product Kits
- Product Attributes

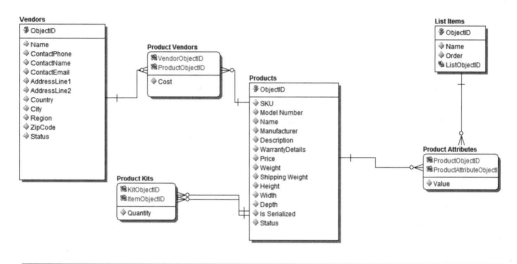

FIGURE 9.3   The Products submodel from the Mountain View Music logical model

This first submodel is pretty simple. Because of the way we created our logical model, we will use all these entities as is and create tables. For example, consider the Product Vendors entity; it exists as a many-to-many join between Products and Vendors, but it also contains the Cost attribute. This attribute allows us to track the cost of a particular product from a particular vendor, and the many-to-many relationship allows Mountain View Music to set up multiple relationships with vendors for each product. Without the cost attribute, this might have been modeled as a many-to-many relationship without the joining entity, in which case we would have had to add the join table to the physical model. That's only a brief aside to let you know what to look for; in this case, however, we will make each entity a table, so all that remains is to rename them in our physical model. Figure 9.4 shows what the physical model looks like at this point, with only tables and primary keys.

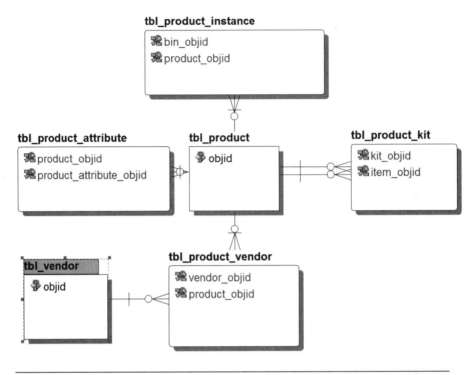

FIGURE 9.4   The beginning of the physical model for Mountain View Music's products

Notice that we have named the tables using the guideline we discussed earlier. In addition, you can see the implementation of our surrogate primary key, a column named objid in all tables. Tables such as tbl_product_instance have a composite primary key that is made up of the primary keys from the two joined tables. As it happens, this is also how we name the foreign key columns—the shortened table name (no "tbl_" prefix) followed by "_objid." We look at foreign keys in the next section.

Inventory Submodel

Next, we look at the entities in the Inventory submodel. This model is similar to the Products submodel in that we don't have a lot of work to do. The entities we will work with are listed here and shown in Figure 9.5.

- Products
- Product Instance

- Bins
- Purchases
- Purchase Details
- Vendors
- Employees

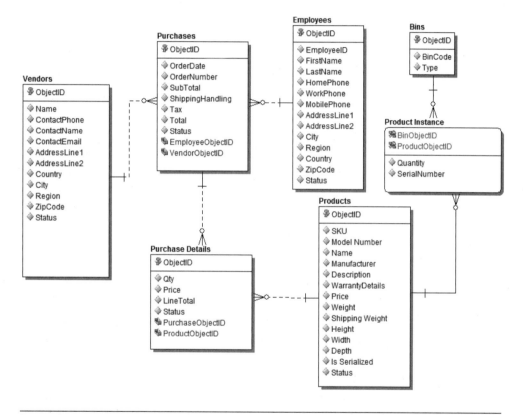

FIGURE 9.5 The Inventory submodel from the Mountain View Music logical model

Again, these entities make nice individual tables so we don't have much to do. Notice that Vendors and Products both appear again in this submodel. We won't need to make any further updates to these tables, and if you are using a good modeling tool, the change you have already made will be reflected in the new physical Inventory submodel. In Figure 9.6 you can see the physical model for the Inventory submodel.

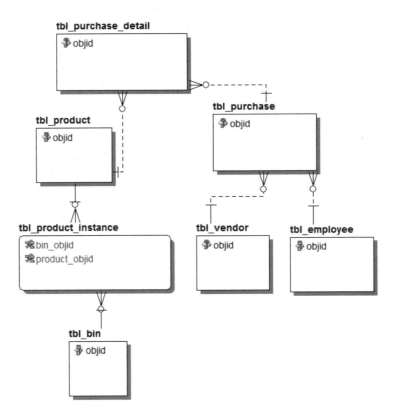

FIGURE 9.6 The beginning of the physical model for Mountain View Music's inventory

Orders Submodel

The Orders submodel contains the most complicated set of entities in the entire model. That's fitting, because the database is centered on customer orders via the Mountain View Music Web site. We have a few decisions to make when building the physical model for these entities. First, let's look at the entities we are dealing with; they are shown next and in Figure 9.7.

- Customers
- Employees

- Orders
- Order Details
- Products
- Shipments
- ShippingCarriers
- Shipping Methods
- Payments
- CreditCards
- GiftCards
- BankAccounts

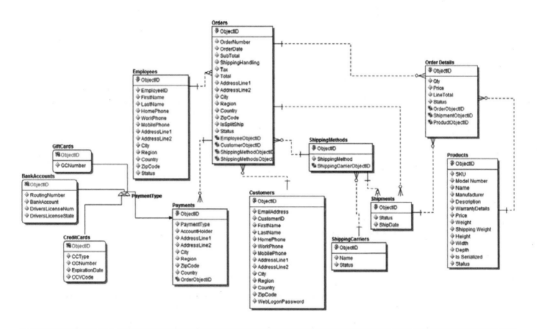

FIGURE 9.7 The Orders submodel from the Mountain View Music logical model

First, let's look at the entities that can be made into tables as is. We have already made tables out of the Products and Employees entities, so those two are all set (with a single exception for tbl_employee, which we look at shortly). Of the remaining entities, Shipments, ShippingMethods, ShippingCarriers, and Order Details can all be made into tables without any major modification other than their names. That leaves us with six entities that still need some work: Orders, Customers, and the supertype

Payments, which includes the subtypes CreditCards, GiftCards, and BankAccounts.

Let's first look at Customers, which on the surface looks like an entity that would work as a single table. In reality, the company wants to be able to store multiple addresses for each customer. If you look at our model, we can store only a single address for each customer. To remedy this, we create a new table, named tbl_address, remove the address information from tbl_customer, and set up a relationship between the two tables. The resulting address and customer tables are shown in Figure 9.8.

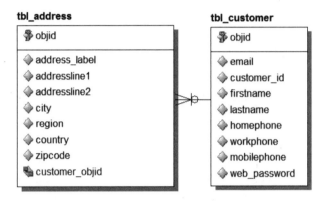

FIGURE 9.8 The newly added address table and the customer table with address information removed

As you can see, we can now store multiple addresses for each customer and keep track of them by providing an address label such as "Home" or "Work."

As it happens, the Orders entity has a similar address problem. If you look at the Orders entity in the logical model, shown earlier in Figure 9.7, you will see that we are storing another set of address information. This is the address that the order will be shipped to. If all our customer addresses are stored in the address table, then putting an additional address in our order table will cause us to have duplicate data, and we would be violating the rules of normalization. Now we can simply delete the address detail from Orders and replace it with a relationship to the appropriate record in the address table.

We have one last change as it relates to addresses: Our employee table also contains address detail. Even though we said that the employee table was ready to go, we need to make a little change for consistency's sake. Adding another relationship between tbl_address and tbl_employee allows us to store employee addresses in tbl_address. Later, when we look at business rules, we will reconcile the fact that we now have two optional relationships in tbl_address.

Last, but not least, we have the subtype construct we modeled for payments. As we discussed in Chapter 3, you have three options when you physically implement subtypes.

- Implement the supertype and all the subtypes in a single table.
- Implement the subtypes as tables, and add the supertype data to each of these subtype tables.
- Implement the supertype as a table and all the subtypes as additional tables.

Which option you choose is dependent largely on the specific data you are working with. In the case of Mountain View Music we will implement a single payment table that will contain all the data from each of the subtypes. This decision is often driven by the number of attributes in each entity. Because the only attributes common to all payments are the account holder and the payment type, we don't want that to be in its own table. Especially with our addition of an address table, that would leave a payments table with two columns.

We could implement each payment as its own table, but that would be a relationship nightmare. It would leave us with three separate relationships to order (depending on the payment type) and three relationships to address (one for each type).

It is for these reasons that we decided to go with a single payment table. This table will contain a relationship to address for the payment address and all the detail from each of the subtypes. When you look at the payments table in Figure 9.9, you will probably notice that many of the columns are optional; that is, they allow NULL data. That could lead to problems because we require certain pieces of information to, for example, process a credit card. We will fix this problem a little later when we look at implementing business rules.

With that, we have looked at all the tables that are related to order and have created the foundation for the Orders submodel, as shown in Figure 9.10. These tables represent the bulk of the Mountain View Music database and were also a bit trickier to derive from our logical model. We

tbl_payment

objid	int	IDENTITY
payment_type	tinyint	NOT NULL
ammount	money	NOT NULL
account_holder	varchar(50)	NOT NULL
gc_number	bigint	NULL
account_number	bigint	NULL
routing_number	int	NULL
license_number	varchar(20)	NULL
license_state	char(10)	NULL
cc_type	varchar(16)	NULL
cc_number	bigint	NULL
cc_expire	date	NULL
ccv_code	smallint	NULL
order_objid	int	NOT NULL
address_objid	int	NOT NULL

FIGURE 9.9 The payment table implemented to model the Payments supertype in the Mountain View Music logical model

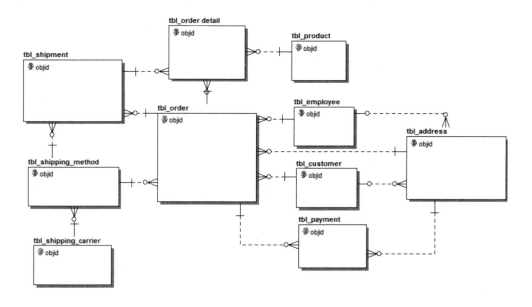

FIGURE 9.10 The beginning of the physical model for Mountain View Music's orders

still have a couple of submodels to look at, but our physical model is quickly taking shape.

Web Session and Lists Submodel

Finally, we have two small submodels that we will look at together. The Web Session submodel has only one new entity, Shopping Cart. This entity acts as a join between Customers and Products so that customers can save items in their shopping carts on the Web site for later purchase. This table is simple. It holds the customer ID and the products that customers have in their cart. In addition it tells us the quantity and the status of each product. This entity is another simple table and is taken as is.

We also have the two tables used for lookup values: Lists and List Items. These tables exist to provide the front-end application a place to store related lists of data such as order status or various product attributes. Again, these tables are physically modeled as is, with only name changes to match our naming standards.

At this point we have looked at all the entities in the logical model and found homes for them in the physical model. In the next section we look at getting the relationships modeled in the physical world as well as getting our primary keys in order and modeling columns based on the logical attributes.

Using Relationships to Model Keys

While modeling our physical tables, we also took care of the primary keys and the foreign keys. As you've seen, we named all the primary keys objid. In the case of identifying relationships—those in which the primary key columns on the table are also foreign keys—we name the columns after the table they reference. Examples are the bin_objid and product_objid columns in tbl_product_instance. Foreign keys, as you may have guessed, are named in the same manner—the referenced table followed by "_objid," such as order_objid in tbl_order_details. This is a simple change; we go through each table and rename these columns to match our standard. Look at Figure 9.11 to see what the Orders submodel looks like with the addition of the foreign keys columns. Each of the other submodels will look similar after you finish renaming the columns.

The next thing we need to do is to ensure that the primary keys and foreign keys conform to our naming standard. Now we are talking about the actual constraints that will exist in SQL Server. Depending on your

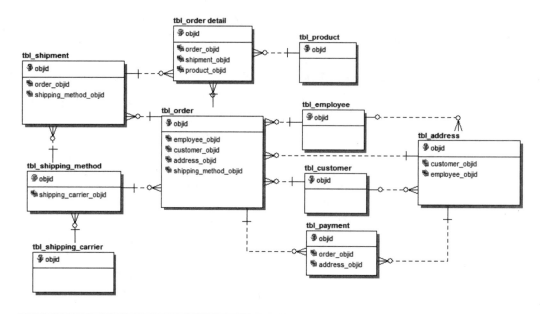

FIGURE 9.11   The physical Orders submodel complete with the foreign key columns

modeling software, this can be done right inside the model; otherwise, you will need to make the changes to your scripts before you implement your tables in SQL Server. Again, go though each table and set the name of the primary key and the foreign keys.

Using Attributes to Model Columns

Finally, we are left with the attributes in each of our entities. Attributes are usually pretty simple. Now that you have all your tables modeled, you need to rename the attributes to match your physical naming standards and place them in the correct table. If you split or combined some of your entities, the bulk of the work comes in splitting or combining the attributes to the appropriate table. One thing to be aware of during this process are your data types. Hopefully, your modeling software understood SQL Server types when you built your logical model, and hopefully you took our advice about using the SQL Server types in your logical model. If these things are true, then your attribute data types should just copy right into your tables.

Most of the work of creating your physical model is simple and straightforward. Usually your data modeling software allows you to generate a physical model based on your logical model. If this is the case, all you have to do is work through any name changes required to match the standards. If your modeling software doesn't support physical models, or if you have been building your physical model right inside SQL Server, then you have more work to do. It isn't complicated; you just need to start from scratch when it comes to creating your tables. All we can say is that, although expensive, good modeling software is worth its weight in gold.

Implementing Business Rules in the Physical Model

One last thing we want to talk about is the business rules that need to be enforced in your model. Many business rules will be set up and managed in the application or in a middle or business tier, but some rules can and should be implemented in SQL Server. We do this for two reasons: First, it makes sense to enforce some things, such as constraints on data, in SQL Server; and second, as database developers, architects, and administrators, we don't trust applications. Is this just paranoia talking? Maybe, but it is still good practice to implement as many business rules as possible in SQL Server.

To be fair, it isn't only because we don't trust applications; other factors push us in this direction. For example, let's say you have a perfect business tier and all the data comes through without failure each and every time; would it then be a good idea to remove all your PKs, FKs, and constraints because the business tier is handling the relationships and data integrity? Some people argue that it is, but we disagree. What happens if for some reason you need to run a bulk import and you do it without the aid of the business tier? You stand to create a lot of integrity problems because of a lack of enforcement in SQL Server. Also, certain features of SQL Server, such as transactional replication, require primary keys. We are firm believers in using any and all means in your power to maintain data integrity inside SQL Server databases. In this section, we look at how to implement business rules using various features of SQL Server and we give examples from the Mountain View Music database for each feature.

Using Constraints to Implement Business Rules

Constraints provide a mechanism inside SQL Server to control the data that goes into tables. We look at three types of constraints: default, unique, and check constraints. **Default constraints** provide a default value for a column in the event that a value is not explicitly specified. **Unique constraints** tell SQL Server that all the data in the column must be unique and must contain no duplicates. **Check constraints** allow you to write a small piece of T-SQL code to do custom data checking against one or more columns. Let's look at each of these a little closer and see how they can be useful in implementing business rules.

Default Constraints

Default constraints are very simple. You provide a value for a column, and when a new row is added to a table without specifying a value for that column, the default value is used. This can be as simple as stating that the status column in tbl_employee should always be 1 unless otherwise stated; or it can be more complicated, such as a function call to generate a new order number. The following code adds a default constraint to the status column in tbl_employee.

```
ALTER TABLE dbo.tbl_employee
ADD CONSTRAINT DF_status
DEFAULT 1 FOR status
```

If you want to call a function to generate your default data, that is done as shown next. This piece of code adds a default constraint to tbl_order to call a user-defined function to create a new order ID.

```
ALTER TABLE dbo.tbl_order
ADD  CONSTRAINT [DF_ordernumber]
DEFAULT dbo.udf_new_orderid() FOR ordernumber
```

Default constraints are useful as long as you document them for the developers who will be writing the T-SQL code. Their functionality can be replaced within stored procedure code, so many people ask why we should bother with default constraints. The answer, which is the answer we give for any question involving the use of data integrity, is that you can't always rely on your stored procedures. What if you develop a SQL Server Integration Services (SSIS) package that writes data in bulk to a table? There will be no stored procedure there to protect you. Similarly, what if a developer gets access to the tables and writes code to insert data directly? This is a bad practice (we look at avoiding it in Chapter 11), but it can still happen, and your database needs to be prepared to stand on its own to maintain data integrity.

Check Constraints

Check constraints are a wonderful tool to help you ensure that the data being loaded into your database is what you expect and require. Using some custom code, you can force data to conform to almost any pattern your heart desires. To check data, you use an expression to look at the data and compare it to some desired result. For example, to ensure that all values in a salary column are greater than or equal to the minimum wage ($5.85, in this example), your expression would be

```
salary >= 5.85
```

Let's look at an example from the Mountain View Music database. As you will recall, we created a table named tbl_customer that holds all the data pertinent Mountain View's customers. The table has three columns for phone numbers called homephone, workphone, and mobilephone. Each of these columns allows NULL values, and this means that a customer could conceivably choose not to provide a phone number at all. The company has decided that it needs to have at least one phone number that it can use to call the customer in the event of a problem with an order. To that end, you need to place a check constraint on tbl_customer to ensure that at least one phone number is provided. Here is the simple expression to check for this condition.

```
([homephone] IS NOT NULL
OR [workphone] IS NOT NULL
OR [mobilephone] IS NOT NULL)
```

This expression, when used in a check constraint, forces one of the phone numbers to be supplied. Failure to supply at least one phone number causes your insert or update statement to fail. To add a constraint to tbl_customer with the expression you use the following code.

```
ALTER TABLE dbo.tbl_customer WITH CHECK
ADD  CONSTRAINT CK_phone_number
CHECK (([homephone] IS NOT NULL
       OR [workphone] IS NOT NULL
       OR [mobilephone] IS NOT NULL))
```

Unique Constraints

Unique constraints are used to ensure that you have no duplicate values in a column. Unique constraints can be attached to one or more columns depending on your needs. If you attach a unique constraint to one column, that single column can contain no duplicated data. If you attach it to multiple columns, then the combination of data between those columns cannot be duplicated in another row. In other words, each column involved in a multicolumn constraint can have duplicates, but when you look at all the columns together you are not allowed to have repeats.

Unique constraints are used frequently in SQL Server. Mountain View Music uses them to ensure that key pieces of data are unique—for example, order ID. If two customers get the same order ID for different orders, they might get the wrong product or no product at all. To avoid this, we add a unique constraint to the ordernumber column in tbl_order.

```
ALTER TABLE dbo.tbl_order
ADD CONSTRAINT UNQ_ordernumber UNIQUE NONCLUSTERED
(ordernumber)
```

Often we see uniqueness in tables enforced only for the primary key. Remember that when you selected your primary key, you evaluated all the candidate keys in the table. Just because you didn't use a candidate as the primary key doesn't mean it should be ignored; these columns are great candidates to have unique constraints.

Using Triggers to Implement Business Rules

Constraints are great, and along with and primary and foreign keys, they go a long way to enforce a lot of business rules on your data. But what if you need to implement something a little more advanced, and constraints and keys just aren't getting the job done? That's where triggers come into play. Using triggers, you can write custom T-SQL code to run after something has happened to a table. Triggers can be set up to run after an INSERT, UPDATE, or DELETE or even instead of one of these actions. Really, the sky is the limit when you use triggers; you can do almost anything, including canceling the statement that fired the trigger.

Keep in mind, however, that triggers fire as part of the transaction that started them, and they fire each time the action occurs. This means that if you insert 100,000 rows into a table, an insert trigger would fire 100,000 times. Be aware of what you are doing in your trigger, and try to keep the code as quick and efficient as possible.

Where does Mountain View Music use triggers? One is on tbl_payment to ensure that we get all the information we need based on the payment type. You will remember we decided to implement payments in a single table even though we can accept three payment methods: gift cards, credit cards, and direct bank draft. To accommodate this, all the columns in tbl_payment that don't pertain to all payment types allow NULL data. Obviously, if the customer pays with a credit card, we require the credit card number, expiration date, type, and credit card verification (CCV) code. To enforce the required data to be present, we use the following trigger.

```
CREATE TRIGGER trg_payment_data
ON dbo.tbl_payment
FOR INSERT, UPDATE
AS

DECLARE @payment_type tinyint
,@cc_type varchar(16)
,@cc_number bigint
,@cc_expire date
,@ccv_code smallint
,@gc_number bigint
,@account_number bigint
,@routing_number int
,@license_number varchar(20)
,@license_state char(10)

SELECT @payment_type = payment_type
,@cc_type = cc_type
,@cc_number = cc_number
,@cc_expire = cc_expire
,@ccv_code = ccv_code
,@gc_number = gc_number
,@account_number = account_number
,@routing_number = routing_number
,@license_number = license_number
,@license_state = license_state
FROM inserted
```

```
IF @payment_type= 1 --Credit Card
BEGIN
     IF @cc_type IS NULL
            OR @cc_number IS NULL
            OR @cc_expire IS NULL
            OR @ccv_code IS NULL
     BEGIN
     RAISERROR ('Error: Credit Card Data is Missing.',11,1)
     ROLLBACK
     END
END

IF @payment_type = 2 --Gift Card
BEGIN
     IF @gc_number IS NULL
     BEGIN
            RAISERROR ('Error: Gift Card Data is Missing.',11,1)
     ROLLBACK
     END
END

IF @payment_type = 3 --Bank Draft
BEGIN
     IF @account_number IS NULL
            OR @routing_number IS NULL
            OR @license_number IS NULL
            OR @license_state IS NULL
     BEGIN
            RAISERROR ('Error: Bank Account Data is
Missing.',11,1)
     ROLLBACK
     END
END
```

As you can see, the trigger looks at the new data and ensures that all the required data is provided based on the payment type specified. If anything is missing, an error is returned and the INSERT or UPDATE statement is rolled back. Again, if you can write it in T-SQL you can manipulate it in a trigger. In fact, you can write CLR triggers using .NET managed code if you are using SQL Server 2005 or later. This really opens the door to what you can do with your triggers and makes implementing business rules for data integrity even more robust.

Implementing Advanced Cardinality

Now let's look at how you can implement advanced cardinality in SQL Server. All relationships you create in SQL Server are one-to-many relationships; there is no such thing as one-to-one or many-to-many in the physical world. We have talked about how you implement M:M relationships in a physical model using two one-to-many relationships and a junction table, but how would you enforce a one-to-one, or even something more advanced such as a one-to-two?

These situations can be tricky, but the good news is that we have already looked at the tools you will need to make this happen. Because the Mountain View Music model doesn't have any of these requirements, let's look at a sample data model for a university. Within a university you often have several colleges; in this case, we have the college of business, the college of science, and the college of engineering. Each of these colleges has one dean, and the university has decided that no one can be dean of more than one college. This requires a one-to-one relationship between college and dean. Figure 9.12 shows what the tables look like when they are set up in SQL Server.

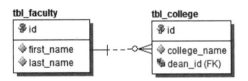

FIGURE 9.12 Tables to hold information about colleges and their deans

As you can see, there is a one-to-many relationship between these tables, but how do we enforce this relationship as one-to-one in SQL Server? For starters, the fact that the dean_id column in tbl_college is required means that we are enforcing the rule that there be at least one dean. Additionally, because the dean_id column exists in tbl_college, each college can have only one dean. But what about the other half of the one-to-one? Remember that each person can be dean of only one college. We can enforce this using a trigger such as the one shown next.

```
ALTER TRIGGER trg_one_dean_per_college
ON tbl_college
```

```
FOR INSERT, UPDATE
AS

DECLARE @college_count int

SELECT @college_count = COUNT(tbl_college.id)
FROM tbl_college
JOIN tbl_faculty
    ON tbl_college.dean_id = tbl_faculty.id
WHERE tbl_faculty.id = (SELECT dean_id FROM INSERTED)

IF @college_count > 1
BEGIN
RAISERROR('This faculty member is dean of another
college',11,1)
ROLLBACK
END
```

As you can see, this code evaluates the number of colleges the faculty member is dean over, and if that number is more than 1, the transaction is canceled.

This trigger evaluates the number of colleges after the actual insert has occurred on tbl_college, so there could be a lot of performance overhead if this were a larger table. To save on this overhead, we could have used an INSTEAD OF trigger to accomplish the same thing. The difference is that we would be able to evaluate the change before the insert occurs, and that would prevent the unnecessary insert if the transaction is rolled back. You can have only one INSTEAD OF trigger in a table for each action, so this may or may not be an option for you.

You see how easy it is to add code using triggers to help implement advanced business rules. Now for a word of caution. Triggers can be great tools, but overuse can cause poor database performance. Although you can implement advanced cardinality using tools inside SQL Server, you need to consider your options carefully. Will the data be unusable if these rules are not followed? The answer is, probably not. Unlike missing credit card data, having too many deans is an easy thing to fix. If you have a real need to conform to some set of cardinality rules, then by all means go ahead and do it, but be careful. In a perfect world, a well-constructed business rules layer in your application will always outperform database triggers. If your application has that functionality, take advantage of it.

Summary

Chapter 9 has included a whirlwind of information, and we've covered a lot of ground. You should now have a handle on naming and creating objects in SQL Server, and you should feel comfortable with creating a physical model given a logical model and some business requirements. At this stage of the game, Mountain View Music has a database, and the only thing left to do is to make sure that it performs up to standards and that our developers have a way to access the information that will be stored in the database. In the final two chapters we talk about just that. First, we look at indexing in SQL Server and then we delve into the creation of an abstraction layer.

CHAPTER 10

INDEXING CONSIDERATIONS

When you hear the phrase "database performance," what do you think it means? Most of us think of how fast a database returns a query. We want to be able to send a query, and, no matter how much data it is returning, we want that query to run instantaneously. Unfortunately, as most of us know, that just doesn't happen. However, performance can be tuned to retrieve data sets in the most efficient way possible. Whether that means getting one row back in less than a second or trying to retrieve 50,000 filtered rows in less than an hour, it can almost always be accomplished. One of the primary ways of speeding access to the data is by using an index.

In this chapter, we discuss what indexes are, how to determine which indexes you need, and how to implement them. We also talk about how information you gathered as far back as the logical modeling step will help shape the indexes you implement in your physical database. Note that all this information is specific to Microsoft SQL Server; however, most of the concepts have parallels in all the other major RDBMSs.

Indexing Overview

Before we can discuss indexes, it is important to have a cursory understanding of how SQL Server 2008 stores its data on disk. We won't go very deep, but we cover enough that you should be able to explain at a high level how data is stored and retrieved. If you are interested in a deeper level of knowledge on this subject, there are numerous books, articles, white papers, and classes on SQL Server internals and data access. For our purposes, we'll take the 15-minute approach.

Because SQL Server runs on Microsoft Windows, all its data is stored in files in the file system of Windows. Every database has at least two files: a file that contains the actual data (known as the **data file**), and a file that contains information about the transactions that have occurred involving that data (known as the **transaction log file**). A database can have more than one of each of these files, but it has at least one of each when it is created. For the purpose of our discussion on indexes, we are particularly concerned with the data file.

Inside the data file is a collection of objects known as extents, which are also collections of objects known as pages. **Pages** are small (8K) allocations of disk space that contain row data. **Extents** are collections of eight pages. Each page generally contains its own identifier, along with rows of data in the order they were inserted into the database. Every table in the database is composed of these pages and extents. Another way to look at it is that tables are designations of extents (and therefore pages) that contain rows of data. It is this basic structure that we are concerned with when discussing indexes.

What Are Indexes?

By default, when you create a new table in a SQL Server database, the server assigns a starting number of extents to that table. When you start inserting data, it adds rows of data to the pages inside the extents. Once a page is full, it begins inserting data into the next available page in that extent. Once an extent is full, it assigns the next available extent to that table and begins inserting data into the first page in the new extent.

Again, by default and without any extra design on your part, the server sorts the rows on the pages in a first-come, first-served manner. This means that unless you tell it otherwise, your data will be sorted based on when it was inserted, period. A table that has been built this way is known as a **heap.** You can think of it as being similar to a pile of laundry; everything has been piled in heap. For a very small table, this might not be a problem (it's easy to find one pair of jeans in a pile of 8 pairs). But for anything with more than a few rows, it can start to be difficult to work with (imagine finding that one pair in 64 piles of 8 jeans each!).

This is where indexes come in. Simply put, an **index** is a referencing set of pointers to rows of data. Additionally, depending on the type of index, it may actually sort the data, giving you faster access to the rows. Indexes physically exist on disk, and thus they take up disk space separately from, and in addition to, your actual table data. There are even special types of pages that exist to manage indexes. We don't cover exactly how indexes are managed on disk; just remember that you'll need to account for them in the overall size of your database. We discuss that basic math for calculating index sizes when we outline the types of indexes.

To understand the performance implications of an index, it is useful to understand how indexes are logically structured. In SQL Server 2008, there are a number of types of indexes based on the types of data each can hold; however, we are concerned primarily with the indexes on the most commonly used types of data, such as strings, numeric data, and so on.

These indexes use a basic structure known as a B-tree. A **B-tree** is a data structure that uses a tree analogy for storing data in parent and child nodes. Figure 10.1 shows a basic B-tree.

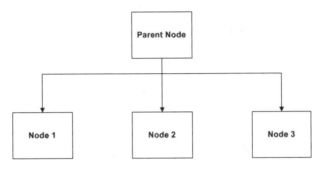

FIGURE 10.1 A basic B-tree structure

Simple, yes? This basic structure can be applied to the very familiar concept of a book index. As you walk through this, it may be useful to actually grab a book with an index (you may in fact be holding a book with an index right now). Flip to any page in the index. Look for a top-level word; often these are in boldface and are left-aligned with the column on the page. These are the **root,** or **parent node,** of the index. The entries beneath the word are indented. For each lower-level entry, the index either gives you a pointer, which is the page number, or more entries even lower in the index. The page number points you to the information you are looking for—the data.

For each word, there can be any number of entries and subentries. For human readability, we rarely see more than three or four levels in a book index. However, in the context of an index on a table, SQL Server can handle reading quite a few levels of an index and can split and manage the index nodes based on the volume of data and the information you've given to it (how you have defined the index). But basically, the index serves the same purpose to the SQL Server query engine that a book index serves for a human; the index helps SQL Server find the data faster than just reading the pages until it finds the information it's looking for.

When you create an index, you define a key value, or a set of key values, that define how the data is separated. For example, when looking at the index in the back of the book, you are looking through the data alphabetically, by the first letters of the highest-level node. In this case, the key value is the highest-level word, which is sometimes derived from the headings and subheadings used in the book. Similarly, when an index is defined on a table, the index must be based on one (or more) columns that tell the index how to arrange the lookups of the data. Unlike a book, a table can have multiple indexes defined to satisfy different types of queries. This allows us to define indexes in order to manage queries from different systems, or wildly different queries against the same data from the same system.

Types

Now that you've seen the very basic structure SQL Server uses for indexes, let's get some context surrounding the kinds of indexes you will actually use in your database. The two basic index types are clustered and nonclustered indexes. All indexes that you define on your tables will be one of these two types. Let's take a closer look.

Clustered Indexes

Clustered indexes actually restructure the data on disk. That is, if you define a clustered index on a table, that table is no longer a heap, because it is actually sorted by the key value you've given it. For example, let's look at the Mountain View Music Customers table, as shown in Figure 10.2.

Customers

ObjectID	INTEGER
EmailAddress	VARCHAR(50)
CustomerID	CHAR(10)
FirstName	VARCHAR(50)
LastName	VARCHAR(50)
HomePhone	VARCHAR(15)
WorkPhone	VARCHAR(15)
MobilePhone	VARCHAR(15)
WebLogonPassword	VARCHAR(16)

FIGURE 10.2   Customers table for Mountain View Music

One of the queries we can imagine being fairly popular for this table would involve finding a customer record based on a customer's last name. If we don't define any index on this table, the records will be inserted first-come, because this table will be a heap. The B-tree structure for this table will be very flat, because we're storing data in no particular order. Figure 10.3 shows the basic structure of this table.

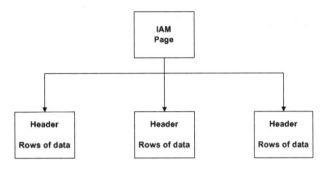

FIGURE 10.3 B-tree for a heap

The **index allocation map** (IAM) page is simply the "management" page for the heap. Each of the child nodes represents pages on disk. There's a simple header that identifies the page (what extent, and object, it belongs to). Then each page stores data as it has been inserted. So if we're looking for a customer with the last name Johnson, we'll start with the first row on the first page in the first extent that was ever allocated to the table. We'll check the last name value for that row. If it is not a match, we'll look at the next one. If it is a match, we'll return that row and then move on to the next row. This process is known as a **table scan.** We'll do this for the *entire* contents of the table. If there are 100 customers, the scan will go fairly quickly. If there are 100,000 customers, then, as you can imagine, it'll be fairly slow.

Now let's assume we don't want this query to take forever, and we know that the vast majority of queries will involve searching for the last name field. It might be useful to store the data, on disk, in an order that facilitates these lookups. Enter the clustered index.

If we define a clustered index on this table, we might define it so that LastName is the only key value. However, we know that the last names may not be unique; there are lots of Joneses and Johnsons and Smiths out there. So we know that we will likely be looking at the first name as well. So we may want to define the clustered index key as LastName, FirstName. The order of the columns is important, because it tells the index to order the data first by last name and then by first name.

When we apply this index, SQL Server will actually reorder the rows of data (if any exist) to list the data in order alphabetically by last name, and, within each unique last name value, it will order the rows alphabetically by first name. Figure 10.4 shows the B-tree structure of the table after the clustered index has been applied.

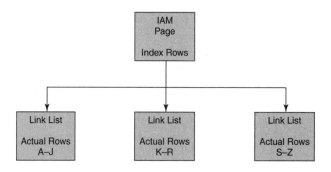

FIGURE 10.4   Representation of a clustered index B-tree

The pages now contain the rows ordered by last name alphabetically. Notice the words "Link List." These pages, unlike the pages in the heap structure, actually contain pointers to the previous and next pages in order by the index. This is because the B-tree can expand to include intermediate levels of pages, which store pointers to the other pages based on values in the key.

For example, if our Customers table has hundreds of thousands of records, the index may need to break down the values by the first few characters, and not only the first character, of each last name–first name combo. Additionally, as data is added, the pages must be reordered to account for values that fall somewhere in the middle of the range of each page. And because the initial management page is an 8K page like all the others, it won't be able to hold all the pointers to the relevant pages in one place. So, as the data grows, SQL Server splits, adds, and rearranges pages as needed. It uses the link list to make sure that it keeps the pages in order.

Because of the nature of a clustered index, there can be only one clustered index defined on a table. As you can imagine, there is a cost to doing this business. We talk about that in a minute, but first we need to discuss the other major type of index.

Nonclustered Indexes

A **nonclustered index** is one that simply stores pointers to the pages that contain the rows of data you are looking for. If table is a heap—that is, if it has no clustered index—then these pointers include the page number and the row identifier for the rows that contain the key value being searched for. If the table has a clustered index, then the nonclustered index has a pointer to the clustered index key for the rows. To put it in a slightly simpler way, a nonclustered index points to the row (for a heap) or to the clustered index key.

One way to remember the difference between a clustered index and a nonclustered index is that a clustered index includes the data pages, and a nonclustered index only points to the data pages. In our book example, a nonclustered index is like the book's index; you find what you are looking for in the index, and it points you to the information somewhere in the book. If the book were a clustered index, all the information in the book would be reordered, as with a dictionary. Remember that a clustered index actually orders the rows on disk according to the key value. A nonclustered index doesn't manage the data; it simply tells you where the data happens to be.

A nonclustered index can be very useful when your data is already ordered—because of either a business rule or a clustered index—but the query being issued doesn't necessarily require the ordered data value. Take a look at Figure 10.5, which shows a simple B-tree, and we'll talk about when you would use a nonclustered index.

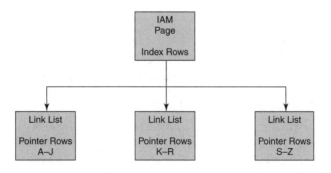

FIGURE 10.5 Representation of a nonclustered index B-tree

In contrast to a clustered index, the B-tree in Figure 10.5 doesn't include the actual data rows. These pages are filled with pointers to the location of the actual rows. Again, for a heap, that is a simple identifier that points to the page number and rows identifier; for a clustered index, the pointer goes to the clustered index key for values that fall in the range of the query.

Why would you want to use a nonclustered index? For the Customers table, you might want a nonclustered index on the EmailAddress field. The data is already ordered by LastName, FirstName, so if you have query that is looking only for the e-mail address, that clustered index may not help (because e-mail addresses don't have to look like a person's name). So we could add a nonclustered index to help those queries look for e-mail addresses by searching ranges of values instead of looking through the entire table. It works by helping break the e-mail address values into specific ranges so that we can scan a smaller number of values to find the matching rows. It also assists in queries to retrieve the last name, first name, and e-mail address of the customer. In more-complex systems, you might see a clustered index accompanied by several nonclustered indexes that help satisfy various types of queries.

Often, indexes are created to handle specific queries; these are called **covering indexes,** because they cover all the fields being referenced by that query. In the next section we talk more about the considerations for using indexes.

Other Index Types

Now that you have a basic understanding of indexes and what they are for, let's take a brief look at some other types of indexes you can use in SQL Server 2008.

Unique

Unique indexes are indexes that specify that the index key be a unique value (or set of values) in the table. Both clustered and nonclustered indexes can be unique; primary keys are always a type of unique index.

Indexes with Included Columns

Starting in SQL Server 2005, designers can specify a new clause when creating their indexes. INCLUDE allows you to specify additional columns in a nonclustered index. This action adds the columns *only* to the final level of the index; there is no reference to the column in the intermediate or root levels. This technique helps minimize the size of the index, while still allowing the query engine to reference those columns when searching data. Consider using this feature when you're building indexes to satisfy very specific queries and the index has gotten too large.

XML Indexes

Because SQL Server supports XML as a data type, it is necessary to include a special type of index that can assist with query performance when you're searching large XML values. These indexes are fairly complicated, allowing for multiple levels of indexing, but it is enough to know that they assist in shredding (the process of taking data from an XML format to a relational format) the XML binary large object (BLOB) by storing rows of data in special storage structures that match each node in the BLOB. In this way, the query engine can reference these special structures to look for the disk location of specific pieces of the XML BLOB, thereby eliminating a full scan of the BLOB and improving query performance.

Spatial

The spatial data types are new to SQL Server 2008, and the introduction of the new data types required the addition of a new kind of index. **Spatial indexes** are built on B-trees, but their purpose is to break down the data into a two-dimensional space, allowing the data points to be indexed and searched efficiently.

Full-Text Indexes

SQL Server provides a special type of index for the full-text engine (FTE) that is built in to SQL Server. (If you're curious, its full name is Microsoft Full-Text Engine for SQL Server [MSFTESQL].) A **full-text index** provides support for the highly specialized and sophisticated word searches inside character data that FTE is designed for. These indexes are actually built on a token-based structure as opposed to a B-tree; they are beyond the scope of our discussion. Just be aware that if you decide to use FTE, you'll need to do some extra research on full-text indexes.

Indexed Views

Technically, an **indexed view** is not a type of index but an on-disk structure. However, in the context of understanding indexes, this is as good a time as any to discuss it. Although views are compiled queries that simply retrieve data sets, the intent is for them to behave like tables. For this reason, SQL Server lets you place an index on them to enhance search performance. When you index a view, you must use a clustered index, which means that the view is materialized. This means that the underlying query is first executed, and then the index is applied to the result set, and the result set is then stored on disk. Therefore, an indexed view is actually a copy of the data from the underlying tables. Keep this in mind when you index views, because you are actually increasing the amount of data being stored on disk, not only because of the index overhead but also because you are duplicating data.

Database Usage Requirements

Once you understand the types of indexes available, you can begin to determine exactly which indexes to use. This means going back to your requirements and looking at your notes about how the database will be used. The key to understanding indexes is to understand the queries that will be run against the data. This means you'll need to talk, probably at length, with the application developer to understand how the application will interact with the data. Additionally, you'll need to account for the other uses of the database: ad hoc queries, reporting, and the like. Knowing the primary use of the database (versus secondary uses) will also help you determine where to cluster your indexes and where to create covering indexes.

Reads versus Writes

Earlier we mentioned that there is a cost of doing all this index business. Here's where it comes into play. When you have a heap, inserting rows into a table is a matter of appending the new row of data to the end of the most recently allocated page. Updating an existing row is a matter of updating the value being changed, something that happens in place on the page where the row exists. And deleting a row means removing the row from the page (there are internal processes for cleaning up the unused space, but we won't go there).

Suppose you've put a nonclustered index on a heap. Now you have a separate object that constantly needs to be aware of where the rows are. Every time a new row is inserted, the nodes of the B-tree in the referencing index must be updated to reflect the existence, and location, of the new row. If a row is updated, the index needs to be updated only if there was a change in the value of the index key field of the given row. Finally, if a row is deleted, the index needs to know that, too. So for every row in a table that has a nonclustered index, some internal processing must occur whenever the data changes.

Now let's look at the case of a clustered index. Once a clustered index has been placed on a table, the data in that table has been physically ordered on its pages on disk to meet the clustering key requirements. In our Customers example, this means that the data has been ordered alphabetically by last name. If a new record is added, that record must be inserted into the correct place on disk, according to the value of the last name.

What if the page that contains the rows immediately before and after the new row is full? We now must *move* the data to keep it in order, correct? Not quite (that would be very inefficient), but there is some processing involved. When this situation occurs, SQL Server allocates a new page to the object (hopefully from the same extent, if possible) and adjusts the link list accordingly. This process takes some resources, however, and is not to be taken lightly. When updates occur, as with a nonclustered index, this processing overhead is incurred only if the update applies to an index key value. Finally, deletions don't incur much overhead that isn't incurred by the heap or nonclustered index.

You can see now that creating and maintaining indexes on a table are not free operations. So even though indexes give you a tremendous performance benefit on your data retrieval queries, you pay the price when inserting or updating the data. The thing to keep in mind is how the database is used. SQL Server has highly efficient index maintenance processes, so inserting records one or two at a time to a table that has an index is usually efficient enough that the benefit of having the index for queries outweighs the cost of maintaining the index.

For operational databases, such as the one we built for Mountain View Music, having the indexes in place will give us a huge performance benefit. The indexes will help the front-end application search for existing customer records, search and display product listings, and generate billing notices. This is because the database has a balanced read versus write usage. We are regularly adding one or two rows to each table, and regularly retrieving one or two rows from each table. It is conceivable that someone would occasionally run a large query, such as to view a comprehensive list of customers, but those queries would be rare, and a covering index would likely ensure adequate performance of that query.

However, not all databases have the same usage. If your database is write-heavy, you will need to carefully consider your index scheme. When a database has data being written to it at very high rates, be sure to include only the indexes that you must include to satisfy the most-used queries. In contrast, if data is added to your database very infrequently but is constantly queried, you can be more liberal with the number of indexes you apply. Remember, though, that there is such a thing as too much of a good thing.

If you find that your database has periods that are write-intensive followed by periods that are read-intensive, such as an OLAP database, you may find yourself actually creating and dropping indexes based on data loading processes. As with anything else, your mileage may vary, but it is often useful to drop your indexes when large data loads are occurring and then re-create them when the data load is finished so that queries can use them to retrieve data. On the flip side of that coin, re-creating the index takes resources. So you must trade off the speed of the load versus the speed of re-creating the index. Sometimes, it is better to leave the indexes in place during the load.

Transaction Data

Way back during the requirements gathering phase, you should have been taking note of general metrics for the system. For example, about how many orders per day are processed? How many employees use the system concurrently? What is the duration of the data that must be kept online—six months? Two years? Knowing these bits of information can help determine what the usage of your database will be. The usage will help further define the types of indexes you place on your database.

For example, in the Mountain View Music database, if we know that 90 percent of the customers use the Web interface and 70 percent of those are returning customers, then we need to make sure that the log-in information lookup is a speedy process. It would be unacceptable for the customer to have to wait 90 seconds for the log-in to complete. Therefore, we can place a priority on the indexing scheme to make sure that this query is fast. In contrast, if we know that once a month the customer service manager will pull a report of all customers who've placed an order in the past 30 days, we can place a lower priority on creating a covering index for that report (if it performs poorly without any help). Knowing these statistics about the usage of your database will greatly increase your ability to index it correctly.

Determining the Appropriate Indexes

After you've built your database and have gathered all the notes about its usage, it's time to start creating indexes. In this section, we cover the key things to think about when you create indexes for each table.

Reviewing Data Access Patterns

As we've discussed, it's crucial to know how your database is being used. Specifically, you need to know how much time is spent writing new data to the database and updating existing data. You also need to know how much data is being removed from the database, and about how much of the data will be kept online at any given time. Then you need to know how much data retrieval there will be. How much data will be queried by the applications versus ad hoc queries? Will there even be any ad hoc queries? How often? These answers will help you produce a logical, efficient index scheme.

From a procedural standpoint, it's a good idea to go through the database table by table—often referencing the data model (for logical reference to the entities)—and ask questions of the users and application designers about the various ways the data is used. Document their responses, and keep those notes handy when you start indexing your tables. Be sure to include both the frequency of the queries being run and an estimate of how much data will be retrieved for each query.

Balancing Indexes

As we've mentioned, there is overhead in maintaining indexes. But the key is to know how many indexes you actually need. Make sure to create indexes in situations where searching and returning the data is painfully slow or needs to be extremely quick. For example, there is no need to create an index on a lookup table of states in the United States. The table will have fewer than 60 records (counting states, D.C., and territories), and the entire table can be searched in subseconds, no matter what. But if the lookup table is states, counties, and cities, it might be worth creating indexes (assuming you don't normalize the table). Remember that no matter what the usage is, you should create only the indexes you absolutely need so that you can minimize index maintenance.

One other thing to keep in mind is the balance between the clustered index and nonclustered indexes on your table. For most operational databases, each table will have a single clustered index on the primary key (whether it is a surrogate or a natural key). This means that the data will be sorted on disk according to its primary usage. Even though you could include non-key columns in the clustered index, it is usually pointless because the lowest level of the index is already the data page; the entire row is actually found when you search the index, regardless of the other values in the query. Thus, the nonclustered indexes are there to satisfy those queries that search the data in a different order from its natural order, or when the clustered key value is not used in the query at all.

In the Customers table from Mountain View Music, we could use a nonclustered index to satisfy the e-mail lookup. Maintaining this nonclustered index is simple, and it can very easily improve the performance of the query. We might also consider nonclustered indexes for the phone numbers. Additionally, we might consider including the phone number fields in either the clustered index (not a great idea) or the e-mail nonclustered index (better). If we create an index with the e-mail, home phone, work phone, and mobile phone, we are creating a wider index, but we are creating a single index that SQL Server can use to search for any of those pieces of data. This is because SQL Server is smart enough to use an index even if the data it's looking for is in a secondary column of the index. The index is still pointing to the data, regardless of the order of the columns defined in the index, so it may still be faster than just scanning the table. What we've created then is a covering index of sorts.

Covering Indexes

By definition, a covering index specifically includes columns from a given query in order to satisfy that specific query. However, in certain situations, such as the Customers table we've just discussed, you can create an index of the columns not included in the clustered index because they might satisfy 85 percent or more of the unknown, or ad hoc, queries. Usually these indexes are created after a database has been in use for some time and a DBA has identified a number of varying queries that could use a common index. However, if you can identify a table that will be the target of these types of queries (based on your notes), then you might consider creating a covering index right out of the gate. Fortunately, indexes can be modified, created, and destroyed after the initial design phase, so this may be a trial-and-error process.

Index Statistics

One often overlooked component of indexes is its statistics. **Statistics** are the pieces of information stored by SQL Server that help it determine whether a given index will be useful and what access method to use to get to the data being requested by any given query. Specifically, SQL Server needs to know the distribution of values in every column and the occurrences of each step in the distribution. In fact, you can keep statistics for any column or group of columns on a table without even creating an index. This capability is helpful when there is no natural index, such as in highly denormalized tables.

Unfortunately, gathering exhaustive statistics on every value in every column could be cumbersome on larger systems, so SQL Server can calculate the statistics based on a sampling of the data. To make sure that the query optimizer has as much information as possible, we can manually force the creation of and updating of statistics on columns. When indexes are created, statistics are automatically created to go along with that index. SQL Server then tries to maintain these statistics (or optionally can be left outdated, in rare circumstances). Most of the time, the statistics on a table are adequately maintained if the indexes are adequately maintained.

Index Maintenance Considerations

We've mentioned repeatedly that indexes must be maintained. What does this mean? Basically, indexes must be occasionally reordered, or defragmented, because they've been updated or changed and SQL Server hasn't been able to keep up with the changes. This includes statistical information being updated. So DBAs must periodically execute some basic maintenance on the indexes (we discuss the specifics later this chapter). What you need to keep in mind when designing indexes is the frequency of changes to the data, and therefore to the indexes. If you've created a clustered index and several nonclustered indexes, you need to take another look at your usage information to determine how often the indexes may need to be maintained.

If you have an extremely volatile database, wherein hundreds of thousands of rows are changing or being inserted daily, you need to work with the DBA to make sure to maintain the indexes quite often. However, if your traffic is primarily read-intensive or if the system just isn't taxed (think fewer than 10,000 updates per day), you may need to have maintenance run on the indexes only weekly. Again, your mileage will vary, but be sure to account for maintenance when the database is deployed. Staying on top of index maintenance from day one will prevent emergency situations later, when the database is huge and query performance has ground to a halt.

Implementing Indexes in SQL Server

Now it's time to start creating some indexes. Although indexes, in some form or another, exist in all of the major RDBMSs, SQL Server has specific syntax and capabilities that are important to know. In this section, we explain how to create indexes on our tables, discuss things to keep in mind, and describe the basic maintenance that must be performed.

Naming Guidelines

As with most objects in the database, a good naming guideline is very important. It helps not only you as the designer/developer but also others downstream. As a basic guideline, establish a naming scheme wherein you can visually identify the index as being clustered or nonclustered and determine the columns it may include. We typically use a combination of a prefix, the table name, and the column name.

For example, on the Customers table, we might have an index named

```
idx_Customer_LastName_FirstName
```

In this case, the `idx` tells us it's an index, and then it's followed by the table name and column names. You could also use `ixc` to denote a clustered index, if the primary key of the table isn't also the clustered index. As with any of the naming standards, the specifics aren't as important as having the standard in the first place.

Creating Indexes

When you create an index on a table, you can specify it either in the create statement for the table (only if it is the primary key or a unique index), or after the table is created using the `CREATE INDEX` statement. Following is a simple create statement showing the most commonly used options (SQL Server 2008 Books Online has an exhaustive reference on the syntax of this statement).

```
CREATE NONCLUSTERED INDEX idx_Customer_LastName_FirstName
   ON Customer (LastName ASC, FirstName ASC)
   WITH (FILLFACTOR = 70,
     SORT_IN_TEMPDB = ON,
     ONLINE = ON)
   N IndexFileGroup
```

This statement creates our index on the Customer table, sorting by last name in ascending alphabetical order and then by first name in ascending alphabetical order. The fillfactor, which specifies the amount of page space to fill with the index information, is set to 70. This means that for all the index pages created to hold the index data, each page will be filled no more than 70 percent. This specification allows for some growth in the pages. By doing this, we leave room for the insertion of rows that will fall in the middle of the ranges of each page. It lowers the overhead of maintaining the index, because we should have fewer pages being rearranged to handle the new rows as they come in.

We then tell SQL Server to do all the sorting of the data for the new index in the tempdb. This moves the processing of the data, which requires temporary physical storage, to the temp database, keeping it out of the actual user database that the index is being created in. Then we tell it to leave the underlying tables online during the index creation process. By default, the underlying tables would be offline, preventing anyone from reading or writing to the tables while the index was being created. Note that this option is available only in SQL Server 2008 Enterprise Edition, so don't try it otherwise. Finally, we specify the filegroup on which to place this index.

Filegroups

Filegroups are a method of storing database data files in a separated fashion. By default, every new SQL Server database has a single filegroup, called Primary, where the first data file lives. Users can create additional files and filegroups and create objects in those files and filegroups. We've specified that there be a user-defined filegroup called IndexFileGroup and that we want the index created there (and not in the same filegroup as the underlying table).

One of the primary reasons to do something like this is to both manage disk space and improve performance. If we separate our indexes from our source tables, we can add disk spindles to satisfy the query, thereby not tying up the same set of spindles to search for the data and retrieve the data. In addition, we can keep an eye on our disk space usage at a more granular level.

Setting Up Index Maintenance

Finally we arrive at the last piece of the index puzzle: maintenance. We've discussed why you need to perform maintenance but haven't said very much about what it is and when you need to do it. As mentioned before, index maintenance is primarily in the realm of the DBA, but if you can provide guidance about the frequency and type of maintenance that is likely to be needed, the DBA will be grateful. Here are the things you need to know.

Indexes, because of the insertion and deletion of data, can become very fragmented. That is, to perform as fast as possible, SQL Server executes these changes in a very efficient manner. Whenever changes are made that require index pages to be split or allocated, SQL Server grabs the quickest available page and allocates it to the index in question. Over time, this means that the index information is scattered throughout the database, in terms of physical location on disk. This in turn has a negative effect on performance. When we refer to performing maintenance on an index, we are referring to fixing this problem.

Rebuilds versus Reorganization

There are two ways to remedy the fragmentation that occurs with indexes: rebuilding the index and reorganizing the index. **Rebuilding** the index means literally that—dropping and re-creating the index. It can be a disruptive process, because it literally drops the existing index and re-creates it, allocating all new, contiguous pages to the new version of the index. This process, however, completely removes fragmentation. In Enterprise Edition, you can execute this online, lowering the impact on users who may be trying to access the table while the index is being rebuilt. However, it can cause the rebuild to take a very long time, so when possible, you should execute it offline.

Alternatively, you can reorganize an index. **Reorganization** simply rearranges the information on the index pages, using only the pages already allocated to the index. Although this doesn't solve the problem of the pages being discontinuous on the disk, it does speed the scanning of the nodes of the index, because they are in order even if they aren't physically next to each other. Reorganization is an online operation by default, regardless of the edition, and thus you can execute it with greater confidence that performance and usability won't be significantly affected during the process.

When should you rebuild versus reorganize? Microsoft, in SQL Server Books Online, recommends that if fragmentation of the index is less than 30 percent, then reorganization will likely suffice. If it is greater than 30 percent, then a rebuild will be required to effectively regain the performance boost of the index. In practice, these numbers hold up for most systems, although it is usually good to rebuild indexes regularly, regardless of fragmentation, to help prevent them from becoming fragmented at an inconvenient time.

Finally, these processes, however they have been set up, should be run on a frequent enough basis that fragmentation never becomes a major problem. It is possible for indexes on very large tables to become so fragmented that it takes 24 hours or longer to rebuild them. In this case, it may be necessary to execute maintenance of different indexes on the same table on different days. However, this situation may indicate the need to remove or archive data from the table; use your judgment when these situations arise. For now, from a development standpoint, just be aware that taking maintenance into account will help you decide how many indexes to implement and balance the pros of the query performance gain against the cons of the maintenance requirements.

Summary

In this chapter, we've taken a high-level overview of using indexes in SQL Server. We've looked at the basic structure of an index and at the various options available to us as developers to help enhance query performance. Remember that usage information gathered early in the project can be a huge help in determining the indexes that should be implemented on your tables. We've also covered the maintenance aspects of indexes. With this insight into the cost of using indexes, you can deliver a well-designed database that performs well under the load it has been designed to handle. In the next, and final, chapter, we discuss some enhanced design techniques you can use to make your database more flexible and easier to maintain.

CHAPTER 11

CREATING AN ABSTRACTION LAYER IN SQL SERVER

Our journey has brought us a long way, and now we're near the end. At this point you should have a fully working physical database complete with all the appropriate indexes. This is the time when many database modelers stop their work and toss the database over the wall for the DBAs to implement and manage. If you choose that course, you may be just fine, but you might also be setting yourself up for failure. In its current state, access to the database will be pieced together by the application developers, and trust us when we tell you that most application developers do not understand how to access a database in the best way.

No, to be complete you have one more step, one last thing to build and that is the topic of this chapter. We look at how you should go about building an abstraction layer on top of your database in SQL Server.

What Is an Abstraction Layer?

Before we get too far along, you need to understand what an abstraction layer is. In general terms, an **abstraction layer** is a way of hiding the complex details about the functionality of a process. It could be thought of as a user interface, although in this case the user doesn't have to be a person. Let's look at a car as an analogy. Your car has an engine, and that engine does many complicated things to make your car move. Do you understand everything that the engine does? For many of us, the engine is just the big apparatus under the hood. The only thing most of us know how to do is look at it and pretend we know what we are looking at. For the common folk, we know that if we put the car in gear and step on the gas, the car will go. That system of the gear shift and the gas pedal is an abstraction layer; it allows us access to the underlying complexity of the engine's function without our needing to know a thing about it.

In computer terms, abstraction layers are often implemented as layers of software that the user or other applications access. Some common abstraction layers include the Windows Hardware Abstraction Layer (HAL), the Open Systems Interconnection (OSI) model, and the Open Graphics Library (OpenGL). All these provide access to the functionality of the underlying objects without providing direct access to the objects.

Now let's look at what an abstraction layer is in terms of our SQL Server database. The complexity we are trying to hide is the **schema,** which includes all the tables, relationships, indexes, columns, data types, and so on. Why we want to hide this complexity is covered in the next section. Our abstraction layer in SQL Server is made up of views, stored procedures, user-defined functions, and a few other SQL Server objects. In a perfect world with a perfect abstraction layer, neither a single piece of code nor a user would have any permission to access a physical table; everything would be handled via an abstraction layer.

Why Use an Abstraction Layer?

Now that you know what an abstraction layer is, it's our job to explain why you would want to use one. Our hope is to make a good enough case that the whole world will understand that a database without an abstraction layer is a problem. As we have discussed, an abstraction layer masks the complexity of the underlying database structure. This is crucial for several reasons. First, it provides a means to manage security without compromising the data in your database. Second, it creates a database that it extensible. Finally, it allows you much greater flexibility than would otherwise be possible. Let's look at each of these in a little more detail.

Security

First and foremost, a correctly designed abstraction layer provides you with more options for the security of your database. By not allowing direct table access, you avoid the pitfalls that come with data changes or over-permissions. To illustrate this let's look at a single table in our database, tbl_customer, as shown in Figure 11.1.

This table contains sensitive data; not only do privacy laws and regulations abound that could create problems if a person's information is com-

tbl_customer

objid	int	IDENTITY
email	varchar(50)	NULL
customer_id	char(10)	NULL
firstname	varchar(50)	NOT NULL
lastname	varchar(50)	NOT NULL
homephone	varchar(15)	NULL
workphone	varchar(15)	NULL
mobilephone	varchar(15)	NULL
web_password	varchar(16)	NULL

FIGURE 11.1   The customer table from the Mountain View Music database

promised, but also this table contains the passwords customers use when they log on to the Mountain View Music Web site. For these reasons we need tight controls that limit who and what can access this table.

For example, let's say that all the customer service employees need to be able to read and write to tbl_customer. If you grant them all read and write access to the table, they will be able to read and write *all* the data in the table. This means that they can see the password, even if it's encrypted. Why let them see it and have the opportunity to change it and affect your customers?

We know what you might be thinking: Permissions can be applied on a column basis, and thus you could prevent them from seeing this information. Although that is true, have you ever tried to manage security to this level? It can be a pain to keep track of who has access to what. Instead, you can create a view as follows.

```
CREATE VIEW vw_customer_detail
AS
SELECT email
      ,customer_id
      ,firstname
      ,lastname
      ,homephone
      ,workphone
      ,mobilephone
FROM tbl_customer
```

This allows your customer service employees to see the data they are meant to see.

In addition, what if you need to add a sensitive piece of information to a table that not everyone needs to see? For example, suppose you need to start storing all your customers' social security numbers; you add a new column to tbl_customer called SSN. Any users who currently have read access to the table can now see this new SSN column, whether or not you want them to have that access. Extra steps need to be taken to prevent them from seeing the new data.

But when you use an abstraction layer, this problem ceases to exist. Adding a column to a table does not automatically add it to your view, provided you didn't create your view using the SELECT * syntax. Now the extra steps would be required to expose the data, and not to hide it. To expose the information, you would need to modify any views you want this new column to appear in, or create new views.

Extensibility and Flexibility

Extensibility refers to the ease with which you can modify your data model as your future needs change. By "change," we mean adding columns to hold new pieces of information, modifying existing columns to change the way data is stored, or even adding or removing whole tables. It's hard to predict what our future needs will be, so it is our job to make the database as extensible as possible so that we can react to future needs as they arise.

We also want our models to be flexible. Although it's similar to extensibility, **flexibility** refers to how much of your model you can change without causing significant or any impact. It is true that flexible models will likely also be extensible, but this isn't always the case. In either event, an abstraction layer is your best friend when it comes to extensibility.

Your abstraction layer allows you to make almost any change you can imagine to the physical tables and not affect a single piece of application code. If all your applications and users are reading data from views and manipulating data using stored procedures, you simply need to update these items as appropriate to prevent problems. How many times have you wanted to make a change to a database, such as splitting one table into two tables, but have not been able to because it would require code to be reviewed, changed, and recompiled? We have been in this boat more times than we care to remember. The problem stems from the lack of an abstraction layer. In the example of splitting one table (TableA) into two tables (TableA and TableB), any code that selects, inserts, updates, or deletes from TableA must be changed to perform its action on both tables. If we have an abstraction layer, we need only modify a few stored procedures and views to accommodate the new structure.

You are probably thinking, "Code will need to be modified either way, so what's the difference?" Although it is true that in either case you need to make a change, the difference is huge. For starters, unlike code in a .NET application, code on SQL Server is not compiled; therefore, if the procedure takes the same inputs and returns the same outputs, you can alter that procedure in the middle of the day while users are online and no one will know the difference. Granted, there are other considerations based on what else you have to change in the database, but we are talking about the transparency of the stored procedure change. The second, and probably the more important, difference in modifying stored procedure code over application code is that there is only one database. If you change application code, you often need to recompile and then have all your users update or reinstall the client application.

Abstraction layers give you the flexibility to make changes for performance reasons, for normalization, and for reasons of extensibility. Future growth and changes are always similar with an abstraction layer.

An Abstraction Layer's Relationship to the Logical Model

When it's time to build your abstraction layer, you should find that it more closely ties to the logical model than to the physical model. You should work back toward your entities if you want things to make the most sense and provide the most benefit. This practice allows applications and users to work with your database in terms that make sense to them. Remember that your logical model is more user friendly than your physical model, which is set up to store data in a SQL Server friendly manner. This means that you should avoid the convention of creating four stored procedures for each table: one for insert, one for update, one for select, and one for delete. You may laugh, but we have seen this done. If you go this route, all you have done is to add an extra layer to a DML statement. Instead, you should look to create procedures for saving a customer entity, procedures that can insert or update and that are aware that the customer entity is stored in more than one table.

SQL Server, especially SQL Server 2008, offers us functionality to simplify the logic in these procedures. We look at this functionality in detail in the section "Implementing an Abstraction Layer." For now, the most important thing to keep in mind is that your abstraction layer should abstract the complexity of the underlying tables, and this usually means that it contains structures that are more closely tied to entities.

An Abstraction Layer's Relationship to Object-Oriented Programming

As you can guess by the name, **object-oriented programming** is a kind of programming that uses objects. **Objects** are representations of real-world items, and in that way they are similar to our concept of entities. When programming an order management system, you will likely have objects that represent orders, order items, and customers. The objects have **properties,** which are similar to attributes. Finally, objects also have **methods,** or actions that the objects can perform. This is a very basic look at objects—we could go on forever about the details—but the goal here is to show the relationship between abstraction layers and object-oriented programming.

Because objects closely resemble entities, the ties are there in plain sight, as is the relationship between object properties and entity attributes. Table 11.1 shows the properties of an Order object as it might exist in an object-oriented programming language, and the corresponding attributes that exist in our Order entity.

Right away you can see the clear relationship between an object and an entity, but what about an object's methods?

Methods are actions that an object can perform. An Order object might have methods to save the order, ship the order, cancel the order, add a line item to the order, and so on, and some of these methods have direct ties back to the database. For example, the method Order.Save may need to insert the order and its related data into our SQL Server database. These methods can be calls to a data layer, or a middle tier, but ultimately a call to a stored procedure in SQL Server will probably be made. This can

Table 11.1 Properties of the Order Object and the Related Attribute from the Orders Entity

Property	Attribute
Order_Number	OrderNumber
Date	OrderDate
SubTot	SubTotal
SH	ShippingHandling
Tax	Tax
Order Total	Total
Address 1	AddressLine1
Address 2	AddressLine2
City	City
State	Region
Country	Country
Zip	ZipCode
Split	IsSplitShip
EmployeeID	EmployeeObjectID
CustomerID	CustomerObjectID
Shipping_Method	ShippingMethodsObjectID

also apply to canceling an order; a stored procedure gets called, and it changes the order's status and maybe triggers a customer refund.

The possibilities are endless, and when you are building your database, you should take them into account. If your database is tightly integrated with an application development project, you may find that an object model exists. We recommend that you use this model as a guide to help you build your abstraction layer. After all, the application will ultimately use the database directly, so the two should be tightly coupled.

Implementing an Abstraction Layer

Implementing an abstraction layer consists of creating objects in the database that act as intermediaries between application code and underlying core database objects. You can use views, stored procedures, and functions to create easily accessible entry points for applications to use.

Views

When you create views, your goal is to display the entity to the end user in a way that makes sense based on the user's requirements. This might mean joining several tables to provide your output, or it might mean querying a single table but not displaying all the rows. A view that returns all the information about a customer is great, but if you also join to the address table, you could receive multiple addresses for that customer and hence receive multiple rows in your view per customer. This isn't necessarily a problem, but the consumers of the view need to understand what they are receiving.

Also, it's a good idea to create views that shortcut application logic. In other words, if the application often pulls a list of all the past orders of a customer to output an account summary page, then a view that joins the customer table to the order table might save time and prevent the application from making two trips to the database and then combining the record sets locally.

Also, avoid using SELECT * syntax or INSERT syntax without a list of values. In fact, *avoid* may be the wrong term; just don't use this syntax. Doing so creates problems and reduces the usefulness of your abstraction layer if changes are made. Either form of this syntax relies on the data being in a particular order. When the application performs a SELECT *, it might be expecting 15 columns of specific data. If you now add a new column before column 5, the application will still get 16 columns, but beginning at column 5 the data will be different from last time.

This kind of unexpected result can trigger a simple problem such as data being labeled incorrectly, or it can create bigger problems, such as application crashes due to incorrect data types, divide by zero errors, item not found in collection errors, and the list goes on. If you select data by column name, the worst the application will do is ignore the new column until you modify the view definition.

Let's look at the views we will need to view our customer data. Remember that the customer entity is made up of both tbl_customer and tbl_address, so we must decide how to return this data. In this case, we will use two views: one for all the customer information except for address data, and the other for address detail. Had we decided to use only one view, we would end up repeating all the customer data for each address in the database. Although this isn't really a problem, it is often easier to reduce the duplication in the view rather than rely on the application to take care of it. For view 1, we use the code shown next.

```
CREATE VIEW vw_customers
AS
SELECT
     objid
     ,email
     ,customer_id
     ,firstname
     ,lastname
     ,homephone
     ,workphone
     ,mobilephone
FROM tbl_customer
```

Notice that the customer view is very simple and returns most of the data from tbl_customer. The only thing left out is web_password, because it was determined that this is a special column and needs to be seen only in rare instances. Next, let's look at the code for the customer addresses view.

```
CREATE VIEW vw_customer_addresses
AS
SELECT
     address_objid = objid
     ,address_label
     ,addressline1
     ,addressline2
     ,city
     ,region
     ,zipcode
     ,customer_objid
FROM tbl_address
WHERE customer_objid IS NOT NULL
```

This view will be similar to vw_customer, which we created earlier, but there are a few key differences. Because vw_customer_addresses returns multiple columns containing objid data from what amounts to the data from different tables, we alias the objid column from tbl_address to address_objid. In this way, there is no confusion about which objid we are talking about.

Second, because tbl_address can hold addresses for either a customer or an employee, we select only rows in which the customer_objid does not contain a NULL value. We select data only from tbl_address in this view. However, in some instances you may find yourself needing to display more customer data in addition to the address data—for example, the customer_id column. If this is the case, you need to join the two tables.

In this instance we have no need for additional information, so we forgo the join and save a little on resources. Because we have these two views, the application developers can decide which one they need to reference in different places in their application and retrieve only the data they absolutely need.

Stored Procedures

The same rule goes for stored procedures as for views. When you create stored procedures, think in terms of the entities they are meant to affect. Doing so will help you avoid the pitfalls we discussed earlier around writing stored procedures to simply insert, update, or delete data. Consider creating standards that govern how and why stored procedures are created, what entities are being affected, and what the potential data manipulations are.

How do you correctly implement stored procedures in your abstraction layer? There are a great many correct answers to this question, because it depends on the environment and on your preferences. We look at some of your options here, but remember that this is not the absolute correct answer in every situation.

A commonly used option is to create a single stored procedure for each entity; the procedure will update or insert data in all the associated tables. This is usually the least confusing option, but it can make for some tricky code. First, let's walk through the logical steps that a stored procedure must perform to save changes to a Customer entity in the Mountain View Music database, and then we will look at some code. When the stored procedure runs, it must first determine whether or not a record already exists. Luckily, you followed good modeling guidelines, so each and every table has a primary key defined, and that makes this step easy. If the record exists it should be updated; otherwise, it should be inserted. In addition, the stored procedure should return any information about what it did and which record was updated.

Sound simple? It can be if you do your job correctly. The following is an example of a stored procedure that performs the process we just discussed for our Customer entity. It writes to both the tbl_customer and the tbl_address table in our database.

```
ALTER PROCEDURE prc_save_customer
@email varchar(50)
,@customer_id char(10)
,@firstname varchar(50)
,@lastname varchar(50)
,@homephone varchar(15)
,@workphone varchar(15)
,@mobilephone varchar(15)
,@addresses CustomerAddress ReadOnly
,@customer_objid int OUTPUT
AS

MERGE tbl_customer AS pri_customer
    USING
    (
    SELECT customer_id = @customer_id
    )
    AS source_customer(customer_id)
    ON
        (
        pri_customer.customer_id =
        source_customer.customer_id
        )
    WHEN NOT MATCHED THEN
    INSERT (email,
        customer_id,
        firstname,
        lastname,
        homephone,
        workphone,
        mobilephone)
    VALUES (@email,
        @customer_id,
        @firstname,
        @lastname,
        @homephone,
        @workphone,
        @mobilephone)
```

```
WHEN MATCHED THEN
       UPDATE
       SET email=@email,
           firstname=@firstname,
           lastname=@lastname,
           homephone=@homephone,
           workphone=@workphone,
           mobilephone=@mobilephone;

SELECT @customer_objid = objid
FROM tbl_customer
WHERE customer_id = @customer_id;

MERGE tbl_address AS current_addresses
    USING
           (
        SELECT customer_objid = @customer_objid,
               address_label,
               addressline1,
               addressline2,
               city,
               region,
               country,
               zipcode,
               is_deleted
        FROM @addresses
        )
        AS source_addresses(customer_objid,
                            address_label,
                            addressline1,
                            addressline2,
                            city,
                            region,
                            country,
                            zipcode,
                            is_deleted)
    ON
           (
        current_addresses.address_label =
        source_addresses.address_label
    AND
        current_addresses.customer_objid =
```

```
                source_addresses.customer_objid
                  )
WHEN NOT MATCHED THEN
         INSERT (address_label,
 addressline1,
 addressline2,
 city,
 region,
 country,
 zipcode,
 customer_objid)
         VALUES (source_addresses.address_label,
                 source_addresses.addressline1,
                 source_addresses.addressline2,
                 source_addresses.city,
                 source_addresses.region,
                 source_addresses.country,
                 source_addresses.zipcode,
                 @customer_objid)
WHEN MATCHED AND source_addresses.is_deleted = 1
         THEN DELETE
WHEN MATCHED THEN
         UPDATE
         SET address_label=source_addresses.address_label,
             addressline1=source_addresses.addressline1,
             addressline2=source_addresses.addressline2,
             city=source_addresses.city,
             region=source_addresses.region,
             country=source_addresses.country,
             zipcode=source_addresses.zipcode;
```

This stored procedure may look a little complex, but it is really simple. Using the MERGE statement, which is new in SQL Server 2008, we can write a single statement for each table. MERGE evaluates the tables based on the provided values to determine whether the record in question is new and needs to be inserted, or whether it is an existing record that needs to be updated. Also notice that one of the parameters being passed is called CustomerAddress. This is a user-defined table data type being passed to the procedure as a table-valued parameter. Table-valued parameters, also new to SQL Server 2008, allow us to pass multiple addresses for a customer using a single parameter.

The really cool thing is that the MERGE syntax works with single or multiple rows of source data, so our single MERGE statement can insert, update, or even delete address records from the address table for the specified customer. Again, we are not saying that you have to use MERGE; you can build all the logic in separate steps, but a single T-SQL statement is likely to be more efficient than anything you can write. We highly recommend that you look at MERGE in further detail.

Other Components of an Abstraction Layer

Although views and stored procedures will make up the bulk of your exposed abstraction layer, you will use many other SQL Server objects in your unexposed abstraction layer. First, let's define exposed versus unexposed portions of your abstraction layer. Simply put, anything that is meant to be consumed by your users or an application is **exposed;** anything consumed only by other elements of your abstraction layer is **unexposed.**

For example, user-defined functions are extremely useful in a SQL Server database, but they typically perform small tasks as part of a larger process. Therefore, UDFs are generally called by stored procedures or used in a view and are not usually exposed to users or applications directly. As you build your abstraction layer you may find that a UDF or a trigger is appropriate for handling a task, and in these situations you should take full advantage of these objects. Just keep in mind that they will probably be called by another object and not the user.

Summary

If you take nothing else away from this book, remember that abstraction layers are extremely important. They provide extensibility and flexibility unrivaled by databases that lack abstraction layers. In addition, abstraction layers provide you with an extra layer of security and are handy during your next Sarbanes-Oxley audit.

At this point, we should have a complete database solution and our customer should be ready to begin using the database. We hope that if you follow the guidelines we have laid out in this book, you will be able to design and implement successful databases. Remember that there are many ways to accomplish the same goals, so take what you have learned here and incorporate it into your own practices and techniques.

SAMPLE LOGICAL MODEL

Logical Orders Submodel

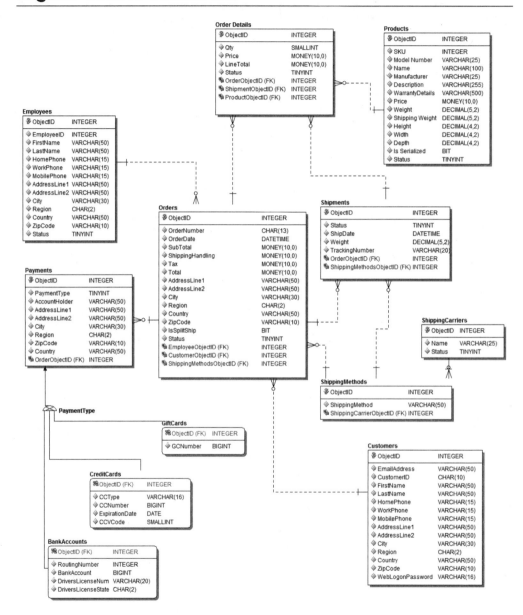

Logical Inventory Submodel

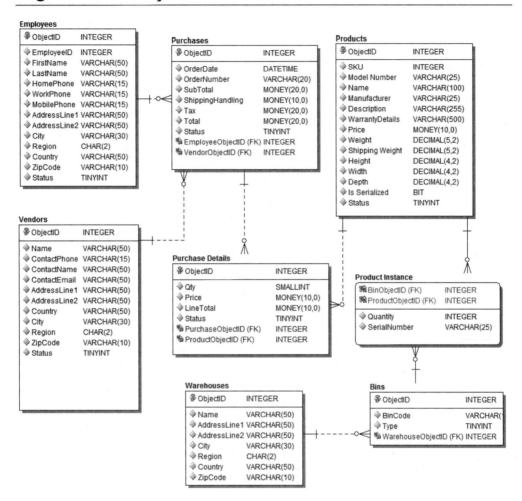

Employees

🔑 ObjectID	INTEGER
◈ EmployeeID	INTEGER
◈ FirstName	VARCHAR(50)
◈ LastName	VARCHAR(50)
◈ HomePhone	VARCHAR(15)
◈ WorkPhone	VARCHAR(15)
◈ MobilePhone	VARCHAR(15)
◈ AddressLine1	VARCHAR(50)
◈ AddressLine2	VARCHAR(50)
◈ City	VARCHAR(30)
◈ Region	CHAR(2)
◈ Country	VARCHAR(50)
◈ ZipCode	VARCHAR(10)
◈ Status	TINYINT

Purchases

🔑 ObjectID	INTEGER
◈ OrderDate	DATETIME
◈ OrderNumber	VARCHAR(20)
◈ SubTotal	MONEY(20,0)
◈ ShippingHandling	MONEY(10,0)
◈ Tax	MONEY(20,0)
◈ Total	MONEY(20,0)
◈ Status	TINYINT
🔖 EmployeeObjectID (FK)	INTEGER
🔖 VendorObjectID (FK)	INTEGER

Products

🔑 ObjectID	INTEGER
◈ SKU	INTEGER
◈ Model Number	VARCHAR(25)
◈ Name	VARCHAR(100)
◈ Manufacturer	VARCHAR(25)
◈ Description	VARCHAR(255)
◈ WarrantyDetails	VARCHAR(500)
◈ Price	MONEY(10,0)
◈ Weight	DECIMAL(5,2)
◈ Shipping Weight	DECIMAL(5,2)
◈ Height	DECIMAL(4,2)
◈ Width	DECIMAL(4,2)
◈ Depth	DECIMAL(4,2)
◈ Is Serialized	BIT
◈ Status	TINYINT

Vendors

🔑 ObjectID	INTEGER
◈ Name	VARCHAR(50)
◈ ContactPhone	VARCHAR(15)
◈ ContactName	VARCHAR(50)
◈ ContactEmail	VARCHAR(50)
◈ AddressLine1	VARCHAR(50)
◈ AddressLine2	VARCHAR(50)
◈ Country	VARCHAR(50)
◈ City	VARCHAR(30)
◈ Region	CHAR(2)
◈ ZipCode	VARCHAR(10)
◈ Status	TINYINT

Purchase Details

🔑 ObjectID	INTEGER
◈ Qty	SMALLINT
◈ Price	MONEY(10,0)
◈ LineTotal	MONEY(10,0)
◈ Status	TINYINT
🔖 PurchaseObjectID (FK)	INTEGER
🔖 ProductObjectID (FK)	INTEGER

Product Instance

🔖 BinObjectID (FK)	INTEGER
🔖 ProductObjectID (FK)	INTEGER
◈ Quantity	INTEGER
◈ SerialNumber	VARCHAR(25)

Warehouses

🔑 ObjectID	INTEGER
◈ Name	VARCHAR(50)
◈ AddressLine1	VARCHAR(50)
◈ AddressLine2	VARCHAR(50)
◈ City	VARCHAR(30)
◈ Region	CHAR(2)
◈ Country	VARCHAR(50)
◈ ZipCode	VARCHAR(10)

Bins

🔑 ObjectID	INTEGER
◈ BinCode	VARCHAR(
◈ Type	TINYINT
🔖 WarehouseObjectID (FK)	INTEGER

Logical Product Submodel

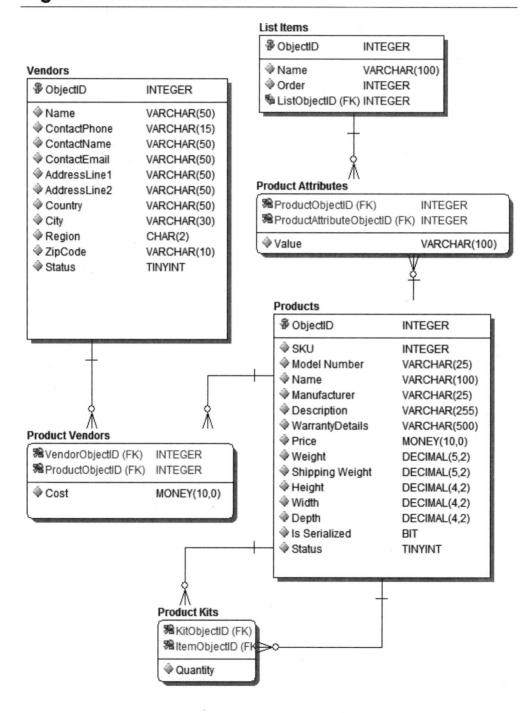

Logical Web Session Submodel

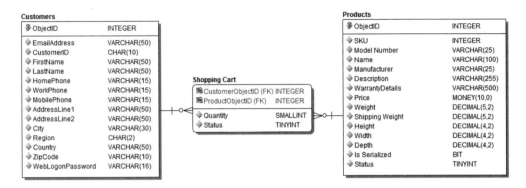

Customers

ObjectID	INTEGER
EmailAddress	VARCHAR(50)
CustomerID	CHAR(10)
FirstName	VARCHAR(50)
LastName	VARCHAR(50)
HomePhone	VARCHAR(15)
WorkPhone	VARCHAR(15)
MobilePhone	VARCHAR(15)
AddressLine1	VARCHAR(50)
AddressLine2	VARCHAR(50)
City	VARCHAR(30)
Region	CHAR(2)
Country	VARCHAR(50)
ZipCode	VARCHAR(10)
WebLogonPassword	VARCHAR(16)

Shopping Cart

CustomerObjectID (FK)	INTEGER
ProductObjectID (FK)	INTEGER
Quantity	SMALLINT
Status	TINYINT

Products

ObjectID	INTEGER
SKU	INTEGER
Model Number	VARCHAR(25)
Name	VARCHAR(100)
Manufacturer	VARCHAR(25)
Description	VARCHAR(255)
WarrantyDetails	VARCHAR(500)
Price	MONEY(10,0)
Weight	DECIMAL(5,2)
Shipping Weight	DECIMAL(5,2)
Height	DECIMAL(4,2)
Width	DECIMAL(4,2)
Depth	DECIMAL(4,2)
Is Serialized	BIT
Status	TINYINT

Logical Lists Submodel

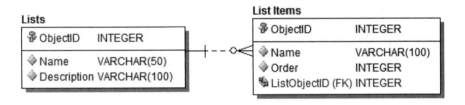

Lists

ObjectID	INTEGER
Name	VARCHAR(50)
Description	VARCHAR(100)

List Items

ObjectID	INTEGER
Name	VARCHAR(100)
Order	INTEGER
ListObjectID (FK)	INTEGER

SAMPLE PHYSICAL MODEL

Physical Orders Submodel

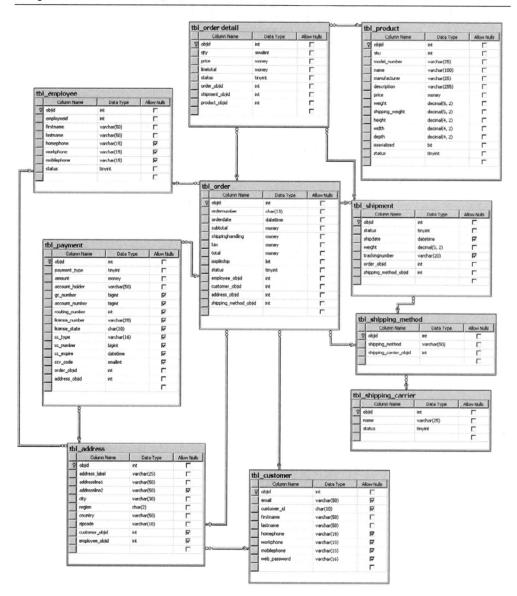

Physical Inventory Submodel

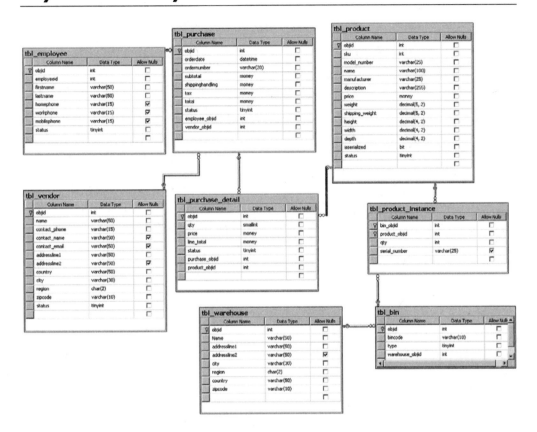

Physical Product Submodel

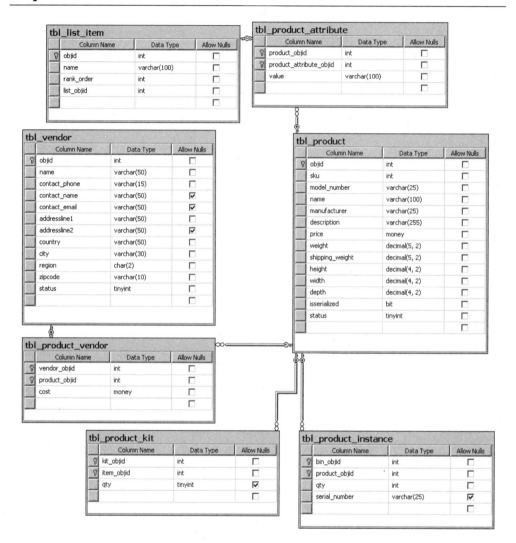

tbl_list_item

Column Name	Data Type	Allow Nulls
objid	int	☐
name	varchar(100)	☐
rank_order	int	☐
list_objid	int	☐
		☐

tbl_product_attribute

Column Name	Data Type	Allow Nulls
product_objid	int	☐
product_attribute_objid	int	☐
value	varchar(100)	☐
		☐

tbl_vendor

Column Name	Data Type	Allow Nulls
objid	int	☐
name	varchar(50)	☐
contact_phone	varchar(15)	☐
contact_name	varchar(50)	☑
contact_email	varchar(50)	☑
addressline1	varchar(50)	☐
addressline2	varchar(50)	☑
country	varchar(50)	☐
city	varchar(30)	☐
region	char(2)	☐
zipcode	varchar(10)	☐
status	tinyint	☐
		☐

tbl_product

Column Name	Data Type	Allow Nulls
objid	int	☐
sku	int	☐
model_number	varchar(25)	☐
name	varchar(100)	☐
manufacturer	varchar(25)	☐
description	varchar(255)	☐
price	money	☐
weight	decimal(5, 2)	☐
shipping_weight	decimal(5, 2)	☐
height	decimal(4, 2)	☐
width	decimal(4, 2)	☐
depth	decimal(4, 2)	☐
isserialized	bit	☐
status	tinyint	☐
		☐

tbl_product_vendor

Column Name	Data Type	Allow Nulls
vendor_objid	int	☐
product_objid	int	☐
cost	money	☐
		☐

tbl_product_kit

Column Name	Data Type	Allow Nulls
kit_objid	int	☐
item_objid	int	☐
qty	tinyint	☑
		☐

tbl_product_instance

Column Name	Data Type	Allow Nulls
bin_objid	int	☐
product_objid	int	☐
qty	int	☐
serial_number	varchar(25)	☑
		☐

Physical Web Session Submodel

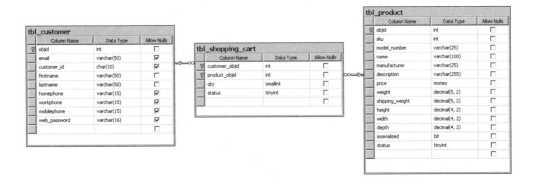

Physical Lists Submodel

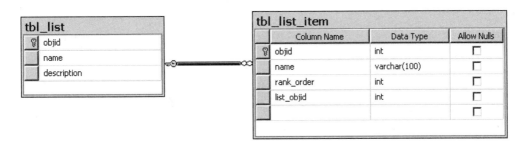

SQL SERVER 2008 RESERVED WORDS

Use of the following keywords should be avoided in any code, column names, or object names. These terms are keywords for the SQL Server engine, and their use could confuse the engine. For more keywords, including ODBC reserved words and a list of possible future keywords, see SQL Server Books Online.

ADD	COLLATE	DELETE
ALL	COLUMN	DENY
ALTER	COMMIT	DESC
AND	COMPUTE	DISK
ANY	CONSTRAINT	DISTINCT
AS	CONTAINS	DISTRIBUTED
ASC	CONTAINSTABLE	DOUBLE
AUTHORIZATION	CONTINUE	DROP
BACKUP	CONVERT	DUMP
BEGIN	CREATE	ELSE
BETWEEN	CROSS	END
BREAK	CURRENT	ERRLVL
BROWSE	CURRENT_DATE	ESCAPE
BULK	CURRENT_TIME	EXCEPT
BY	CURRENT_TIMESTAMP	EXEC
CASCADE	CURRENT_USER	EXECUTE
CASE	CURSOR	EXISTS
CHECK	DATABASE	EXIT
CHECKPOINT	DBCC	EXTERNAL
CLOSE	DEALLOCATE	FETCH
CLUSTERED	DECLARE	FILE
COALESCE	DEFAULT	FILLFACTOR

(continued)

(Continued)

FOR	OFFSETS	SCHEMA
FOREIGN	ON	SECURITYAUDIT
FREETEXT	OPEN	SELECT
FREETEXTTABLE	OPENDATASOURCE	SESSION_USER
FROM	OPENQUERY	SET
FULL	OPENROWSET	SETUSER
FUNCTION	OPENXML	SHUTDOWN
GOTO	OPTION	SOME
GRANT	OR	STATISTICS
GROUP	ORDER	SYSTEM_USER
HAVING	OUTER	TABLE
HOLDLOCK	OVER	TABLESAMPLE
IDENTITY	PERCENT	TEXTSIZE
IDENTITY_INSERT	PIVOT	THEN
IDENTITYCOL	PLAN	TO
IF	PRECISION	TOP
IN	PRIMARY	TRAN
INDEX	PRINT	TRANSACTION
INNER	PROC	TRIGGER
INSERT	PROCEDURE	TRUNCATE
INTERSECT	PUBLIC	TSEQUAL
INTO	RAISERROR	UNION
IS	READ	UNIQUE
JOIN	READTEXT	UNPIVOT
KEY	RECONFIGURE	UPDATE
KILL	REFERENCES	UPDATETEXT
LEFT	REPLICATION	USE
LIKE	RESTORE	USER
LINENO	RESTRICT	VALUES
LOAD	RETURN	VARYING
NATIONAL	REVERT	VIEW
NOCHECK	REVOKE	WAITFOR
NONCLUSTERED	RIGHT	WHEN
NOT	ROLLBACK	WHERE
NULL	ROWCOUNT	WHILE
NULLIF	ROWGUIDCOL	WITH
OF	RULE	WRITETEXT
OFF	SAVE	

RECOMMENDED NAMING STANDARDS

Object Type	Prefix	Example
Table	tbl_	tbl_customer
View	vw_	vw_open_orders
Stored Procedure	prc_	prc_save_order_detail
User-Defined Functions	udf_	udf_new_orderid
Triggers	trg_	trg_new_order
Index	idx_	idx_customer_name
Primary Keys	pk_<table name>	pk_tbl_address
Foreign Keys	fk_<foreign key table>_<primary key table>	fk_tbl_address_tbl_customer
Default Constraint	df_	df_customer_status
Check Constraints	ck_	ck_customer_phone_number
Unique Constraints	unq_	unq_customer_email

Index

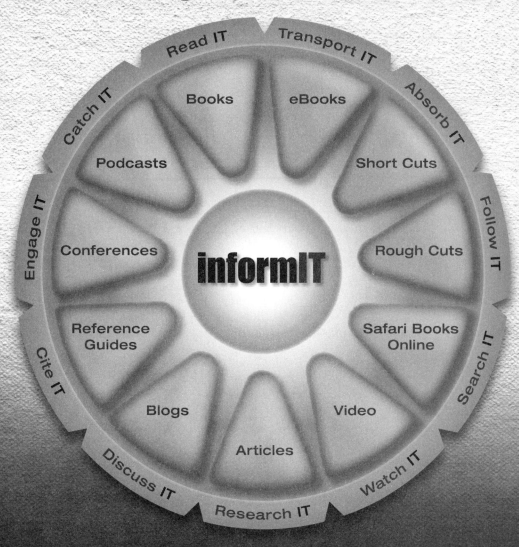

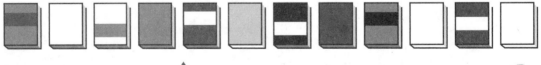

BOOKS ONLINE
ENABLED

THIS BOOK IS SAFARI ENABLED

INCLUDES FREE 45-DAY ACCESS TO THE ONLINE EDITION

The Safari® Enabled icon on the cover of your favorite technology book means the book is available through Safari Bookshelf. When you buy this book, you get free access to the online edition for 45 days.

Safari Bookshelf is an electronic reference library that lets you easily search thousands of technical books, find code samples, download chapters, and access technical information whenever and wherever you need it.

TO GAIN 45-DAY SAFARI ENABLED ACCESS TO THIS BOOK:

- Go to **informit.com/safarienabled**

- Complete the brief registration form

- Enter the coupon code found in the front of this book on the "Copyright" page

If you have difficulty registering on Safari Bookshelf or accessing the online edition, please e-mail customer-service@safaribooksonline.com.